THE ARAB UPRISINGS

ALSO BY JEREMY BOWEN

War Stories

Six Days

THE ARAB UPRISINGS

The People Want the Fall of the Regime

JEREMY BOWEN

**SIMON &
SCHUSTER**

London · New York · Sydney · Toronto · New Delhi

A CBS COMPANY

First published in Great Britain by Simon & Schuster UK Ltd, 2012
A CBS COMPANY

PICTURE CREDITS
Getty Images: 1, 3, 8, 10
Alamy: 2, 9, 11
Darren Conway: 5
Etienne de Malglaive: 12

The author and publishers have made all reasonable efforts
to contact copyright-holders for permission, and apologise
for any omissions or errors in the form of credits given.
Corrections may be made to future printings.

1 3 5 7 9 10 8 6 4 2

Simon & Schuster UK Ltd
1st Floor
222 Gray's Inn Road
London WC1X 8HB

www.simonandschuster.co.uk

Simon & Schuster Australia, Sydney
Simon & Schuster India, New Delhi

A CIP catalogue record for this book is available
from the British Library

ISBN: 978-0-85720-884-2 (Hardback)
ISBN: 978-0-85720-885-9 (Trade Paperback)
ISBN: 978-0-85720-887-3 (ebook)

Typeset in the UK by M Rules
Printed and bound by CPI Group (UK) Ltd, Croydon, CR0 4YY

To Mattie and Boatie, so that they will know why
I wasn't around much when they were ten and eight.

To my friends, who made life on the road
during the Arab uprisings possible.

CONTENTS

A NOTE ON THE TITLE

When Tunisians were overthrowing their dictator president Zine al-Abidine Ben Ali at the very beginning of 2011, demonstrators came up with a new chant. In Arabic it has a nice rhythm: *Ash-shab yurid isqat an-nizam.* The people want the fall of the regime. It caught on across the Arab world, sometimes with local variations, sometimes with the classic words. It became part of the soundtrack of revolution, which is why it is part of the title of this book.

Prologue

BEFORE THE SPRING

The day after Hosni Mubarak resigned as president of Egypt tens of thousands of people packed Tahrir Square in central Cairo and celebrated their elevation from subjects to citizens by cleaning it up. They brought brooms and buckets, paintbrushes and scrubbing brushes and set about demonstrating that they were the new owners of the city. Around the fringes of the square a shingle beach of rubble and rocks had been deposited during eighteen days of protests, thrown in spiky black clouds by thousands of hands at those supporters of the ex-president who had tried to break in to stop the revolution. Now the beach was shovelled into bags and taken away – except for the granite cobblestones that had been Tahrir's heavy artillery, which were picked out of the rubble and put back in their original spots.

The political symbolism of the clean-up was in the mind of everyone who was there. For years Egypt had felt like a country drowning in difficulty. But, that morning, not only was it bliss for them to be alive; there was also an extraordinary sense of the possible. People lined up to tell me that they had done the job of removing the president themselves. Their determination and their steadfastness had made the difference. They were taking control of their own political destiny and regaining their dignity: so different to 2003, when any satisfaction at the fall of Saddam Hussein, the tyrant of Baghdad, was outweighed by humiliation that Americans and their Western friends, not Arabs, had deposed him. Day one, year zero of the new Egypt – 12 February 2011 – was so full of euphoria and sheer outright happiness that they brushed aside, very cheerfully, anyone who tried to remind them of one iron law of revolution: that the hardest job is not overthrowing the dictator; it is making the new order.

This book does not pretend to be a comprehensive account of the turbulence in the Arab world since the end of 2010. I have concentrated to a very large degree on what I experienced myself – and I discovered during those remarkable months that too much was happening in too many places for one individual to witness it all. I have tried, as much as telling the story allows, to concentrate on events I saw first-hand. But, since I think I have seen as much as anyone, I hope the reader can get an idea not just of why the Middle East has been convulsed but also why it is happening. At the time of writing in some places revolution has happened, in others it is happening and in others it is still something for the future. If this is a five-act play, it's getting towards the end of act two, and the play's authors, the people themselves, are still trying to work out where the story ends. It is not too early, though, to conclude that Arabs from the Mediterranean to the Arabian Sea have embarked on a process of real, historical, revolutionary change. The old certainties have gone. No country is immune.

Arab dictators, generals and kings presided over countries that were under severe economic, political and social stress. Removing the old leader, or trying to, didn't take away all the other problems. It was not a magic cure. It even sharpened them sometimes. The police states that kept the old leaders in power had acted as a dampener, a limiter. They scared people into accepting the by-products of authoritarian rule, especially corruption and the feeling that the states' agents could get anyway with anything they liked. The longer that went on, the more discontent increased. In the places where the intimidating weight of the police states was removed, issues that had been buried surged to the surface.

When Hosni Mubarak stepped down it looked as if the Arab dominoes were going to tumble as fast as the communist ones had in Eastern Europe in 1989. Less than two months earlier, a Tunisian market trader, Muhammad Bouazizi, had set fire to himself after being humiliated by government inspectors once too often. His death started a protest movement that spread to Tunis, the capital, by the end of the year and forced the authoritarian and corrupt president, Zine al-Abidine Ben Ali, in power since 1987, to flee to Saudi Arabia. That was sensational enough, but Mubarak's fall in Egypt, the traditional centre of gravity in the Arab world, energised protestors across the region. They rose up in Libya, Bahrain, Yemen and Syria. Governments in Jordan, Morocco, Algeria and Oman were forced into rapid talk of reform. Even Saudi Arabia redirected a huge chunk of its oil revenues to education and welfare items the king hoped would buy off any new discontent. The speed of events made some predict a transformation of the Middle East by the summer. It has not been that simple, and it has not been at all easy. How could it have been, after the years of authoritarian rule, and the accumulation of so many layers of economic, political and social problems?

In 2011 Arabs across the region – not just the Egyptians who took their mops and brushes to Tahrir Square – pushed to be citizens, not subjects. Citizens of any country want to be able to choose their leaders and to sack them if they do a bad job. They tend to prefer leaders who know what they are doing and can make decisions that work and make the lives of the people easier. Arabs, like everyone else, do not want rulers who depend on fear, who wield power based on police states that terrorize the people.

One day towards the end of 2011 I was talking about the way politics in the Arab world works with one of Britain's top diplomats in the Middle East, Sir John Jenkins. At the time he was ambassador to Libya, and was preparing to move on to do the same job in Saudi

Arabia. We were walking through the ruins of the official British residence in Tripoli, the Libyan capital. The British had taken over a floor of a hotel because the ambassador's house and the embassy, which were in two halves of one of Tripoli's most historic houses, had been burnt out by a mob of Gaddafi's supporters after NATO started bombing at the beginning of March that year.

Jenkins said that governments in the Middle East operate at the 'intersection of legitimacy and consent. A lot of governments in the region have pretty low levels of legitimacy, but moderate levels of consent'. In other words, many people had for years received just enough from repressive states to keep them from taking active steps to bring their governments down. If anyone wavered, the police state would give them a sharp reminder of who was boss. You could tell, Jenkins said, when consent rose, because people felt a bigger stake in their societies. That was why thousands of Egyptians turned up in Tahrir Square with the contents of their broom cupboards. Public spaces in Arab countries could be filthy. Most homes, however poor, were immaculate, but their residents had no compunction about chucking their garbage into the street.

As we walked round the residence that he could not use, past the skeleton of the charred 1920s snooker table, our shoes stirring up clouds of ash, Jenkins suggested that a garbage index could be a measure of change. Under the dictators 'consent never stretched far enough to get the people to do something about the rubbish or clean the streets up [...] It sounds a bit odd to say that you can tell how successful a revolution is when people start picking the bags up outside their houses, but in a way you can.'

The Arab people wanted to seize the big chance they had in 2011 to change the game, to find a better way, without leaders who in some cases were turning dictatorships into dynasties. President Hafez al-Assad had set the precedent as he prepared the succession in Syria in the 1990s. He groomed his son Basel to follow him and when Basel was killed in a car crash in 1994 he was replaced as heir apparent by another son, Bashar, who left his studies in ophthalmology in London to return to the family business. Bashar took over what looked increasingly like a throne when his father died in 1999. In Egypt, it looked as if Gamal Mubarak, who was the younger of the president's two sons, was being fast-tracked into politics. By the time Gamal, an investment banker, turned forty in 2003, he was in charge of the state's privatisation programme and looked to be his father's candidate for the succession, though both men denied it. Gamal busied himself ticking the necessary boxes. One problem was that he had never married. That box was ticked in 2007 when he had a highly publicised celebrity wedding to the beautiful twenty-three-year-old daughter of one of Egypt's richest businessmen. As President Mubarak became older and sicker, Gamal was rumoured to be taking many of the daily decisions, with the help of one of a new class of oligarchs, Ahmed Ezz, a steel tycoon who had been enriched by privatisation. In Yemen, too, there was a family-succession plan. President Ali Abdullah Saleh, in power since 1978, would drop occasional hints about retirement but there was also an assumption that he would be handing over the national enterprise to his sons and family.

Many of the people who rose up against the old order in 2011 took action when they realised that not even the death of their aging despots would free them. The demonstrations were dominated by a generation of young people who were more politically conscious, more aware of the outside world and better connected to it than their parents and grandparents had been. Arab police states obsessively tracked threats to their regimes. But they could not defuse the biggest bomb of all – demography. No statistics in the Arab uprisings of 2011 were more important than those concerning population growth. The exact numbers vary from country to country, but getting on for 60 per cent of the population was under the age of thirty; sometimes the percentage was greater, sometimes it was a little less. The under-thirties were in the vanguard of all the Arab uprisings. They had been born in the 1980s, when relative prosperity and better healthcare produced a baby boom. Even in places where there was still high infant mortality, like Yemen, the population rose. By the turn of the century the Arab boomers were coming to maturity and finding a world that was not at all to their liking. They wanted their share of the national cake, but it was shrinking at a time when more people wanted a slice. The people at the top took their own huge cut, while the people further down the pecking order concluded that they could wait forever for their turn, but it would never come. By 2011 the boomers had had enough.

Economic problems powered their discontent. In 2010 world food prices rose sharply. Wheat and maize went up by a third. Food prices rose 21 per cent in Egypt in the last year or so before the uprising against Hosni Mubarak. The price of tomatoes, supposedly cheap and plentiful in season, hit almost record levels. In 2008 food prices had caused riots in twenty-eight poor countries around the world. The global problem magnified local crises. In Syria a severe drought between 2006 and 2011 ruined the livelihoods of at least one million people. Arab states subsidised some staples, but rising prices increased the pressure on people who were already discontented and close to their breaking point. As food prices went up, unemployment was also rising. The economies of many Arab countries had been hobbled by corruption and the years of under-investment. Many economies appeared to be expanding but they were not creating jobs for the new generation entering the labour market, and most of the profits went into the hands of a small elite. By the time Mubarak fell, 700,000 young people were joining Egypt's workforce every year. But only around 30,000 new jobs were available. In Tunisia around half the population was under thirty and 30 per cent of them did not have jobs. In 2011 nearly 38 per cent of young Tunisians had never been employed and 66 per cent of college graduates were still jobless eighteen months after graduation.[1]

In a small, dusty, forgotten Tunisian town called Sidi Bouzid, Muhammad Bouazizi, born in 1985, was an archetypal representative of his generation, dissatisfied by the prospect of a life that would neither make him richer nor give him enough political freedom to make him believe that he could influence his own chances. Early, incorrect reports from Tunisia, claiming that Muhammad Bouazizi was a university graduate who had been forced to sell fruit and vegetables because he could not get a job, were seized on by educated, impoverished Arabs who saw in Muhammad a mirror image of their own lives. In fact he had been forced to leave high school before he took the baccalaureate, the leaving examination, to go to work to support his family. He had no chance of getting close to university. One day in December 2010 inspectors confiscated his produce and, much more seriously for a poor trader, his cart and his weights, which were the only capital in his business. Muhammad went to the governor's offices in Sidi Bouzid and set light to himself, inflicting terrible injuries that eventually killed him. His act of rage, humiliation and frustration touched off the political storm that is still howling through the Arab world.

They felt like revolutions, even looked like them. In the narrow streets to the east of Tahrir Square, the epicentre of protest against the Egyptian regime, there is a small mosque where a first-aid station was established during the protests against President Mubarak. At the height of the stoning and brawling, men with improvised stretchers – sheets of metal, doors torn out of shops, or just linked arms – were bringing casualties in about every twenty seconds. They laid them down in the street, because the mosque had run out of space, and went back for more. The doctors carried out triage in the gutter and on the pavement, assessing who needed urgent treatment and who could be left for a while. They said the injuries were caused by shotgun pellets and knives as well as stones and clubs. One of the doctors kept working on a cut head as he talked about the patient he had just put in an ambulance, a seventeen-year-old boy with a ruptured globe, a tear in the surface of the eyeball.

I kept getting reminders, perhaps absurdly, of heroic, idealised engravings of nineteenth-century revolutionaries with their bloody dressings and their flags, flashes of the Paris commune reborn 140 years later in the narrow streets around Tahrir Square. Bandages crusty with dried blood were worn like campaign medals, left on long after they were necessary. It was a perfect revolutionary moment, unity in a city where life was often hard enough to drive people apart, as dramatic, tragic and triumphant as an opera. And there was the setting; the buildings, the backstreets around the dressing station, a rotting stage of urban revolution planted in what was once Cairo's European quarter, canyons of steep art-nouveau apartment buildings off grand avenues, balconies choked with junk behind finely wrought, broken balustrades. Every time I was in those streets in 2011, with the blood and the bandages in the spring and, later, in the autumn, when heavy clouds of teargas hung like mist, I wondered about the buildings when they were new, in the years before the First World War. That was a time when Arabs were not in revolt from the modern world but were taking steps to be part of it, when there were aspirations to parliamentary democracy and when the rich got richer by investing in their own country rather than channelling their cash into safe havens abroad that no taxman or revolutionary could ever touch. The streets they left behind around Tahrir Square were not even all that poor by the lavish standards of poverty in Mubarak's Cairo, but were still a crumbling symbol of an entire country's decay and stagnation and the dead hand of a corrupt dictatorship.

Other Arabs had their perfect revolutionary moments too. In Benghazi, only a week after the fall of Mubarak, tens of thousands of Libyans took over their city, tore down the images of their dictator, Colonel Muammar al-Gaddafi, and took up arms to drive him out of the rest of the country. Others believed they were changing their countries, until the forces of the old order reasserted themselves and made it into a war of attrition. In Bahrain protestors tried to create their own Tahrir, at the Pearl Roundabout in Manama, until they were driven out. Yemenis in Sana'a, the capital, set up a tented village outside the university, which they called Change Square, and stayed there even after they were attacked. Photographs of people killed in the protests, revolutionary martyrs, were everywhere. In Benghazi they took up an entire wall of the courthouse.

They died not because they wanted to be part of a Pan-Arab revolutionary movement – there wasn't one – but because they wanted to change their own lives, and those of their families, for the better. Most Arabs are nationalists. They identify strongly with their own countries. It is a mistake to try to find much in common between what happened in, say, Libya in North Africa, and Yemen in southern Arabia. Every country had its own reasons for discontent. Revolutionary politics are local. But the idea that the people could bring down the regime spread much more easily through a part of the world that shared a language and culture. Arabs can disagree, sometimes violently, with their neighbours. But authoritarian governments create the same kind of problems, so when they took to the streets they called for the same kinds of change, chanting slogans against regimes that oppressed and humiliated them, demanding freedom and justice and an end to corruption. Some eminent Arab thinkers have declared that the uprisings in 2011 were not fully fledged revolutions because a settled new order has not yet emerged. It is true that the job has not been finished, and in some parts of the region it has barely started. But I like the word revolution, because there is no going back to what there was before. The process of change continues. A revolution has happened in the thinking of people in Libya, Syria, Egypt, Bahrain and Yemen, and it is brewing elsewhere. A man in Tahrir Square summed it up when I suggested that a hard future lay ahead.

'We've got problems,' he said. 'But we know – and the government and the army know – that if everything else fails we know the way back to Tahrir Square. We will not stand for another dictatorship.'

*

In 2011 millions of Arabs decided that they had wasted enough time being oppressed, frightened and excluded in their own countries, and finally called time on their dictatorships. It was hard to believe that deeply unpopular regimes had started out with a lot of popular support, in a wave of what were called revolutions in the Middle East after the Second World War. In the late forties and early fifties the Arab world was in ferment, reeling after the humiliating failure to destroy the new Israeli state. Britain and France, the imperial powers in the region, were in decline. There was an opportunity and it was grabbed by military officers who seized power and made big promises about a new age of Arab glory. They did not deliver, but concentrated power in the hands of a few and started to build the regimes that the people finally lost patience with in 2011.

In the fifties, just as in 2011, what happened in Egypt was crucial. In 1952 Egyptians were directing their rage and humiliation at the British, who were retreating from their Middle Eastern Empire but still in control of the Suez Canal Zone.[2] Egypt was at the centre of the storm because it was the state that most influenced other Arabs. It had more people and its politics and culture set the tone for the whole region. By the last weekend of January 1952 strikes and riots gripped the country. The prime minister, who was a nationalist, abrogated the treaty allowing Britain to base troops in the Canal Zone. The interior minister went one stage further, urging the Muslim Brotherhood to use force against the British occupiers. Forty-six Egyptian police were killed and seventy-two wounded in a shootout after they refused to surrender their police station to the British army in Ismailia in the Canal Zone.[3] The next day furious crowds filled the same elegant boulevards in central Cairo near Tahrir Square that were the epicentre of the uprising in 2011, and set about burning down all the symbols of British power and the Western way of life they had transplanted to Cairo. The offices of Thomas Cook were torched, so were cinemas; the Shepheard hotel, with its famous terrace and a men-only bar that was a home from home for the British officer class, was burnt to the ground. Other targets included Groppi's, an elegant cafe where the British, as well as the Egyptian elite, liked to have tea and cakes, along with dozens of other restaurants and bars. The turmoil opened the way to a coup d'état later in the year by a group of young military officers, led by Colonel Gamal Abdel Nasser. They overthrew the king and, in the next few years, delivered British imperialism a mortal blow at Suez in 1956, made an alliance with the Soviet Union and became the standard bearers of Pan-Arabism, a dream of unity that never materialized. There was a short-lived union of Egypt and Syria, and attempts by Nasser to overturn the established order by overthrowing the West's Arab allies in Jordan, Iraq, Saudi Arabia and Lebanon. In the turmoil the Iraqi royal family was overthrown and slaughtered, and to stop the contagion Britain sent the Parachute Regiment and a Royal Artillery unit to Jordan and US Marines landed on Lebanon's Mediterranean beaches. By 1958 the Arab world seemed to be on the brink of historic change, just like in 2011; but, as the historian Avi Shlaim says: 'history failed to turn'.[4]

Instead Arab states settled into a long period of authoritarian rule, led by the men who had come to power in uniform. Claims were made that a uniquely Arab form of socialism would restore the region to the place it deserved to be in the world. In Arab capitals from Baghdad to Cairo you can still see some of the architecture from that heroic, deceiving time: white walls and sharp edges rotting slowly next to the crumbling buildings left by European imperialists. Their boasts that they had created a new age of Arab power were crushed in 1967 with another Israeli victory in another war. In desperation Nasser's Egyptian regime, which had led the Arabs into another military disaster, lied to the people that it was winning until the truth became impossible to hide. By then, Pan-Arabism was already dead and after the Israeli victory even secular nationalism began to be questioned. The answers coming from the mosques were increasingly compelling for a generation that did not want any more humiliation. The idea that Islam was the solution to the Arab world's decline had been around since the nineteenth century but after 1967 it began to move into the mainstream. Since political parties that opposed authoritarian regimes were not allowed to operate, the mosques had the priceless advantage of often being the only places where it was possible for a group of people to get together and talk without breaking the law.

Political Islamists, often in prison cells as well as mosques, had long-running, bitter debates about the right way ahead. At the most extreme end, by the 1980s Arab jihadists were trying to find quick and violent ways to unseat regimes they believed were ungodly. Iran had its Islamic revolution and they wanted one too. But other Islamists, like those in the Muslim Brotherhood, which started in Egypt and spread abroad, were playing a long game, building support through providing education and healthcare, nurturing communities who over years grew to trust them. The Islamists' other big virtue for many – which really mattered when free votes became possible – was that they were not usually corrupt. The contrast with the people in and around the old regimes could not have been greater.

Nasser died in 1970, having been hugely popular on the streets until the very end – even though he had led the Arabs to the catastrophic defeat by Israel in 1967. A year before Nasser's death he was still influential enough to inspire a young officer who wanted to take over his country in the way that Nasser had seized Egypt in 1952. The officer's name was Muammar al-Gaddafi, and, with a group of his contemporaries from Libya's military academy, he overthrew King Idris. Among his first acts was to demand, successfully, that the United States and Britain give up their bases. Gaddafi was a devotee of Nasser's until his own death. Right until his downfall in 2011, Libyan state television would show black-and-white pictures of the young and skinny Gaddafi being congratulated by Nasser, the man who had defied the West. Nasser's death brought Egypt to a grief-stricken standstill. Among the Arab leaders who came to Cairo to pay his respects was a member of the Syrian military junta, Hafez al-Assad.

The death of Nasser, who had dominated the Arab world since he took on the British and French at Suez in 1956, must have been a sign to Assad that it was time for a younger generation to make its move. He returned to Damascus from the funeral and seized sole power. His first visitor was Colonel Gaddafi. When Assad went to meet him at the airport, apparently he quipped, 'It's a good thing you didn't arrive half an hour earlier.'[5] Gaddafi had been in the air while Assad was finishing the statement announcing that he was the new man in charge. The young men of 1970 and their anointed successors were still holding power when Muhammad Bouazizi immolated himself.

The Arab authoritarians who dominated the region from the 1950s to the first decade of the twenty-first century had a tacit deal with the people. The state would provide jobs and cheap food and fuel, and in return the people would not complain about the absence of freedom or demand the right to change their leader. If they did, the growing, pervasive and vicious police state would show them where they had gone wrong. The regime's challengers could expect a painful incarceration and perhaps an early death. A grand network of subsidies and patronage, which descended deeper into corruption every year, developed alongside the apparatus of coercion and repression in Arab police states. They were equal halves of the same system of control. Countries lucky enough to have oil, like in Libya, Iraq and the Gulf, could pay the bills themselves. Others relied on their powerful superpower patrons.

The Middle East was one of the most important battlegrounds in the Cold War, which meant that the United States and the Soviet Union competed for influence and supplied weapons as well as cash and political support to their clients. After the collapse of the Soviet Union, the Americans were the dominant foreign player in the region. Western countries did not write the old rules in the Arab world, but the rules lasted as long as they did because they suited the West. The most powerful countries in the world found it useful to have some rough friends to police an unstable but highly strategic place. Stability in the Middle East was a price worth paying in broken heads, torn-out fingernails and the denial of basic freedoms. The United States and the British and their Western friends forgot their scruples about the rule of law and the representation of the people because they reckoned that with allies like the Mubaraks and, eventually, the Gaddafis, and others, their enemies would be taken care of nicely. Secular leaders from the military took up the fight against political Islam with relish and this suited the Americans, who were haunted by the humiliations inflicted on them by Iranian revolutionaries. It seemed even more vital after the 9/11 attacks by al-Qaeda on the United States to have Arab friends who could take jihadist movements on, perhaps infiltrate them, and promise to destroy them. It was not just easy for America, Britain and their Western allies to turn a blind eye to the repression and brutality perpetrated by their Arab friends. It was necessary and useful.

Jihadist suspects were captured and even abducted under a programme that was given the euphemistic name of 'extraordinary rendition', and were sent to Arab countries where there were none of the tiresome legal constraints that made life difficult in Western democracies. A former CIA agent called Robert Baer said, 'If you want a serious interrogation, you send a prisoner to Jordan. If you want them to be tortured, you send them to Syria. If you want someone to disappear – never to see them again – you send them to Egypt.'[6] Jordan and Egypt were American allies. Syria was not. But accepting a suspect was an easy way for President Bashar al-Assad to do the Americans a covert favour, and perhaps open up a channel of communication. In 2002 a Canadian-Syrian businessman called Maher Arar was detained at Kennedy Airport in New York then deported to Damascus, where he was tortured and detained for a year. No Arab state had a more brutal or ruthless police state than Syria's, but cooperation on some security matters helped to develop an idea that the country was a potential ally. For a short time it was a Western pariah after a UN investigation leaked suggestions that the regime of

President Bashar al-Assad might have been responsible for a huge bomb that killed the former Lebanese prime minister Rafik Hariri in Beirut in 2005. But in a world of realpolitik, Syria's pivotal position in the region meant that only a few years later President Assad could choose from a dance card of Western suitors. They had concluded that he could unlock peace in the Middle East as long as he dropped his friends in Iran and Hezbollah, the powerful Lebanese Shia militia that had fought Israel to a standstill in 2006.

In Libya Colonel Gaddafi was a bogeyman for years, condemned and sanctioned for funding and perpetrating attacks on Western targets. Persuading him in 2003 to pay compensation to the victims of the Lockerbie attack, and to give up Libya's attempts to build weapons of mass destruction, was seen, rightly, as a big success for British and American diplomacy. But no attempt was made to make him change the repressive and violent policies that were at the heart of his regime, or to trade Western help for political reform. Instead Gaddafi's prison system was incorporated into the extraordinary-rendition network, and suspects were sent to Tripoli for what they said was torture.

Egypt's Hosni Mubarak had another important role, as a heat shield for Arab – especially Palestinian – anger against the Israelis. Whenever the Palestinian-Israeli conflict heated up, Palestinian leaders would be dispatched, with Western approval, for pep talks in Cairo. Mahmoud Abbas, the Palestinian president, became so dependent on his trips to see his friend President Mubarak that he attempted to defend him when protestors occupied Tahrir Square. Perhaps it was commendable loyalty, but it put the Palestinian president further out of step with his people.

The US and Britain and other Western powers tailored their policies towards the Middle East to their broader needs. They forgot their opposition to political Islam when it came to Saudi Arabia, which is a strict Islamist state. The Oxford University academic Tariq Ramadan pointed out that the Western allies' desire to court Saudi Arabia showed they could set aside their suspicion about political Islamism if it suited their economic interests.[7] It was not just a question of buying oil. Saudi Arabia was a huge market for Western weapons, and the Saudi ruling family saw al-Qaeda as their enemy too.

Middle East dictators had their uses for America, Britain and their Western friends. Politicians and diplomats, on the rare occasions on which they were questioned about the company they were keeping, would argue that they had to be realistic and pragmatic, clear-sighted and not at all naïve about the realities of one of the toughest parts of the world. When the excesses of regimes were too egregious to ignore, some mild criticism might emerge; but this did not affect the core of the relationship. They realised what they were doing. Condoleezza Rice, then US secretary of state, summed it up in a reproachful speech in Cairo in 2005.

> For sixty years, my country, the United States, pursued stability at the expense of democracy in this region, here in the Middle East, and we achieved neither [...] Throughout the Middle East the fear of free choices can no longer justify the denial of liberty. It is time to abandon the excuses that are made to avoid the hard work of democracy.

It was all too little too late for its intended audience. The invasion of Iraq in 2003 had contaminated anything the Bush administration would ever want to say about the Middle East in the eyes of most of its Arab residents. Anyway, the Americans soon pulled back from the high noon of Dr Rice's rhetoric. Less than a year later supporters of President Bush's so-called 'freedom agenda' realised that offering Arabs unsupervised democracy could be dangerous. They might vote for the wrong candidates. On a freezing winter day at the beginning of 2006, Palestinian elections produced a victory for Hamas, the Islamic Resistance Movement, over the pro-Western secular Palestinian nationalists in Fatah. President Bush had refused pleas by the

Israelis and the Fatah Palestinians to postpone the election, which was signed off as fair by the European Union. Elections, it seemed, were all very well unless they produced the wrong government. Hamas refused to accept a demand to stop using violence and recognise Israel, and was sent into isolation. Not long after Dr Rice's speech about democracy, a very senior American diplomat sat back in his chair in the State Department in Washington and told me cheerfully that 'of course our top objective is getting that Palestinian election overturned'.

Years of Western support for Arab autocrats meant that millions of Arabs considered Europeans and Americans to be part of their problem. That feeling was magnified enormously by the invasion of Iraq and its disastrous fallout. Western policies helped prepare the ground for political extremism in the region. Even among well-educated, Westernised, secular intellectuals in Arab countries there was more or less a consensus that the West, led by America and Britain, was waging a war on Muslims in Iraq and Afghanistan. When friends of the West, especially President Mubarak, were sent packing, millions of Arabs believed that their enemies in the West had been struck a serious blow.

The late-afternoon British Airways 747 to Cairo on Wednesday 26 January 2011 did not feel like a flight into a revolution, but it was. Wealthy Egyptians were heading home with carrier bags from London's top stores. A few pale-faced British tourists were flying out to look for the sun, and Egypt's antiquities, some of them dressed in light clothes and sandals that they would regret in the chilly late-winter evenings in Cairo. Across the aisle an old man was on his way to the grave of his brother, who had died in Egypt as a child in the 1930s. He hadn't managed it while he had been a soldier there during the Second World War, so now the man's wife and daughter were taking him for a last nostalgic trip. And there were a few reporters and camera crews – the only sign that something was not quite normal.

The Middle East had been having its usual disproportionate share of wars since 2006 – Gaza and Iraq were running sores – but much of the region had been full of fires that smouldered but rarely blazed. Political problems would not go away but were being deferred or evaded, never resolved. It meant that the region was tense, and most people in the Middle East had a life that, while being perhaps a little quieter, was no more secure or relaxed. There wasn't much for a reporter to witness. Television journalists need drama and strong stories in order to connect with their audiences. Convincing programme editors, let alone the people at home, that they needed to care about what happened in the Middle East was getting harder. I thought at the very start of the year that the most likely flashpoints in the next twelve months would be in Yemen, where the local affiliate of al-Qaeda was assertive and ambitious, and that Israel might go through with its threats to attack Iran's nuclear installations.

But that Wednesday Egypt was the obvious place to go for the journalists on board the plane. The previous day Cairo had been brought to a halt by a huge demonstration against President Hosni Mubarak's regime. For a while, the people had even occupied Tahrir Square, the centre of Cairo and the symbolic key to control of the city. While the British Airways cabin crew brought smiles and glasses of wine, protestors in Cairo were trying to reignite the streets. The Interior Ministry warned that they would be met with force. Thousands of riot policemen were deployed across strategic parts of the city, at junctions, at places that could be used as rallying points and on the bridges across the Nile. It was not the first time that the regime had faced crowds of protestors, but it was bigger and more significant than usual because twelve days earlier Tunisian revolutionaries had set Arab minds racing by deposing their hated president, Zine al-Abidine Ben Ali, not even a month after the start of the popular uprising that followed Muhammad Bouazizi's attempt to burn himself to death.

It was going to be a remarkable year. But that afternoon I couldn't see it. I was out of love with journalism, full of New Year blues on the flight to Cairo, and expecting to be home by the weekend. President Mubarak's police state just seemed to be too strong. Surely it couldn't crumble in the way that Ben Ali's regime had in Tunisia? The fractured Egyptian opposition was planning a big anti-Mubarak demonstration for the coming Friday. I was expecting it to be crushed. I thought the demonstration might not even sustain a whole piece, so I planned to try to join the dots – comparing what had happened in Tunisia and what might happen elsewhere. All the twenty-two Arab states were different, but ideas crossed borders between them, powered by social media and television, especially al-Jazeera. The Egyptian police state, I reckoned, had been taken by surprise by the protests the day before. By Friday the hard end of the Mubarak regime would be ready. The police and the riot squads and the regime's plain-clothes thugs would not make the same mistake twice.

The wife of the old man across the aisle on the plane adjusted his blankets. I told his daughter not to worry. A flurry was coming on Friday, a few broken heads perhaps, but their trip should be fine as long as they stayed away from the centre of Cairo. The country was not about to erupt. President Mubarak's opponents had tried to make it happen before, and the same thing always occurred. They got squashed. The power of the Egyptian state was ugly – and depressing for anyone who believed in freedom – but it was at the very least predictable.

On that flight I had not grasped the size of what was starting, not just in Cairo but in the year to come, on the revolutionary roadshow of the Arabs in Libya, Bahrain, Yemen and Syria. Perhaps I would have had a better sense of it had I been covering the Tunisian revolution. But I had missed the fall of Ben Ali in Tunis on 14 January because I was testifying against the ex-leader of the Bosnian Serbs, Radovan Karadžić at the former-Yugoslavia war-crimes tribunal in The Hague. For the best part of two days I was cross-examined by Karadžić himself, thinner than in Bosnia, less ebullient, his extravagant politeness failing to cover up his contempt for anyone who dared to challenge his version of history. He was on trial for genocide, persecution, extermination, murder, deportation, hostage-taking and terror. I caught glimpses of the Tunisian revolution on TV as I was escorted back and forth to the witness box. But in court the Arab tumult faded away, obscured by my first journalistic love, Sarajevo and its ghosts, the city of bullets and shells, the indomitable, the villainous and the dead. The tribunal had helped to set a precedent that national leaders might have to account for what they had done in court, and the Karadžić trial was my third time in the witness box in The Hague.

Still, it did not occur to me that the legal principle of accountability would ever be applied to Arab leaders. Apart from anything else, too many of them were too useful to powerful Western countries. But within two months Muammar al-Gaddafi, the Brother Leader and guide of the Libyan Revolution, the man who had been embraced by Tony Blair and kissed by Silvio Berlusconi, would be charged with crimes against humanity. He never had his day in court, thanks to the Libyan fighters who captured and killed him with the brutality his regime had meted out thousands of times and then put his body put on display in a walk-in fridge so the people had proof the monster was dead. By the summer Hosni Mubarak was on trial for his life for corruption and ordering the killing of protestors, wheeled into a cage in a Cairo court in a hospital bed, alongside his sons and some of his henchmen. Many Egyptians were disgusted when the court gave him a life sentence and not execution. Ex-president Ben Ali, his wife and key members of his family were put on trial, in absentia, in Tunisia. He was safe in exile in Saudi Arabia, but was also given life, for his part in the killing of demonstrators.

Ten months after that flight into the Egyptian revolution I sat at a tea stall in Tahrir Square with a man called Wael Abbas to try to work out why 2011 had turned into the most dramatic year in the modern history of the Arab people, and why opponents of Mubarak and the others had broken through when in the past they couldn't. It was a bright day in late November and demonstrations and street battles had started again in Cairo. Egypt's revolution was not going the way that the revolutionaries had hoped. A couple of hundred yards away, at the other end of the square, teargas was drifting out of Muhammad Mahmoud Street, where protestors were fighting police riot squads. Ambulances pushed out through the crowds, lights flashing, sirens screaming. Wael Abbas is one of Egypt's best-known and most sensible bloggers. We were balancing on rickety plastic stools opposite the museum where Egypt keeps the treasures of its pharaohs, on a stretch of road that Cairo's street vendors were trying to turn into the revolution's food court. Men dressed in grubby robes and white turbans roasted sweet potatoes in wood-burning ovens made from oil drums. Corn popped in glass-sided carts, sinister-looking liver sandwiches turned up their edges and *kusheri*, my favourite Egyptian fast food (a mess of rice, lentils and pasta topped with fried onions and a spicy tomato sauce), was being ladled into tubs. The operator of a rival tea stall across the way arranged a bunch of fresh green mint in a jar, flicking drops of water on to it from a bottle. He held the mint out and inspected it. It must have still looked too dusty to float in a glass of strong, sweet Egyptian tea. So he took a big swig of water, and sprayed it out of his mouth over the leaves. He repeated the process a couple of times, producing a fine high-pressure jet from his pursed lips until he was satisfied that the mint had been given a good enough rinse.

A mental note never to buy a glass of mint tea from that stallholder spluttered its way into my head, along with a metaphor for the tarnished revolutionary hopes of the Spring. Plenty of people in Tahrir Square were feeling as if someone had been spitting all over their revolution. Back on 11 February, when President Hosni Mubarak resigned from office, hundreds of thousands of Egyptians in the square had been filled with joy by the power and beauty of what they had done, a political event that seemed to them to be as perfect as anything in nature. So much euphoria was always going to cause some kind of hangover when their world, inevitably, failed to change fast enough. By the time I met Wael for that glass of tea, the revolutionaries were despairing. The future of Egypt was looking more and more as if it was going to be a struggle between Islamists and the military. That was not what so many hysterically happy people in Tahrir Square had been expecting on 11 February.

Wael and I were getting occasional whiffs of teargas from the other end of the square, but I was less interested in what was going wrong a few hundred yards away than in working out where it had all begun. One starting point was the way that the internet was changing everyone's lives. Wael Abbas was one of the first Egyptians, one of the first in the Arab world, to recognise that the internet had the power to outmanoeuvre a police state and to amplify and magnify public outrage, and to help them recognise that other countries did not do things the same way. Another kind of life had to be possible, Wael said, because they could see it existed elsewhere.

'I felt there was something wrong with the country. It's not like we see and hear in other countries, in European or American movies, when you see people throwing stones and tomatoes and eggs at the officials, and swearing at the president and criticizing the government and we don't have the same here. That was my impression as a child.

'I started late 2004. I found that I could publish as much as I want, as much text as I want. I can post videos, I can receive comments from the people about what I write, their opinion, their reactions, so it wasn't reactive [...] You could have instant interaction.'

I suggested that this meant he could also have instant interaction with the security police. His answer showed how slow they had been to recognise the threat that came from the internet.

'Back then they were not really that active. They didn't take the internet seriously. They didn't take us seriously. They thought that we were some kids in pyjamas sitting in their bedrooms and trying to say smart stuff and talking to people of our kind and we had no audience. But then they started taking us seriously once we took to the streets, once we organised [...] Because bloggers in Egypt are different than those in anywhere else. I always said we had one foot in the street and the other on the internet.'

But Wael Abbas and Egypt's other internet pioneers were creating a new politics of protest with their computers. The regime took them very seriously after they scored a rare and early victory against the regime of President Hosni Mubarak in 2006. It was much more than a hint that the regime was not immutable. It was a sign that there were cracks inside the edifice of his power that could be widened. The bloggers' first victory happened because brutal and arrogant local policemen, puffed up by years of impunity and the belief that they could get away with whatever they wanted, had made a video of them torturing Imad Kabir, a twenty-one-year-old minibus driver they had arrested at a bus stop. Back at the station one of them used his phone to film Imad being sodomised with a broomstick. The police attacked him after they had stripped him from the waist down, tied his feet together and hoisted them into the air so that only his back was touching the ground. On the video you can see his agony, fear and humiliation, and hear the panic as he screams, 'No, *pasha*, no', and begs them to stop. The police not only did not stop. They distributed the video in Imad Kabir's home patch, a scruffy neighbourhood not far from central Cairo, as a warning to others. Boasting about their own brutality has been a common tactic by the internal security forces in Arab states, known usually by the generic term 'mukhabarat', for many years. The Syria security services under the Assad regime made a habit of returning the mutilated corpses of people they had tortured to death to the bereaved families. Across the region the men who were hired to keep regimes in power wanted their subjects to know what they were capable of doing, and to come to the right conclusions about the way to behave in the future.

The tactic worked well when it was a matter of intimidating small, relatively defenceless groups of people, like the minibus drivers who worked with Imad Kabir, who would then have even more reasons to pay bribes to the police. But the equation changed once the video that the police had so arrogantly taken to Imad's colleagues was uploaded to the web and shared, and shared again, because the more people who saw it the more the anger grew. Everyone knew that torture was routine in Egyptian police stations. It was a major reason why the police were held in such contempt and usually they could get away with it. But a video of torture by sexual assault, complete with close-ups of the agonised face of the victim, put the authorities under such pressure that eventually they had to react, and two policemen ended up in jail.

The scandal surrounding the video was part of the drip feed of discontent that led to revolution in Egypt. Before 2011 there had always been Egyptians who opposed the regime openly but there were never enough of them to shake it, let alone bring it down. Groups of middle-class intellectuals formed political groups, the most prominent of which was the Egyptian Movement for Change, known by its Arabic slogan *Kifaya,* which means 'enough'. I went to some of its demonstrations in Cairo after it emerged in the run-up to the 2005 presidential election. Activists, often dozens rather than hundreds, would try to assemble, vastly outnumbered by squads of riot police, then if they were lucky they would have a few minutes of chanting in front of the TV cameras before they were carted off. But Kifaya and the other groups never built a significant political base, slid into internal political bickering and most importantly of all failed to find a way to work with the Muslim Brotherhood, the most significant mass movement in Egypt outside the regime. The Brotherhood had the numbers to threaten the regime. But it was conservative, working within a system in which it was officially illegal in the hope that the time would come when they could transform Egypt into an Islamist state.

Some Egyptians had a proud tradition of standing up against President Mubarak's regime. But the power of the police state had always prevailed. What changed in 2011 was the formation of a critical mass that was too big to be intimidated on its way to sweeping President Mubarak aside. The Tunisians led the way, Wael believed.

'It gave people courage to do something similar. Because they saw that it was possible. Other people did it. This small country that beats us in football, in African tournaments, has removed its president. Why the hell can't we do that? Let's do it. And they did it.'

And Arabs in every other part of the Middle East and North Africa were watching what was happening in Egypt live on television, and seeing no reason why they couldn't try to do the same thing.

When I did my first trip to the Middle East after Iraq invaded Kuwait in 1990 I heard some reporters with a lot more experience saying that Arabs like a strong leader. Apparently that trait explained the survival of the likes of Saddam Hussein, even though they imprisoned and often killed their subjects. I realised almost straight away that despots ruled through violence and fear, and that the notion that Arabs liked it was absurd, but I am ashamed to admit that the line might have crept into a few scripts before my brain kicked in. Another colleague, an experienced man lecturing a greenhorn, told me when I moved to Jerusalem to be the BBC Middle East correspondent in 1995 that my timing was perfect. Not only was there going to be peace between the Israelis and the Palestinians, but also the generation of Arab autocrats who had emerged in the sixties and seventies was getting old. Change was coming – it was ripening; you could feel it – and I would have the privilege of watching them bring in the harvest. Some hope. The Israelis and the Palestinians did not make peace, and Arab political life sank deeper a repressive malaise. The only dynamism came from some kinds of political Islam. President Mubarak gave up Egypt's position as the Arab world's natural leader in favour of his version of stability, a brutal, corrupt stagnation that allowed him to stay the West and Israel's best Arab friend, especially when he fought jihadists.

And Arabs, after all, liked and needed a strong leader. Everyone knew that. Westerners lapped up stories about their toughness. Over the years I heard plenty about the guile of Arab autocrats, like the story about the first President Assad plying an American secretary of state with endless glasses of sweet tea during marathon diplomatic talks and then relentlessly continuing the negotiation without bathroom breaks.

But guile counts for nothing when the people lose their patience, and then lose their fear. Leaders were toppled – or, as I write, are fighting for survival (literally, not just politically) – because a younger generation of Arabs realised that the old systems were offering nothing to compensate them for their lack of freedom. Don't forget that 60 per cent of Arabs were under the age of thirty. Cutting up the existing cake was no longer an option. It wasn't big enough and the wrong people were counting the slices.

It was always wrong to think that change in the Arab world would be easy or quick, or would turn brutal autocracies into the Netherlands or Spain overnight. Some of the dissident elite, who Western reporters like to interview, often educated in the West and as comfortable in English as they are in Arabic, might have wanted their countries to be more like the EU. But the way that Arabs have voted in their millions for Islamist parties when they have had the chance suggests that plenty of them have no desire whatever to fall in behind the dreams of Western liberals. They have decided that the best choice available to them is religion, as expressed by political Islam. By the end of 2011 even those who hoped the Arab world could model itself on Turkey were getting to be disappointed. Since the election in 2002 of Prime Minister Recep Tayyip Erdogan, an Islamist who was also a democrat, Turkey had turned round its economy and transformed its relations with Europe and the Arab world. Egypt was supposed to be the best candidate to be an Arab Turkey, but a year after the fall of President Mubarak it was submerged in the consequences of an unfinished revolution. Syria was close to outright civil war. The weak central government in Libya was struggling to deal with its fractious, heavily armed tribes and city states.

In 2011 we were also shown how much influence the United States and its Western allies had lost since the hubris of catastrophic invasion of Iraq in 2003. The US still had enormous wealth and military power. But when it was confronted with the challenges of the Arab uprisings it realised how few answers it had, and how much leverage it had lost. Since the 1950s it had poured power and cash into creating a Middle East that was as far as possible politically compliant, as keen to sell oil to the US and its friends as they were to buy it, a land where Israel would face no unanswerable threats. After the Egyptian people rose up against President Mubarak, the Americans lost their best Arab friend and became spectators in a headlong political dash to a new future.

If 2011 was a year of revolution, 2012 showed that the revolutions were still unfinished. The huge drama of the spring had turned into a long and sometimes bloody slog. Some of the change that had looked so definitive in February and March now seemed to be only half the story, as in many places old political, military and economic elites still had power and influence. But at the same time the region changed irreversibly. Arab people, in huge numbers, decided that they should have the big say in their own futures. A new habit of public protest was learnt. Fear still exists in plenty of places. But it is no longer an effective weapon. Arabs have rediscovered the power of crowds, and the slogan about the people wanting the fall of the regime has not been retired. As someone in Cairo said to me, 'We still know the way to Tahrir Square.'

The Arab world has had some seismic moments in the last century or so. The first came after the Great War, when Britain and France carved up the Ottoman Empire in the Middle East and drew the borders of the region's modern states. The next big upheaval came when British and French imperialism waned after the Second World War, when Israel was created and inflicted such a severe defeat on its Arab neighbours that they were plunged into a decade and a half of revolutions and coups. Israel's victory in the 1967 war with the Arabs ended with Jewish rule over all of Jerusalem, and twisted the most intractable conflict in the region into a new, even more painful shape. The new revolutions that started in 2011 will have consequences that are at least as significant, and it might take a generation for a new equilibrium to emerge. The Middle East is being remade.

1

REVOLUTION

M uhammad Sakher al-Materi was proud of losing weight. Ever since he had married the daughter of the president of Tunisia, and his business career had taken off, he had struggled with the temptations of the table. For a twenty-eight-year-old, he had been getting tubby. But Muhammad had a gym built in his house, and liked to work out – which was only wise, considering the skills of their chef. On 17 July 2009 the Materi kitchen was in overdrive, because Muhammad and his wife, Nesrine, were having an important dinner. The American ambassador to Tunisia and his wife were coming. The chef was preparing around a dozen dishes, including turkey, octopus, and a special fish couscous. For dessert there was going to be ice cream and frozen yoghurt that Muhammad had brought in on his private jet from St Tropez, as well as blueberries, raspberries and chocolate cake. Not bad for a man still on the right side of thirty. While Muhammad was in the gym his staff were burnishing the house, a freshly renovated white villa in Hammamet, one of Tunisia's best-known beach resorts. The architect had included touches echoing the history of the town. Roman columns were set into the walls of the villa's clean, modern lines and water gurgled from the gaping mouth of a stone lion's head into the infinity pool. The house was at the centre of a compound guarded by government security men, so Muhammad, Nesrine and their friends didn't have to worry about unexpected visitors when they were enjoying the fifty-metre terrace overlooking the Mediterranean, or feeding Pasha, the pet tiger that had been part of the family since he was a cub only a few weeks old. Hammamet was beautiful, but not convenient for the capital. So Muhammad and Nesrine's builders were working on another seaside house, a little less modest, in the picturesque village of Sidi Bou Said, all whitewashed walls and blue shutters, on the edge of Tunis. The new house was very close to the official ambassadorial residence of Robert Godec, the guest of honour, so they were neighbours-to-be as well as a top diplomat and a prince of the ruling house.

Muhammad had plenty of good reasons to be close to Tunis. He was rich and getting richer, fortunate from the moment he had been born into a wealthy family with connections at the very top of Tunisia's business and political elite. His father was one of the country's most successful industrialists, and his uncle had been an ally of Tunisia's first president, Habib Bourguiba, in the fight for independence from France. Connections mattered in Tunisia. Without them, you didn't stand a chance. Muhammad had made the best connection of all. He had married Nesrine, the youngest daughter of Bourguiba's successor, Zine al-Abidine Ben Ali.

Later in the evening, as course after course was delivered to the dining table, his egalitarian American guests noticed there were some harsh words for the dozen or so staff, including a butler from Bangladesh and a nanny from South Africa, but Muhammad made sure that he deployed all his charm towards the ambassador's wife, who was disabled. He seems to have wanted to be thought of as a man who made an effort to get on with people less lucky than he had been in life's lottery – a rare quality in Tunisia's aloof ruling family, though there were limits when it came to the servants. The young hosts declared how they loved America. Nesrine was devoted to Disney World, but she had put off a trip earlier in the year because of the fear of a global pandemic of bird flu. Muhammad had just got back from the States, where he had been to Illinois to buy another plane.

When they moved on to business Muhammad told the

ambassador that he would be glad to help McDonald's establish itself in Tunisia, though as a newly minted enthusiast for the gym he pointed out that fast food was making Americans fat. When the ambassador asked whether his host had any ideas he could pass on to the White House for the newly inaugurated president, Barack Obama, the conversation moved on to the environment. Muhammad said that his wife liked to keep their family projects as green as possible. She wanted everything in the new house in Sidi Bou Said, even the paint and varnish, to be organic.

After the dinner Ambassador Godec was amused, appalled and intrigued enough by what he had seen to write a cable that was sent back under the heading 'Secret' to the State Department in Washington.[1] One of the ambassador's previous jobs had been to work on the transition of power in Iraq after the Americans and their allies overthrew Saddam Hussein in the 2003 invasion. Pasha the tiger, in his cage in the Materis' garden, living on four chickens a day, reminded him of the lion that Uday, Saddam's notoriously sadistic eldest son, kept in his garden in Baghdad. The families of Arab leaders often had a liking for unusual, sometimes carnivorous pets. Saadi al-Gaddafi in Libya also had lions. His brother Saif al-Arab was on his way back into his house from feeding his antelopes when it was flattened by a NATO air raid in April 2011. He was killed by a collapsing wall.[2]

The ambassador's report of the dinner party linked the excesses of the Tunisian ruling class with growing discontent in the country. The house in Hammamet was 'over the top', and there was enough food 'for a very large number of guests'. Materi was 'clearly aware of his wealth and power, and his actions reflected little finesse. He repeatedly pointed out the lovely view from his home and frequently corrected his staff, issued orders and barked reprimands.' Ambassador Godec concluded that the Materis were living 'in the midst of great wealth and excess, illustrating one reason resentment of President Ben Ali's in-laws was growing'.

The point about the in-laws was crucial. Some Arab autocrats, like Hosni Mubarak in Egypt, encouraged economic reforms, especially privatisations, and used them to enrich a whole class of their fellow countrymen, giving them a big stake in the survival of the regime that had given them access to an orchard of money trees. But Ben Ali liked to support family business, which meant the business of his own family. By 2011 some estimates said that half of the Tunisian economy was in the hands of his family, and that of his second wife, Leila Trabelsi.

Ambassador Godec was well aware of the wealth and corruption of President Ben Ali's extended family before he accepted the invitation to the dinner in Hammamet. Just under a month earlier, on 23 June, he had composed a cable he called 'Corruption in Tunisia: What's Yours is Mine'.[3] The ambassador wrote that 'corruption in Tunisia is getting worse. Whether it's cash, services, land, property, or yes, even your yacht, President Ben Ali's family is rumored to covet it and reportedly gets what it wants.' Not only did the president, his wife and their large extended families control huge sections of the economy, but they had also put themselves above the law. The Ben Alis, he said, were often regarded as a 'quasi-mafia', with two of the president's nephews on one occasion brazenly stealing a yacht belonging to a prominent French businessman. One of the ambassador's sources 'lamented that Tunisia was no longer a police state, it had become a state run by the mafia. "Even the police report to the Family!" he exclaimed. With those at the top believed to be the worst offenders, and likely to remain in power, there are no checks in the system.' Corruption was stopping Tunisians investing in their own country, which weakened an economy that suffered from endemic unemployment, and it was fuelling unrest. Protests in a mining region were a symptom of discontent that was buried under the surface. The government had based its legitimacy on delivering economic growth, but a growing number of Tunisians believed the people at the top were keeping the benefits for themselves.

Ambassador Godec's cables provide an icily accurate and remarkably prescient analysis of Tunisia and its leader. If Godec's political masters in Washington, DC, had paid it more attention the United States and its allies might not have been as blindsided as they were when the revolution started in Tunisia. In the cable sent on the day he had dinner with Muhammad Sakher al-Materi, Ambassador Godec wrote that Ben Ali and his regime:

> . . . have lost touch with the Tunisian people. They tolerate no advice or criticism, whether domestic or international. Increasingly, they rely on the police for control and focus on preserving power. And, corruption in the inner circle is growing. Even average Tunisians are now keenly aware of it, and the chorus of complaints is rising. Tunisians intensely dislike, even hate, First Lady Leila Trabelsi and her family. In private, regime opponents mock her; even those close to the government express dismay[4] at her reported behavior. Meanwhile, anger is growing at Tunisia's high unemployment and regional inequities. As a consequence, the risks to the regime's long-term stability are increasing.

When the patience of the Tunisian people snapped a few of them took hairdryers to demonstrations to mock Leila's old job as a hairdresser, which she did until she married and set about making the people she loved seriously rich. Her only competition for the position of most hated person in the country was her brother, Belhassen Trabelsi. He was believed to be a billionaire, with businesses that included banking, airlines, radio and television, construction and the local Ford dealership. After the revolution the Trabelsis' houses were looted and burnt. Dozens of videos are on the internet showing people wandering in and out of the houses, carrying pieces of furniture, marble sinks, cooking hobs, and strange pieces of junk that took their fancy. Cars were left burning in their garages, garbage was thrown into the swimming pools. Someone found a stash of Belhassen's family videos and put them on the web too. Viewers can watch Belhassen's wife giving us a tour of a holiday home, from kitchens where retainers were grilling lamb chops and making salads to the family table where she teases her husband about his weight, zooming in on his multiple chins and his expansive belly spilling over the waistband of expensive beach shorts as he reaches for another glass of wine.

The corrupt way in which the ruling family had accreted power and wealth created a parallel and impoverished and resentful universe in the rest of the country, which was suffering from the regional inequalities and high unemployment mentioned by Ambassador Godec. A prime example was on display in Sidi Bouzid, a small town in the Tunisian interior, around a three-hour drive from Muhammad al-Materi's luxurious villa in Hammamet. In the year or so after his opulent dinner party with the American ambassador, Materi's business career went from strength to strength. In Sidi Bouzid Muhammad Bouazizi, a man only a little younger but with a life that was profoundly different, was struggling to support his mother and younger siblings. They lived in a tiny house made of breezeblocks, with a small back yard behind a high wall. Muhammad Bouazizi, who was twenty-six, was not at all unique, and neither was Sidi Bouzid. It was a typical town, and there were men like Bouazizi not just in Tunisia but across the Arab world, full of resentment at being trapped in lives that had been stalled by chronic unemployment and corruption. Resentment was turning to anger as they watched the favoured classes – or, in Tunisia's case, favoured families – getting richer.

On Friday 17 December 2010 Muhammad Bouazizi could not take it any longer.[5] For most of his adult life he had been earning a living from selling vegetables from an unlicensed cart in an informal market, which meant he was face to face with the corruption that had trickled through Tunisia from the top to the bottom. Having a licence would have made things easier, but to get one Muhammad would have had to bribe an official, and he did not have the money. When inspectors from the local municipality came to check for permits, Bouazizi and the other traders used to sweep up their produce and make a run for it. But on 17 December 2010 something inside him made him stand his ground and turn to face them, raging at his lot in life and the way that his chances of making it better were being crushed. The inspectors confiscated his cart, his scale and weights and some boxes of pears. Bouazizi stormed off to the office of the governor of the region, which was only a short walk from the market. But he was rebuffed. After that final humiliation Muhammad doused himself with an inflammable liquid (some reports say petrol; others say it was paint thinner) and set himself alight. By the time the fire was put out he had the horrific burns that killed him on 4 January. I asked one of the traders who sold vegetables alongside Muhammad Bouazizi what he was like.

'He was just a poor guy who set himself on fire because of injustice and pressure. The government officers pushed him into doing it.' He talked of injustice as if it was one of life's immutable facts, like the weather, or growing old.

Muhammad Bouazizi and the government inspectors had started a chain of events, on a winter day in Sidi Bouzid, that were about to spark a revolution in Tunisia and uprisings right across the Arab world. From the very beginning the details of what happened were made known to thousands, and then millions, through television and the internet. And this is where some confusions and contradictions come into the story. Twenty-first century communications constantly shift and disseminate huge amounts of data. Stories flash around the planet in seconds. That doesn't always make all of the details true; and, because one story is often based on others, the easiest version to understand and explain can become a modern gospel very quickly. Like most international journalists, I was slow to pick up the details of what was happening in Tunisia. In the Western world it was nearly Christmas, and broadcasters like the BBC were shortening news programmes for more seasonal delights and letting their staff head off for the holidays. I realised the significance of what was happening in Tunisia only when I was prompted by an email from a Tunisian academic at Oxford University in early January asking why the BBC was not taking the uprising seriously.

By then the internet was carrying many reports that Bouazizi had been slapped by Feyda Hamdi, the only woman on the inspection team, and then wrestled to the ground, and perhaps beaten, by her male colleagues. Bouazizi was also widely reported to be a university graduate who had been forced to sell fruit and vegetables. It is always hard to know how truthful people are being. Walid Sattouti, a local journalist, said the inspectors were within their rights to ask a trader for a licence, and that Bouazizi had become extremely angry and had been 'rude to the lady and obstructed justice'. He had been fined and had stormed off to complain to the governor's office, where no one would listen to him. So he came back to the market and set himself on fire.

When I met Feyda Hamdi six months after the death of Muhammad Bouazizi she was sitting with her three male colleagues, who flanked her protectively. She was wearing a tightly wrapped yellow headscarf, rubbing her forehead and weeping, denying that she had ever touched him and remembering with a shudder the 110 days she spent in jail. One of Ben Ali's last acts as president was to have her locked up, a few days before Bouazizi's death, in what appears to have been a crude attempt to corral some of the popular anger against him. She was charged with assault and public slander, which carried a sentence of up to five years in jail. In the end she had her day in court.

She said: 'I felt like Saddam Hussein. But it was a fair trial, though I had to go on hunger strike for a month to get it. They dismissed the case after three hours.

'On 17 December 2010, eleven a.m., we were going to check a construction licence, then check out the illegal carts. Everyone except the military or government institutions needed a licence to trade. All the vegetable carts were illegal. We found a group of sellers, they ran away, but Bouazizi stayed and started to scream. We were just talking to him but he was yelling and I tried with my colleagues to confiscate his cart, but he wasn't cooperative. I took the box of pears, he took it again, and grabbed my shoulder, and took off my official badge. He was protesting and kept yelling violently.'

She dried her tears, and the four government inspectors relaxed. It looked as if they did not like her crying. With all the plodding bureaucracy of Ben Ali's police state, they explained why they had to act. One of the men, a beefy individual called Saber Guizani, who Feyda said had helped her with Bouazizi, made it sound as if the first hero of the Arab Spring was a recalcitrant street urchin.

'In law, if he's an illegal seller in a forbidden area, our duty is to confiscate the cart. The area where he was selling is close to the municipal police station, and the governor's office, and there is no doubt about it: it's not allowed. But he came on a Friday and stood there, and she went to him and asked him to move out of there, but he told her, "No, I'm staying." [...] He was resisting. We didn't even reach the cart; we were trying to get the box of fruit.'

I asked the inspectors why Bouazizi set fire to himself. Guizani said it was nothing to do with them.

'He set himself on fire two hours later, not straight away. We confiscated the box of fruit when I had reinforcements from my colleagues, and we went to the police station because I wanted to file a complaint, and he was there too. It's only 800 metres away from where he was standing. Nobody beat him [...] Though we did confiscate his cart when he left it in front of the police station. Between taking his cart and the incident there was more than two hours. We were leaving work by the time he was setting fire to himself.'

It is of course possible that the inspectors have worked out their version of the truth, and that they are sticking to it. But, had they been as brutal as some of the more lurid versions allege, it is doubtful that they would still be able to live and work openly in Sidi Bouzid. The precise details do not really matter. It turned out that thousands of Tunisians in Sidi Bouzid and millions more Arabs around the region were waiting for a symbolic moment that would create a channel and a spark for their anger, and it was provided by Muhammad Bouazizi, his terrible act of immolation, and what must have been his agonizing and lingering death.

Word spread only slowly in Sidi Bouzid that the young man from the fruit and vegetable market had set himself alight after a confrontation with the hated inspectors and the corrupt municipal authorities. Most people heard not by word of mouth but when they saw a report of what had happened on the Pan-Arab TV news network al-Jazeera. A trade union, the UGTT, fed information to the broadcaster and then organised a demonstration for the next day, Saturday 18 December.

By noon on Saturday what one witness called a 'huge' demonstration had gathered in front of the governor's office, where Bouazizi had suffered his last humiliation. It stretched from there for hundreds of yards down the main boulevard that runs through the town, which is now named after him. The chanting was aimed squarely at the regime, and activists from the UGTT union were prominent in the crowd. The slogans smashed the boundaries of what was permissible in Ben Ali's Tunisia, calling for jobs, freedom and demanding that 'the gang of thieves' running the country get kicked out. The demonstration appears to have taken the authorities by surprise. Hardly any police were on duty as the police gathered. A lawyer called Dhafer Salhi, who had seen Muhammad burning, had sensed there was trouble ahead. According to one report he urged the local police chief to meet the Bouazizi family because the rage on the streets was growing fast. The policeman refused.[6] But the size of the demonstration, and the direct verbal attack it was making on the regime, and the rocks that some people started throwing at the governor's office, guaranteed a response from the riot police. According to Walid Sattouti, the local journalist, 'to start with there weren't many police, but then the riot squads arrived in big numbers, and attacked the crowd, and fired teargas, and it went crazy.'[7]

It turned into a full-scale riot. The police killed two people. Activists, as well as friends and relations of Muhammad Bouazizi, posted videos on Facebook, which were picked up by al-Jazeera. The disturbances spread, and by 27 December they had reached Tunis.[8] From the outset, President Ben Ali's security forces used force, their favourite tactic, and it fed the spiral of protest and violence. Every time the police killed a demonstrator there was a funeral, and every funeral led to another march, and more violence, and more shooting and more unconfined anger. President Ben Ali must have realised that matters were deteriorating – or perhaps years of wealth and power had not blunted all his political instincts – and he visited Muhammad Bouazizi in hospital on 28 December. If he hoped to look sympathetic, it did not work. Ben Ali looked more distant than ever as he stood in his dark suit, talking to the doctors at the patient's bedside. Bouazizi's whole body, including his head and eyes, was trussed up in heavy bandages. Many Tunisians who saw pictures of the whole uneasy tableau decided that it looked as if the perpetrator was taking one last advantage of the victim.

President Zine al-Abidine Ben Ali had been one of the West's favourite Arab leaders, a secular bulwark against Islamist extremism despite the weaknesses that Western diplomats like Ambassador Godec recognised. He had been head of state since 1987, when he deposed his patron, Habib Bourguiba, in a bloodless palace coup. Bourguiba was old, and slumping into his dotage, but he had cultivated for himself a powerful cult of personality based on his past as the hero of the struggle for independence from France. Ben Ali seemed to be a much blander proposition. Every night the evening news on state television had opened with a shot of Bourguiba taking his daily dip in the Mediterranean, watched by his drab lieutenants. Ben Ali was one of them, dutifully turning out at the beach to watch.[9] As the new president, Ben Ali kept Tunisia on the path to economic modernisation and firmly in the Western camp. Women's rights were guaranteed by law in ways that were unknown elsewhere in the Arab world. He cracked down, hard and frequently, on political Islam and, by the standards of the region, religious minorities, even the Jews, were able to pray unmolested. Tunis and much of the Mediterranean coast felt more than half way to Europe. The French-speaking bourgeoisie strolled the boulevards of Tunis, families went to the beach (working hours ended after lunch in the summer to make that easier) even the petrol stations looked and felt European, selling baseball caps, sandwiches and espresso as well as fuel. Ben Ali's Tunisia had about the best economy in North Africa, growing at 5 per cent every year either side of the turn of the century. Phones worked, banks functioned, the roads were good, and the people were getting reasonable education and healthcare. Millions of foreign tourists visited Tunisia's Mediterranean beaches.

In the 1960s Arab rulers, Bourguiba included, formulated a social contract. The regime would provide. In return the people would stay out of politics, at least out of any politics that did not exalt the name of the leader. Bourguiba built up a cult of personality, and once the previously anonymous Ben Ali took over he replaced it gradually with one of his own. It deepened as the years passed and so did Ben Ali's determination not to let the people interfere with the way he ran the country. From the point of view of his powerful Western friends, he kept Tunisia mostly quiet, seemingly prosperous, and that made him an ally worth having.

But corruption and nepotism were eating away at Tunisia like a cancer. The contradictions of an authoritarian ruler trying to square the circle with economic growth were showing badly by 2009, when the American ambassador dismissed Ben Ali as aging, without a clear successor, at the head of a sclerotic police state with little freedom of expression and serious human-rights problems.[10] Perhaps the ambassadors of other states whose political leaders counted Ben Ali as a friend – Ben Ali had been rewarded with a state visit to Washington, DC, as early as 1990 – were just as scathing in their top-secret dispatches home. But Ambassador Godec's views had an utterly different impact because his cables were released by WikiLeaks and publicised worldwide just as the uprising in Tunisia was starting. For someone daring to demonstrate against Ben Ali, in the certain knowledge that the risks included a beating or a bullet, the first thing that was necessary was to feel brave enough to take the risk, to break the barrier of fear that police states raise by using violence and intimidation and maintain with arbitrary arrests, fists, boots and worse. In the past senior American diplomats had made statements praising Ben Ali's 'moderation and tolerance'.[11] The knowledge that in private, for at least 18 months, the American ambassador had been enthusiastically reflecting their view of the president and the first lady helped them feel braver. Not because they thought the Americans might rescue them, but because they guessed, correctly, that the Americans and Ben Ali's other Western allies had no desire to rescue the regime. It was a conclusion that cut across the whole Tunisian population, an exhilarating experience for the enemies of Ben Ali, deeply worrying for the regime's loyalists who saw their world changing in a fast and painful way.

Six months after Bouazizi's terrible death, Sidi Bouzid was still full of men killing time, still frustrated and angry that they can't earn money for their families. A passer-by saw the BBC team unloading camera gear and, without breaking step, said, 'It's not a revolution. Nothing's changed.' That was not quite accurate. Tunisia in half a year had gone from being a police state to a state where the police were almost invisible. The only one I saw in Sidi Bouzid was a senior officer standing in the sun outside a government building. Lawlessness was becoming a problem. The night before there had been fights on the streets between rival gangs, and a local prison had been torched. The police still had a bad reputation as Ben Ali's corrupt enforcers, so when they patrolled at night they had to do it jointly with the army, who were more popular. Sidi Bouzid is a traditional town and not many women were ever visible, but just like every small town in Tunisia it was striking how many men were on the streets killing time during what should be working hours. Graffiti in Arabic, French and English commemorating the events of December 2010 were daubed on the whitewashed walls around the governor's office that Muhammad Bouazizi left in despair to set himself alight. Its status as the place where the first demonstrations of the Arab uprisings started makes it sacred revolutionary ground for locals who are proud of what they did. But the exhilaration of the winter had long gone. Sidi Bouzid was oppressed by the summer heat and the dullness and despair of lives without the prospect of improvement. Elections were on the way, but on their own everyone knew they would not magically produce jobs. The Cafe Samarkand was a scattering of tables in the shade of trees, close-clipped in the French colonial style, on the pavement of main avenue through Sidi Bouzid, which, when I was there, was still named after independent Tunisia's first president, Habib Bourguiba, and which is now called Boulevard Muhammad Bouazizi. Dozens of men sat nursing small coffees, or tiny glasses of sweet black tea. 'I'm in the cafe all day – at noon, at one, two, at five, at ten, eleven,' complained Hisham Laabidi, a nineteen-year-old who said he had occasional work polishing marble. 'I drink fifty coffees a day [...] I want to have a job, build my life, be rich, and work.' His brother Mongi, ten years older, worked from time to time in construction. 'The problem is that I'm afraid that what we're dreaming of won't be realised. A real revolution should include and change many things like things in education, health, employment, more justice, more freedom.'

One man confessed how embarrassed he was that his parents still gave him pocket money at the age of twenty-eight. He looked ten years older. He must have used his time wisely, because he delivered a sharp analysis.

'We can't go back to a regime like Ben Ali's, because after the revolution no one would accept it. We'd get back on the streets. We're always ready for another revolution. It boiled up over ten years, because a decade ago there were fewer graduates, and a smaller population, so unemployment was less of a problem. But the regime made the economy stagnate. They were robbing the country. There were many rules to stop people running businesses. The wealth wasn't distributed fairly; sometimes they'd deliberately neglect an area. And investors weren't interested because the government agents here were so corrupt that projects and contracts would only go to their people.'

At the vegetable market where Muhammad Bouazizi worked, the traders were close to boiling point, demanding more change more quickly, while also being nostalgic for the quiet streets that used to be part of being in a police state. A man wearing a farmer's straw hat against the sun said they wanted stability and security again. Revolutions started because the old Arab world could not satisfy the people. Under his straw hat he still wasn't happy.

'We are disappointed. That's normal. What are revolutions for Arabs? Arabs are known throughout history for living through disappointment and drama, meaning things will never get better.' The man next to him chimed in that it didn't matter what had started in Sidi Bouzid.

'Even if the whole world is set on fire we don't care. We just want this country to be fixed.'

Their lives in the market had improved in one significant way. Feyda Hamdi and the inspectors who had tipped Muhammad Bouazizi into a suicidal rage were no longer bothering them. The inspectors were in their office, a small whitewashed building with Tunisia's ubiquitous sky-blue shutters, sheltering from the sun and from a reputation that had flashed around the world. They had defended themselves by saying that they were only doing their jobs. Rules were rules. But then the four sticklers for procedure admitted, or maybe just claimed, that they could feel the pressure for a revolution too. Our hearts, they said, were full of anger, and it was sharpened by Bouazizi's suffering. Feyda Hamdi, the woman who denied humiliating him with a slap, spoke more than the men. Her notoriety seemed to have made her the leader.

'You can't imagine how much repression there was, how little freedom, everything. We as officers weren't happy. But you had to work that way. You had to follow orders you didn't like.

'Bourguiba left us with two good things: education and health. Even in little villages people are educated. Menzel Bouzaien [a small town near Sidi Bouzid] has 3,000 jobless young people with degrees. With this terrible social situation and the bad economy, and the bad political environment, it's like a tsunami in the hearts of people. It's not because of Bouazizi or me, or x or y; people were already mad. Plus the administration and the government were just robbing people.'

Her beefy, protective colleague Saber Guizani chipped in.

'As officers we didn't have even a 1 per cent part in his death. Imagine if everybody sets himself on fire when you confiscate his cart: everybody will be dead.'

The words kept tumbling out of Feyda. I asked her if she thought things in the region would have been different if they had not confiscated the vegetables.

'No, no, no! The revolution was going to happen in Tunisia [...] because everyone was so frustrated. We didn't know when exactly, but we knew it was going to happen. It was like a full glass of water, and Bouazizi was the drop that made it overflow.'

And when the frustration and anger flooded the country, Ben Ali's regime fell fast. The deaths of scores of protestors across the country at the hands of the security forces made the demonstrations spread. Once the protests reached Tunis bigger and bigger crowds gathered in the centre of the capital, and would not go home. The army made a crucial intervention that helped push Ben Ali out. It put itself and its tanks between the people and the regime's guns, protecting the demonstrations and giving them the confidence to stay in the streets. It was the culmination of years of animosity between the armed forces and the president. Ben Ali and Bourguiba before him had never trusted the military, as they feared a coup d'état. They built up the paramilitary National Guard as the regime's military wing, and periodically imprisoned senior army officers. Ben Ali came up through the army, ending up as a general and head of internal security, but moved against it when he became president, purging the high command after more accusations of plots and plans for coups in 1991. In retirement, he might be wondering if that was a mistake.[12]

In his last twenty-four hours in power Ben Ali attempted to make concessions that simply made the crowds more determined to throw him out. On Thursday 13 January he said he would not stand again for office when his term ended in 2014. The next afternoon he promised elections in six months. Less than two hours later Prime Minister Muhammad Ghannouchi went on television to say that he was in charge. Ben Ali was on a plane, heading for exile in Saudi Arabia. Five months later, in a statement read at his trial in absentia for embezzlement and the misuse of public funds, Ben Ali claimed he had been the victim of a trick. He said that Ali Seriati, his head of presidential security, had convinced him that he had uncovered a plot to assassinate him and talked him into leaving the country for his own safety. Ben Ali's wife, Leila Trabelsi, gave her version of their last day in Tunis in an interview with a French magazine.[13] She said it was not a matter of public protests. Instead it was 'an orchestrated, masterminded and planned coup d'état, but I don't know who led it'. Ben Ali had rung her suggesting visiting Saudi Arabia for a pilgrimage to 'let things calm down'. Trabelsi said Seriati talked her husband into it: 'My husband was already at the airport and Ali Seriati did everything to convince him to leave, even though he didn't want to. We had no luggage, money or passports.' In the statement at his trial in absentia Ben Ali complained that his pilots had taken him to Saudi Arabia and then disobeyed an order to wait, making it impossible for him to return home. His testimony did not stop the court sentencing the former president and his first lady to thirty years in prison and a fine of more than forty million pounds. Later, other courts added another twenty years for inciting violence and murder, and life for the killing of hundreds of protestors.

In Libya, Tunisia's eastern neighbour, Colonel Muammar al-Gaddafi felt moved to go on television too. 'You have suffered a great loss,' he told Tunisians. '[...] there is none better than Zine to govern Tunisia. Tunisia now lives in fear.' It was more accurate to say that Arab autocrats were feeling the fear. Their subjects, who had seemed cowed and quiescent, had been stirred to anger. Gaddafi, quixotic, impulsive and ruthless, was voicing what must have gone through the minds of every Arab leader on the evening of 14 January 2012. They were being challenged. The only question was who would be next.

2

CAPTURING TAHRIR

Zyad Elelaiwy woke up in his flat in Cairo feeling excited, and a little nervous. He was tall and slightly plump with untidy hair and glasses, still looking like a student even though he was a lawyer in his thirties. It was 25 January 2011, Police Day, a public holiday originally granted to commemorate Egyptian police officers who had fought against the British in 1952. Zyad and his friends had a plan for what was still, almost sixty years on, a day off for Egyptians lucky enough to have a proper job. It was not to celebrate the police. They had stopped being national heroes a long time ago. Instead they were the notoriously corrupt and brutal tools of President Hosni Mubarak. He was plunged into the job in 1981, after his predecessor Anwar Sadat was assassinated by Islamist extremists inside his own praetorian guard, as a summary punishment for the peace he had made with Israel. Mubarak, an air-force general who was vice-president, was sitting next to Sadat when he was killed. Bodyguards hustled him away, flecks of blood on his dress uniform, into thirty years of repression. Almost his first move was to impose a state of emergency that he never lifted, which gave the police and the security services sweeping powers and thirty years of impunity. By 2011 the police and the security services were secure and arrogant, confident that they were above the law.

Mubarak's ideology was stability, as measured by his friends in the United States. He fought political Islam, and Egypt's jihadists, upheld the unpopular peace treaty with Israel, and made sure that the armed forces kept their position as Egypt's most dominant institution. He allowed parts of the economy that had been nationalised by his revolutionary predecessors to be privatised, which pleased economic liberals in the West and enriched a small class of Egyptian tycoons. Mubarak became Mr Reliable, the West's necessary man in the Arab world, the leader who kept the Palestinians in check and reassured Israel. One of Israel's leading political analysts told me once, only partly joking, that the first job every morning in the foreign ministry in Jerusalem was to say a prayer for Hosni Mubarak's health. The price for popularity in the White House, Downing Street and Israel's security cabinet was repression and political stagnation at home. Corruption was endemic. Extracting services, permissions, rubber stamps and almost anything else from the state often required a bribe.

The president and his complacent coterie were confident that they had the Egyptian people exactly where they wanted them. The rich, including the ruling family itself, were getting richer, and the fact that the poor were getting poorer did not seem to be a threat to the established order. They were controlled by State Security and food subsidies. Any anger left after the men with the guns and clubs had done their job could be mopped up by cheap bread. Dogged trade unionists organised strikes, but the huge disenfranchised and impoverished underclass was so tied up with the struggle to get enough food to see them through the day that they appeared to ignore politics altogether.

And there were plenty of conventional political reasons to get angry, which would be recognisable in any country in the world – even in those that did not also have corrupt and violent security services and a poisonous disdain for human rights. The privatisation programme that had started in the 1990s brought in foreign investment and the economic-growth numbers looked good. In 2008 the Egyptian economy grew at the rate of 8 per cent. But almost none of the wealth trickled down to the poorer parts of society. Most

Egyptians had to work extremely hard to survive. A Peruvian econo-mist called Hernando de Soto established that, however hard they worked, would-be entrepreneurs found it extraordinarily difficult to do well because Egypt's inadequate legal system denied them prop-erty rights and wrapped them in red tape. Starting a business legally, de Soto found, meant dealing with fifty-six government agencies. The opportunities for officials to extract bribes were endless. The result was a burning sense of alienation from a system that enriched a small minority, and guaranteed a life of struggle and poverty to the major-ity. The only surprise was a revolution did not happen sooner.

By December 2010 the regime was so unconcerned with public opinion, so confident that the Egyptian people had been bludgeoned into submission by poverty and repression, that it barely bothered to cover up the blatant rigging of a parliamentary election. Ahmed Ezz, a model citizen of Egypt's new plutocracy, a billionaire who con-trolled the nationalised steel industry, was in charge. Egypt's oligarchs were stroking the hand that fed them. The president needed a com-pliant parliament, as his biggest priority at the beginning of 2011 was arranging the succession of his son, Gamal, which was still not a done deal. Many Egyptians still thought Mubarak's preferred option was to stay in power forever, even though he was eighty-two, and ailing, which generated a lot of jokes. In one of them Mubarak was on his deathbed. An aide asked him whether he had a last message. *Who for?* asked Mubarak. *For the people, sir,* said the aide. *They need a farewell.* Mubarak couldn't understand it. *Why?* he said. *Where are the people going?* In March 2010 rumours of his death when he was being treated in a clinic in Germany were so strong that state TV had to film him in his dressing gown, chatting to his doctors. Short of showing him reading that day's edition of *al-Ahram*, the official newspaper, it was almost the same kind of video that hostage-takers circulate to estab-lish that their victim is still alive.

For Zyad Elelaiwy and other Egyptians who had grown up hoping for a better and freer life, the thought that even the death or retirement of the president would not release them from the Mubaraks was the last straw. Zyad was part of a loose group of old friends and new political associates who had been using Facebook to organise a demonstration that they hoped would make Police Day 2011 a festival the regime would never forget. The plan was to march into the centre of Cairo from a number of different locations, encouraging others to join them along the way. Zyad was already a veteran of political protest against the regime, and knew all about its hard hand.

'To be honest, we thought we'd last about five minutes. We thought we'd get arrested straight away. I reckoned I'd end up in the back of a police van getting a kicking. It had happened before, after all.'

But it did not happen in 2011. He was speaking to me three weeks later, next to long queues of Egyptians waiting patiently to get through the security cordon that protestors had set up around Tahrir Square. His eyes were still full of disbelief and wonder at the way that Cairo was being taken over by the demonstrators. Not far from where we were standing, on one of the bridges over the Nile, the head-quarters of Mubarak's ruling party was a blackened ruin, burnt out by demonstrators (they had also targeted and sacked the corporate headquarters of Ahmed Ezz's conglomerate.) Zyad and the others had started organizing their protest before the revolution in Tunisia. But the abrupt departure of President Ben Ali from Tunis had diluted their realism with a speck of hope. Tunisia was much smaller than Egypt, but both countries had fierce and vindictive police states, and presidents who were so useful to Europe and America that Western leaders were prepared to forget their rhetoric about human rights, justice and democracy and turn a blind eye to corruption, stag-nation and brutality. Ben Ali, on his last day in power, had offered wild concessions, including elections in six months, which had only inflamed the protestors on the streets in Tunis and delivered the mes-sage to everyone in the Arab world that tyrants could be overthrown if the people pushed hard enough.

The possibilities that Tunisia opened up generated thousands of messages and exchanges on the internet. Egypt's press was allowed a certain amount of freedom, more than in many other Arab countries – Syria was the most censored country in the world, along with North Korea and Eritrea – but across the Middle East the web bypassed any attempt by the government to control information. Google surveyed its searches and found that internet users in the Arab world were fifteen times more likely to use the web to search for news and politics than people in the United Kingdom or Poland. Dozens of Facebook groups communicated in the virtual world where the police and intelligence services found it hard to keep up. One of the biggest was the page of the April 6 Youth Movement. Activists founded it to support an attempt at a general strike in April 2008 by textile workers in Mahalla, the tough industrial town in the Nile Delta. Thousands of people signed up to the page. The strike in 2008 was, as usual, broken by the power of the police state. But people who did not like the regime had a new way to organise, and to protest, and they knew it. One prominent Egyptian blogger, Nora Younis, told a reporter from *The New York Times* in January 2009 that Mahalla was 'a rehearsal for a bigger thing [...] right now, we are just testing the power of each other.'[1]

A bigger test came after two plainclothes policemen in Alexandria, Egypt's second city, beat a young man called Khaled Said to death in June 2010. The authorities had attempted to cover up what happened. They told his mother that Khaled had died because he had swallowed a bag of drugs he had been trying to sell. But witnesses said that the police had picked on him in a cafe, beaten him, slammed his head into a marble table and left him dying. Khaled Said's brother saw his body in the mortuary: a corpse with the agonised expression of a man who had died in terrible pain and despair, some of his teeth gone, and his face smashed and twisted. The brother took out his mobile phone, one of the most potent weapons for revolutionaries in the new century, snapped a photograph and uploaded it to the internet. The contrast between the photograph of Khaled Said after his terrible death with one of him alive, a young man in a grey sweatshirt with an open, hopeful smile, was not just poignant. It became politically devastating. Wael Ghonim, an Egyptian living in Dubai who was an executive at Google, started a page called We Are All Khaled Said, which rapidly became one of the main vehicles for dissenters against Hosni Mubarak. It attracted tens of thousands of followers, and then hundreds of thousands more. The relative anonymity of the internet was a crucial part of breaking the grip of fear that the regime's forces always tried to maintain. The big numbers of people involved felt safer online than being part of a small demonstration in the streets, yards away from the clubs and guns of the police.

The security services in Egypt, and other Arab countries, were behind the curve, still looking to intimidate and control through breaking bones and spilling blood, still able to inflict terrible damage if they could get their hands on a suspect, but struggling because their tried and trusted methods were being outflanked by modern digital technology. The point was rammed home throughout 2011. Countries that once could be sealed, with the great mass of their people kept in ignorance, exposed only to government propaganda, had become porous. Governments had lost their monopoly of information. Knowledge fed the frustration of young and growing Arab populations, which knew more about the outside world than any generation before them had done.

The irony for the aging, out-of-touch Hosni Mubarak was that back in the fifties, when the regime was young, Gamal Abdul Nasser was at the cutting edge of the mid-twentieth-century's revolution in communications. He was charismatic, dashing in a uniform, elegant in one of his beautifully cut Western suits, and he understood the power of image and propaganda. Sandy Gall, one of the top British foreign correspondents of the era, saw Nasser in his prime in 1967: 'physically he was an impressive man, tall for an Egyptian, well-built, handsome and with a film-star quality that turned heads and made him the centre of attention. But his most noticeable feature was his smile. It came on like an electric light, the shiny white teeth flashing on and off.'[2] Nasser invested big money in high-powered radio transmitters at a time when mass opinion was emerging in the Arab Middle East for the first time, thanks to radios in cafes and village squares that were often tuned to highly partisan broadcasts from Cairo. By the 1960s Bakelite or teak-encased wirelesses were being succeeded by cheap transistor radios that were portable and personal, and often still tuned to Nasser's mouthpiece, Voice of the Arabs. Nasser, and other Arab leaders concluded, correctly most of the time, that they could manipulate the way people thought.

Not anymore. Pan-Arab satellite TV started tearing away at taboos about what could be discussed in the mid-1990s. Rulers could not shut countries off anymore. But often they continued to behave as if it was still 1960. By the time the Egyptian police killed Khaled Said social media meant everybody with a computer could join in the conversation. The people who used the social network – mainly educated middle-class professionals in their twenties and thirties – had a lot in common, and they seized it to help them organise.[3] The web, along with satellite television, was a critical factor right across the region in making them the most knowledgeable and connected generation of Arabs in history. They knew what was wrong with their lives, and they knew that not everyone in the world suffered in the same ways. Facebook became a political slogan and a symbol of rebellion once the revolution started, but the activists who were organizing the Police Day protest realised its limits as a political tool. It had the potential to reach only a small part of Egypt's eighty-three million people[4], because more 40 per cent of them were illiterate and more than that were too poor even to pay money to internet cafes, let alone buy a laptop. That did not mean the poor and uneducated were politically ignorant, as televisions are everywhere in Egypt, but it meant that reaching them was going to need some old-fashioned political foot-slogging.

Sally Moore, an Egyptian doctor with an Irish father, was another organiser, and a close friend of Zyad Elelaiwy. She had wanted to do something big against the Mubarak regime for months. Sally and her friends decided that if they were going to have a successful protest – in early January 2011 it seemed far too ambitious to talk about touching off a revolution – they needed the poor. A protest without them, without the majority of the country, would not scratch the regime. They fanned out across the poorer parts of Cairo, where there was anger they hoped to channel, caused by a life that was never easy, always overcrowded and overshadowed by corrupt police and officials who had to be paid off to carry out the most routine job. To make lives even harder, food was getting more expensive, thanks to the worldwide demand for commodities. Since Egypt imported more than half its food, rising world prices, even with food subsidies, hit the poor disproportionately. Sally Moore went to Omraneya, a hard-up district near the pyramids where the local Christian population (10 per cent of Egyptians are Christians) had long-running, blood-fuelled grievances against the police. A row over the building of a church had led to demonstrations in which the police had killed protestors, and the Christians had attacked police stations and burnt vehicles. Sally tried to give out leaflets publicizing the march on 25 January but found that preaching wasn't necessary. The locals were already converted. 'They said, "Don't bother." They said, "We know about it and we're coming because we have a vendetta against the police." We knew they were going to come out against the police. We didn't know it was going to escalate.'

On the morning of 25 January feeder demonstrations started across Cairo, moving towards the centre of the city. It was a strange mix of people. As well as the young activists who had linked up with Facebook, there were trade unionists and Islamists, and football fans known as 'ultras', who had been making their own plans. A man called Abdullah Elnuazhi, from the Zamalek White Knights said, 'we had many meetings to discuss the revolution before it started. We discussed that we must play an important part for Egypt, we must support Egypt.' It also meant a chance to settle a few scores with the security forces. The Ultras liked fighting, were good at it, and wanted to cause the police as much damage as possible. Throughout the weeks ahead, they gave the protestors their hard edge.[5]

Sally Moore found it hard to tell how many of them were walking from Omraneya, because the streets were narrow and winding. The holiday meant more people than usual were on the streets. Local journalists reported the next day that plenty of them stepped off the pavements and joined the marchers, sometimes families with children as well.[6] Sally had her first inkling of the size of what they had started only when they reached Gameat al-Dowal Street, which is a long straight avenue. 'I looked back and saw there 20,000 people marching. And that was just one of the demonstrations. It was a sea of people. By then I felt that something big was going to happen.' The organisers spoke to each other by phone, and realised that tens of thousands, maybe hundreds of thousands were on the streets of Cairo. Around 3.30 in the afternoon Sally and the other organisers decided to head for Tahrir Square.

'Things were escalating. We had succeeded in gathering all these people. What do you do with them? People need something. Every time you clash with the police and every time you meet them you escalate and escalate. And it's also the adrenaline, and the will of the people, and it was showing on the streets. It was magical.'

The slogans changed. The first ones were against the police. By the afternoon they were chanting 'Tunis' and demanding the fall of the regime.[7] The security forces tried to force them back with batons and teargas but for a few hours that evening they managed to stay in Tahrir Square, until another assault with teargas and rubber bullets in the early hours of the morning. The Tunisian virus had spread to Egypt, the most populous Arab state. The battle was starting. One in four Arabs is an Egyptian. If so many people turned on the mighty police state built by Hosni Mubarak and his predecessors, no regime was safe.

I saw the pictures on the evening news that night, caught a plane the following morning, and was out and about on the streets from early on Thursday 27 January 2011. Something was up. Lines of black police vans were positioned near the bridges over the Nile, at important traffic junctions and outside government buildings. I headed for the Journalists' Union headquarters in central Cairo. It was seen as a nest of trouble and was surrounded by riot squads. Occasionally someone would be dragged away and arrested, and the chant that started in Tunisia, *Ash-shab yurid isqat an-nizam*, the people want the fall of the regime, would break through the traffic noise. It still seemed like dissent in the old Egypt – a noisy group of mainly well-educated activists outnumbered by riot police, with passers-by looking on but not getting involved. But across the country the authorities were struggling to restore order. In a small town in the Sinai a group of young men taunted the police and were answered by live fire. You can hear the bullet that killed one of them, a young man called Muhammad Atef, on the video that one of his friends filmed on a phone and uploaded to YouTube. The politically impossible suddenly wasn't. And the Tunisian virus wasn't just infecting Egyptians. In Jordan there were demonstrations, and in Sana'a, Yemen's capital, crowds gathered to demand the end of the regime of President Ali Abdullah Saleh, who had been in power since 1978.

In Washington, DC, the Obama administration, already reeling from the events in Tunisia, was struggling to find a coherent response to the speed of events. The Middle East was shifting under its feet, and it was not a feeling that made American policymakers comfortable. Since the 1950s the US had protected its interests in the Middle East by making alliances with regimes that were reliable and would, to a greater or lesser degree, do as they were told. In return the United States would not make much fuss about the unsavoury methods its friends used to stay in power. Now the White House was in two minds. The president commented that violence on the streets was not the way ahead. But no American leader could condemn the slogans about freedom chanted by crowds in Tunisia, Egypt, Jordan, Yemen and other countries too in those first few weeks of January, even if they were directed at men who Washington saw as vital parts of its strategic jigsaw. Hosni Mubarak was America's lynchpin in the Arab Middle East. He had made Egypt into a vital pillar for the United States, earning the two billion dollars or so of aid that the US had provided every year since Mubarak's predecessor, Anwar Sadat, made peace with Israel in 1979. Only Israel received more US aid than Egypt, and most of it – at least $1.3 billion a year – was for the Egyptian military. If Mubarak was going to go the way of Ben Ali, the United States was going to have to make some very hard decisions.

Early in the evening of 27 January at Cairo airport the usual crowds waiting for friends and family, the dozens of touts for freelance taxi drivers who besiege bewildered foreigners and the ever-present uniformed police and plainclothes security men were joined by a mob of reporters and cameras. It was a classic stakeout, an ambush of someone in the news. Their quarry was Mohamed ElBaradei, the man who a year earlier had emerged as the most public critic of the Mubarak regime. He had declared an interest in running for president, an ambition that seemed at the time highly unrealistic. But now it looked as if his moment might be arriving. ElBaradei flew in from Vienna, where he had lived and worked for many years for the United Nations. He was a Nobel laureate, holder of the Peace Prize for his work with the UN's nuclear regulator and watchdog, the International Atomic Energy Agency. ElBaradei is bespectacled, bald and looks every inch the high-UN official, well-dressed in a quiet, expensive way, part of the international business-class elite. The fact he had spent so long abroad made him, the Mubarak regime claimed, a stranger to his homeland. The president's allies in the press tore into

ElBaradei, claiming he was to all intents and purposes a foreigner, who had even forgotten how to speak Arabic properly.

He was courteous and stubborn when he ran the IAEA, irritating the Bush administration in the early years of its 'war on terror' by refusing to rubber stamp its analysis of the nuclear ambitions of Saddam Hussein's Iraq and then Iran. I met him for the first time in his new life as a would-be Egyptian leader in April 2010 at his villa in a gated community near the pyramids. Closer to the city centre Cairo was its usual self – sprawling, chaotic, noisy, dirty and magnificent. It is the Middle East's city that doesn't sleep, exploding with human energy. For Cairo's poorest citizens – and there are an awful lot of them – most of that energy goes into extracting a life out of very unpromising circumstances. Foreigners who turn up expecting to get things done can end up deeply frustrated.

Deep frustration, followed by a swift return to Europe, is probably what President Mubarak wanted for ElBaradei. But he did not go away and his supporters started yet another internet campaign to make him a credible presidential candidate. We sat in the garden of his villa, which was elegant and spacious, though relatively modest by the standards of the Egyptian elite. We didn't discuss the chances of an uprising by the people. The police state that sustained Hosni Mubarak seemed far too strong. ElBaradei was relaxed about the roasting he was getting in parts of the official media.

'I think they're panicking by the increasing snowball effect of the call for change [...] You see the vilification of me. I thought I was vilified by the Bush regime. Compare that to the vilification I am getting in my own country. I am the devil incarnate!'

ElBaradei was friendly and straight-talking, laying into the regime of Hosni Mubarak. He said he might run for president, but not until the rules were changed. For him there was no point in trying to compete on a playing field that had been designed to let Gamal Mubarak, the son of the president, win the succession. ElBaradei, like every other Egyptian I had asked, was certain that the rules of the game were designed to deliver Gamal what increasingly looked less like a presidency and more the throne of Egypt.

Nine months later ElBaradei was incredulous when he heard the US Secretary of State Hillary Clinton's first reaction to the Police Day marches, which was a reflex defence of American support for Hosni Mubarak. She said that Egypt's government was stable and 'looking for ways to respond to the legitimate needs and interests of the Egyptian people'.

> I was stunned to hear, you know, Secretary Clinton saying the Egyptian government is stable. And I ask myself: at what price is stability? Is it on the basis of twenty-nine years of martial law? Is it on the basis of thirty years of ossified regime? Is it on the basis of rigged elections? That's not stability; that's living on borrowed time. Stability is when you have a government that is elected on a free and fair basis.[8]

The word went out on the internet that Friday 28 January was supposed to be a day of rage, which is a familiar billing in the Middle East. I was still sceptical about the power of protest against Mubarak's security state. During the night the authorities cut access to the internet and the mobile-phone networks. Belatedly they had woken up to the way in which the wired world magnified and amplified protest. One activist out on the street looked up in exasperation from his BlackBerry, his thumb still jabbing at the useless 'send' button as he spoke.

'They've blocked everything around us. No telephones, no nothing, internet. We need people outside to know what is going on here. If you look around it's a ghost town [. . .]' The streets were packed, so it was hardly a city of ghosts. What he meant was that Cairo felt as if it had been cut off from the outside world. A generation of young people who were used to being in constant contact with each other suddenly found themselves silent in the world's noisiest city.[9] It wasn't easy for journalists, either, even those old enough to remember when mobile phones and email were science fiction. Assuming that there would be a lot of confusion and that I would be cut off from any source of information that wasn't standing right in front of me I decided that we had to start the day with ElBaradei. Some Egyptians – rightly – complained later that he had more exposure in the West than his position in the country justified. But on what became one of the most decisive days in the revolution he was going to be the focus of the first flashpoint. The police drew the same conclusion. ElBaradei was going to pray in a mosque in Giza, on the road to the pyramids. Dozens of black police vans were drawn up in a car park close to the mosque by the time that news people started to arrive. Egyptian police vans are like the country – old, battered and overcrowded. They are big steel cabins attached to the backs of lorries and crammed with riot police with their helmets, armour, shields and clubs.

I strolled past and managed to count about forty vans, each with about thirty men in and around them, before someone told me get out. Westerners were highly conspicuous. But so were the secret police. The place was crawling with obvious-looking men from the General Intelligence Service as well as their uniformed colleagues. Plainclothes Arab secret policemen might as well be dressed in a uniform. The ones who have arrested me in different places over the years have usually been wearing leather jackets and sunglasses and carrying cigarettes, which they smoke aggressively. Sometimes they have mean-looking short submachine guns poking out of their jackets, which they flash like a highly intimidating business card. That morning in Giza, and right across Cairo, the regime was putting on a big show of force. The officers who were commanding the uniformed police looked calm. It was another day's work. It wasn't going to go wrong. They tolerated the presence of news teams if they were just looking on. The minute anyone tried to do any active filming, or interviewing, they risked arrest.

A few groups of demonstrators merged together and started to chant. A couple of hundred riot police, a human warhead of shields and clubs, scattered them back into the Friday-morning crowds. It was just a taster. Everyone was waiting for the real action after the prayer. Behind the mosque were lines and lines of more police in riot gear, waiting to stop the march they knew was coming. We had to get up somewhere high to have a chance to film what was going to happen without getting arrested. Raouf Ibrahim, the BBC's long-serving and streetwise driver, went off to find a roof and came back a few minutes later, grinning, with a set of keys. At a scruffy building with a broken lift across the road he gave the doorman a few grimy Egyptian bank-notes as he hustled us up flight after flight of broken marble steps to a locked door. Raouf's magic keys did the trick and we pushed it open. The cameraman Rob Magee squatted down next to a low wall that ran around the roof. Then he started, as discreetly as he could, to film.

The mosque down below was so full that more than 1,000 men were lined up to pray outside, on a patch of grass, ringed by lines of riot police. It was a crude attempt at intimidation, which looked as if it could work. The Egyptian police state had perfected its methods. The morning's orders were about dealing with defiance, and all the men planning to take on the police were able to take a long look as they prayed at the clubs and the shields and the boots that would be aimed at them if they did not go home quietly.

On the surrounding balconies and roofs the neighbours were getting ready for the show as well. The area was dilapidated by Western standards, but for Cairo it was not badly off. Families, old men and ladies with headscarves had set up chairs and tables and were sitting in the warm winter sun of Cairo. They were curious, not partisan, calm but engaged, like neutrals at a big football match. It struck me that the men I had seen getting ready to pray at the mosque looked more prosperous than the Cairo average. If they were going to have any success they were going to need the poor people too.

The moment the prayer ended, the worshippers turned into demonstrators and started chanting slogans against Hosni Mubarak and his regime. The police moved forward immediately, swinging their clubs and firing teargas. Mohamed ElBaradei was inside the mosque, dressed in the smart but casual clothes you see in Vienna at the weekends. In an expensive-looking khaki pullover he shook some hands, smiled, still learning how to be a candidate, excited and nervous. When the pack of television camera and photographers made it impossible to move forward, he appealed to the world outside to 'practise what they preach, to defend the rights of Egyptians to universal values, freedom, dignity and social justice'. No one needed to go more than a few steps into the world just outside the mosque to confirm that the Mubarak regime would not surrender any of its prerogatives without a fight. The chanting grew louder and more angry. The police were firing teargas, which was leaking into the mosque, and the people near the doors were starting to cough and move back. ElBaradei's staff tried to get him out. As they hustled him towards the exit it took the full blast from the police water cannon and they had to retreat.

The next day I spoke to ElBaradei again in his garden in Giza. The pyramids close by had tanks parked next to them. He believed he had been singled out to send a message.

'I was targeted and hit by water cannon [...] they kicked out and crushed the cameras of the foreign media, and they clearly have done it on the specific orders of the government to say if we can do that to ElBaradei then you'd better be careful [...] The regime has failed to deliver, economically, socially; it's a socially fragmented society, it's politically repressed, it's economically stagnant. Mubarak needs to go. The regime has failed and we need a change.'

As ElBaradei sheltered from the water cannon a secret policeman burst on to our roof, yelling. He ran at Rob and went to grab his camera. Raouf blocked his way and tried to calm him down. Rob was bent double over his camera, his back towards the policeman. I realised he was switching tapes, putting a new one inside the camera and hiding the one with the pictures. It is an old trick, which doesn't work very often. Most police these days are media savvy enough not to accept a blank tape. They insist on seeing what they're getting. Rob slipped me the tape with the pictures on before the secret policeman could get to him. I sidled out through the door, stuck the small plastic case of the videotape into my sock and ran down the stairs. Leaving my colleagues was not exactly heroic but we were there to report what was happening and without pictures that would be impossible. I knew Raouf would look after Rob and talk them out of any trouble in the end. His voice, coaxing the policeman off his pillar of rage, had faded away into the stairwell by the time I reached the bottom and plunged out into the chaos, noise and violence of the riot.

Clouds of teargas were drifting across the square outside the mosque. The crowd had been broken up into smaller groups, but they were still there and still chanting. I went to the edge of an elevated highway to see what was happening. The water cannon opened up again, spraying a crowd of a couple of thousand people. Hundreds of them ran forward over the wet road, chanting, punching their fists in the air. More people were arriving, jumping out of minibus taxis to join in. Some of them were waving Egyptian flags. They were determined to be the patriots, not to let national symbols be hijacked by the regime they believed had betrayed their country. The police fired volleys of teargas grenades, which bounced around where I was standing. The water cannons did not let up, but they weren't stopping the crowd. The people around me were angry and excited, shouting for ElBaradei, cursing Mubarak, demanding a new life. And then I realised that these were not just the middle classes, what one protestor, flashing his own expensive watch, described to me as the 'Rolex brigade'. Poor people were there too, and that really mattered. It meant the demonstrators had a chance. The regime could always handle angry middle-class liberals, but it was not them surrounding the police vans. The police inside looked terrified as the crowd pelted the vans with stones, smashing the windows, rocking the vehicles on their axles. Even old men were there, punching their fists in the air. Another volley of teargas came in, and with hundreds of others I retreated into an alleyway, coughing, spluttering, tears burning down my face and snot pouring out of my nose. The trick with teargas is not to touch your eyes, no matter how much they sting, because it only makes it worse. Someone shoved a half-squeezed lemon into my hands, and I rubbed my face with it. It's supposed to help. I still hadn't opened my eyes properly in the couple of minutes since I had taken in a lungful of the stuff. I had the impression of a crowd around a water standpipe, half of them like me, bent double, coughing, spitting, mess pouring out of their noses. We lined up like supplicants looking for salvation and a man ladled water into our cupped hands. Then they turned and went back to the fight in the square in front of the Giza mosque, and felt more like citizens with every chant and every stone.

I found my colleagues, who had talked their way off the roof and away from the secret police. We went off to see what was happening in the centre of the city. The security forces were deployed, in massive force, at every important intersection and across the approaches to every bridge over the Nile. The most important crossing in the uprising, the direct route to Tahrir Square, is Qasr al-Nil Bridge. Black-uniformed men in riot gear stood three and four deep between the stone lions that guard the bridge. A line of vehicles was drawn up behind them. No one was being allowed through. Groups of demonstrators, in their hundreds and sometimes a couple of thousand strong, were everywhere, trying to find a way across, to link up with the others, to get a critical mass that could challenge the regime. I had not yet realised it, but weight of numbers was overwhelming the police. Sometimes preconceptions can fight the evidence of your own eyes. I was still very sceptical about the demonstrators' chances against Mubarak's security forces. There just seemed too many of them – too well armed, too well organised – for the protestors to succeed. But to win a fight you have to believe in your chances, and it helps if you are desperate enough to risk everything. Passers-by were not just watching. When they saw the mass of demonstrators coming their way you could see them making up their minds in a moment and joining in, men chanting for freedom, a boy in his late teens screaming into a TV camera, in English, 'This is a corrupt regime!' and then repeating it because he liked the sound of the words, and being with so many others stopped him being afraid.

Raouf took us over the 6 October Bridge, which leads to the other end of Tahrir Square. The police were making their stand on the far side, blocking the way down to the square and to the Nile Corniche headquarters of the ruling party, the National Democratic Party (NDP). Lines of police fired volleys of teargas. By now we had some primitive masks but it was still very painful. And it wasn't just gas. Stones and pieces of pavement were flying in all directions. Someone came up asking for us to take photos 'so all the world can see what's happening here in Egypt'. An alarmed bystander asked if the police were firing into the crowd. I told him that the flat bangs he was hearing came from teargas launchers. It struck me that the police were not using as much force as I had expected. As usual at an Arab demonstration, the chants were a running commentary on the mood of the crowd. Arabs like to chant. It's always rhythmic, sometimes seething with fury, at other times funny or based on a clever pun. For a while some protestors tried to charm the police by chanting at them that all Egyptians were brothers. At that point, in the early afternoon near the NDP headquarters, the people in the crowd were holding back. It was almost as if limits were being observed, for a while. The main targets of the chants were the regime of Hosni Mubarak, his son Gamal and the blatantly corrupt and fixed parliamentary elections of December 2010. Then there was the classic, heard in every anti-regime demonstration I went to throughout 2011 across the Arab world, 'The people want the fall of the regime.' President Mubarak's heir apparent was a big target: 'Gamal, you're the son of your father. Go to him because we hate you.'

In Egypt there is a huge gulf between better-off, educated people and the urban poor. Some young men, tears from the gas coming out from under their fancy Italian sunglasses, were enjoying the rare moment of social solidarity. One of them, a little plump, wearing jeans with the kind of rips and holes that you can get only in really expensive shops, looked over at a crowd of threadbare, shabby, skinny and furious Egyptians.

'We've had thirty years of the rich getting richer and the poor getting poorer. This is inequitable distribution at its best. What I'm not calling for is a socialist revolution; I want people to have jobs, I want this country to have food on the table for every single person, and that's why I'm here today.' And then he said something that summed up how the Mubarak regime had failed. Even people like him, getting educated with the chance of decent jobs, were fed up.

'[...] all of us here are going on to universities abroad. The idea is that these people can't find a way to express themselves [...] our parents, older generation, didn't have a way. It was very, very suppressed. Now there is Facebook and Twitter. You are able to get out. What happened on Tuesday broke the fear [...]'

I asked him whether Arabs in other countries would see what they were doing and be inspired to start their own protests.

'They should, but everyone has his issue. We're trying to solve our issues here. OK? This is our nation, this is our country; we need our rights, we need to survive this place.'

A middle-class woman looked at a much poorer mother, dressed in traditional clothes, who had brought her young son to see what was happening. The richer woman did not try to speak to the poorer one – in fact I thought she was more comfortable talking to me in English than trying to communicate with someone from a very different background in the same city. But what she said to me suggested that the display of solidarity against Hosni Mubarak had made her regret the rigid social divisions and huge gap between the rich and the poor in Cairo, and the brutalizing impact of the regime. 'We're trying to show we are human beings and they need to value us as human beings.' I asked her if she thought the uprising would work. She took another look at the poor woman and her child.

'Yes, I have faith in the Egyptian people.'

Not everyone was as friendly. From the very beginning in the Egyptian revolution some people in the crowds vilified America, Britain and their allies for supporting the Mubarak regime for so long. Foreign news teams, as usual, got the blame as the nearest available Westerners. My chat with the young man in expensive jeans ended when a furious guy of about the same age butted in, screaming that it was all our fault for not telling the truth. A cloud of teargas drifted by and shut him up, and we went our separate ways, choking and spitting.

Throughout the day, right across the country, demonstrators and the police had been hammering at each other, generally in protests that were smaller than those in Cairo but just as violent – sometimes more so. Government imams, without much success, told worshippers to stay off the streets. In Suez protestors took on the riot squads as soon as the noon prayer ended. In the violent, teargas-fuelled confusion some luxuriated in all the ways that they could protest. Two men shinned up a lamp post to tear down a poster of Mubarak, then decided to set fire to it instead. Police stations were burnt and looted, just as they were in Cairo. In the crowd some men had weapons they had taken from the police.

In Cairo, by half past three there were no more friendly attempts to chant the police into changing sides. It was getting angrier, and more violent. From where I was standing on the 6 October Bridge I could see a pitched battle going on for control of Qasr al-Nil, the next bridge down. Teargas was belching off it across the Nile, some of it fired from police boats. On the bridge a line of black police vehicles ebbed and flowed with the protestors who were trying to break the police lines to get through to Tahrir Square, only a few hundred yards away on the other side. The 6 October Bridge, leading into the other end of the square, was better defended. A police vehicle, its engine revving hard, careered up one of the 6 October's ramps, firing teargas canisters into the crowd at point-blank range. Volleys of broken paving stones cascaded on the truck, which retreated abruptly in reverse. People who were hit by the canisters staggered away bleeding. Lines of police advanced on foot, scattering the protestors. Another van drove at the crowd, with a policeman, his head and shoulders poking up through a trap door in the roof, firing a pump-action shotgun at the people, repeatedly reloading and firing again. The people who took the blasts of birdshot had dozens of small, bleeding cuts over their faces and bodies. I saw a lot of wounded. The BBC's only casualty was the left wing mirror of Raouf's elderly Dodge Durango truck.

The radio announced that a curfew was being imposed at six in the evening. Everyone was to leave the streets or they would face arrest. But by six the police were falling back from the bridges, and tens of thousands of increasingly exultant protestors were milling and surging around the streets of central Cairo. Rob, Raouf and I approached Qasr al-Nil Bridge cautiously. There was no need. The riot squads had gone. Their lorries, now burnt-out skeletons, smouldered in the gutters. The regime had lost the most important bridge to Tahrir, Cairo's central square and the symbol of control of the city. It was the same as demonstrators in London taking over Westminster Bridge on the way into Parliament Square. Excited people were everywhere, desperate to talk. A man was stripped to the waist, his torso covered with bloody dots caused by shotgun pellets. 'We're going to do everything and we're going to make it. We're going to make it.' He kept on repeating the mantra as someone poured water from a small bottle on to his wounds. Any pain that he might have been feeling was masked by the revolutionary intoxication that was seizing all of them. It was stoked by what they could see over to the right, just up river. The NDP headquarters was on fire. The flames were coming out of the windows on the upper floors and black smoke was all over the night sky. Immediately rumours started that the regime had sent its thugs into the building to start the fire. One version had it that the plan was to discredit the revolutionaries by making them look like vandals; another said the order had been given for the party to burn its secrets.

Rob, Raouf and I pressed forward into Tahrir Square. It was dark and confusing. People were milling around, shouting, running, arguing with each other, and all along the road there was the debris of a riot; rocks, rubble, empty teargas canisters, and burnt-out cars and police vans still smouldering, hot to the touch, smelling of burnt plastic and petrol fumes. A miasma of teargas hung over Tahrir, not so acute that it was impossible to function but enough to make eyes and skin sting and scratch. Most of the square was in the hands of the people. The police had retreated to the south-eastern corner, where they were defending the streets leading down to government buildings. Hundreds of demonstrators were throwing stones at them, and being answered with more teargas and birdshot. The pellets pinged off the heavy iron railings that separated the people from the traffic in what was in normal times Cairo's busiest road junction. Now the only cars left in that part of the square were on fire. Scores of people had picked up pieces of broken paving and were banging them on the iron railings. The cliché rhythm became the Tahrir tattoo in the next few weeks, sometimes a steady drumbeat, then wilder and more urgent when the people thought they were in danger of attack. They were still using it at the end of the year, when they were back in the square, with the euphoria that had started on 28 January long since turned into bitterness, division and disappointment.

Not long after ten in the evening, President Mubarak appeared on television. The government, he said, would be resigning that night, and a new one would be appointed in the morning. No suggestion came from the president that he would go too. As I was waiting to go live on the BBC *News at Ten* that night a voice from the London studio said that there were rumours on the internet that Mubarak was on a plane to Paris. I told them not to believe it. Change in Egypt would not come that easy.

*

The next day Mubarak's men still controlled a lot of the streets behind the eastern side of the square. A line of riot police was stopping the demonstrators moving towards the Ministry of Interior down Muhammad Mahmoud Street, a straight, not particularly wide street lined with handsome, crumbling buildings that once were grand. Bad things happened in Muhammad Mahmoud Street. You can blame a lot of that on the squatting, evil presence of Hosni Mubarak's Ministry of Interior in the Abdeen quarter near the road. The ministry was a place where people were tortured. On 29 January, the day after the revolutionaries seized Tahrir Square, I had my first encounter with the dark side of Muhammad Mahmoud Street. The riot police in their black uniforms were firing continuous salvoes of teargas and buckshot back towards Tahrir. The Ministry of Interior was their citadel, and they did not want anyone getting close to it. The flat bangs of the teargas launchers and the percussive shotgun blasts beat time around the square. Our BBC team decided to try to outflank them, so we drove in a wide loop from Tahrir to come out behind the men with the teargas and the guns. I could see them, shoulder to black shoulder, helmets almost touching, a couple of hundred yards up Muhammad Mahmoud Street in the direction of the square, firing volleys of gas. At the crossroads where we stopped a crowd of agitated people swirled around one side of a roadblock. I was not relaxed either. It was obvious it was not a good place to be. The mood of an Egyptian crowd when it is tense and even dangerous can change fast. I saw an alleyway that worked round the back of the roadblock. Rob, the cameraman, and I put on our flak jackets and left the rest of the team with the car while we went off to try to get some shots of the police firing and then get out. I did not realise that the alley was almost directly opposite the entrance of the Ministry of Interior. We were arrested in less than four minutes. Two plainclothes security men detached themselves from a knot of tough-looking men behind the police lines and came jogging towards us. Other journalists were already reporting nasty experiences at the hands of State

Security. I began to regret going anywhere near Muhammad Mahmoud Street.

The man who grabbed me was a bit more than six feet tall and extremely strong. He took my arm and shoulder and I knew I was only going where he wanted me to be. Rob's guy looked just as proficient. They were shouting, demanding the tape that Rob had popped out of the camera and stuck into one of his pockets when he saw them coming. By the time we were across the road and heading for the door of the ministry I decided we had better offer them the pictures as we were going to lose them anyway. They calmed down once they had the tape. Then I realised that in their own way they had been as frightened as we were. Mubarak's Egypt, and his security services, dealt in fear. The thought of what might happen once they got us through the door of the ministry made us cooperate. They were aggressive because they knew that if a Western TV network got hold of pictures of a street they were supposed to have secured they would be in big trouble. Once my secret policeman took the vice off my arm the noise of the street, the teargas grenades banging up the street into the square, faded back up into my brain. A lot was happening. They let us go.

While we were away the crowd near the roadblock had spotted the car. About thirty people were around it. Raouf, Cairo as they come, and the BBC producer Jeannie Assad, a Palestinian, were trying to look friendly and keep them calm. But as soon as they saw two Europeans the mood of a few of the people around the car flipped from wary to hostile. Some of them had seen us being dragged off towards the ministry and ticking into their minds came state TV's propaganda message that foreigners were responsible for the confusion and were conspiring to show Egypt and its beloved, patriotic president in a bad way. A few people tried to say we were welcome, but one man, the most angry, pulled a big knife out of his waist band and pointed it at my chest. I doubted that he intended to use it, but my blood was pumping from the arrest and the noise and I could still feel the secret policeman's iron hands on my arm. Another nanosecond of thought raced through my head. I was still wearing my flak jacket. Maybe he didn't know what it was. If you stab me, I thought, stick the knife into my chest, where the Kevlar is good and thick. If it stops high-velocity bullets a knife shouldn't be any kind of problem. But already someone was pulling him away, and Raouf was hustling us into the Dodge; then we were gunning away fast from the kerb and back to the safety of the square and the revolutionaries.

It took two more weeks for Hosni Mubarak to resign. What happened in that fortnight did a great deal to shape what happened in the rest of the year and beyond. The military asserted itself once it decided that its own position in the country was in jeopardy, giving Mubarak the final push off the throne to protect its own prerogatives.

The senior generals in the military council, who were Mubarak's appointees, took the job of running Egypt after he stepped down. A government and a cabinet still existed. But the military council was in charge.

The armed forces have been at the centre of political life in Egypt since Nasser and the Free Officers seized power in 1952. Unsurprisingly for soldiers in politics, they are conservative, instinctively against rapid change, and in the last sixty years have created a state within a state. Egyptians used to say that the military wanted to rule without governing. They found when they had to govern that they were neither enthusiastic nor very good at it. Field Marshal Muhammad Hussein Tantawi, the head of the military council, feared that the new role was creating strains inside the military, especially for middle-ranking majors and colonels, which could severely damage it as an institution. Diplomats said that Tantawi told a visiting Western foreign minister that he wanted to get the military off the throne and back to where it had always been, wielding power from behind it. The military has a huge role in the Egyptian economy. No official figures exist to show exactly how many factories and businesses it controls, but some estimates go higher than 30 per cent. They have a good business reputation. I sat once with an academic, a leading intellectual inside the old regime's ruling party, inside a four-square faculty building in Cairo University. He tapped the walls appreciatively. 'The army built this. One of their construction businesses, actually. They charge a little bit more than some other companies but you know they're not going to let you down and they're going to do a good job.'

Hosni Mubarak found that, while his regime had been born out of the military, generals he had appointed and favoured were not prepared to be the regime's protector once they realised that there was a critical mass of people in Egypt that wanted the president out. Bucking the mood of the people was not a good option for the generals. Mubarak discovered to his cost that, as far as his military brothers were concerned, no man is indispensable if the institution is in danger. The interventions of the armed forces in the Tahrir protests were crucial, and without them Mubarak might even have survived. But for the first few days after the occupation, the military council under Tantawi had no clear strategy. As they debated where they wanted the country to go, the soldiers they deployed in Cairo complained that they had no clear orders, no plan of action, just a vague instruction to secure the streets.

One of the favourite chants of the crowds in the square was about the unity of the people and the soldiers. There were times when it felt like wishful thinking. On the first Sunday of the occupation, 30 January, a column of modern American-designed Abrams battle tanks rolled into Tahrir Square. The protestors blocked them, sitting down in the streets to stop them going further. Some of the more religious men who were there lined up and started praying in front of the tanks. Some suspected (others were convinced) that the tanks had arrived to force them to go home. A senior officer emerged from the lead tank and tried to reassure them. After about half an hour he gave up and drove off in his tank, presumably to talk to his superiors, leaving the rest of the armour behind. At least part of the high command was prepared to rattle their sabres for the president. In the afternoon war planes screamed in low over the square, buzzing the crowd and causing something close to panic. Mubarak, they feared, was preparing to use force against them. Tahrir Square might become Mubarak's Tiananmen. I didn't feel very safe either, and went to the car to get our team's flak jackets. 'Today Egypt will be free, or we'll die here, we'll die here,' one man kept saying.

A woman started shouting: 'The world should ask why he is putting planes in the sky. I am a doctor and I have extracted live bullets from the wounded. Live bullets!' The rest of what she said was drowned out by roaring jet engines as they made another pass. But the tens of thousands in the square did not leave, and more arrived to support them. A clumsy attempt to intimidate them had failed, thanks to the number and tenacity of the demonstrators in Tahrir Square.

The next day the armed forces made a decision. The military council issued a statement saying its men would not allow protestors to be harmed. That reassurance was hugely significant. The atmosphere in the square relaxed. Twenty-four hours after Egyptian jets were buzzing the square, parents felt safe enough to stroll around it in the afternoon sun with their small children. The protestors in Egypt found themselves with the same protection that those in Tunisia had enjoyed. The army had positioned itself between the regime and the people. It was far too neutral for many of the protestors, but its statement said that the people had legitimate grievances and had the right to demonstrate. It was a critical moment and the importance of it became very clear once the uprisings started in Libya and Syria. In both countries the army did not have the same sense of itself as an institution sworn to defend the people and the country. The mission was protecting the regimes. Demonstrators had to deal with the full force of the military. They responded by picking up guns and fighting back, and uprisings turned into wars.

One evening I visited the home on the edge of Cairo of a senior officer who had agreed to speak on condition of anonymity. He warned that they were under strict orders from the military council not to speak to outsiders and that he would face dismissal if his superiors knew what he was doing. Over tea and homemade cake I asked him whether there was a feeling in the army that they were protecting the people from the regime.

'Of course. The army comes from people [...] They're our families. We trained to die for the country and for our families, for these people. How could we kill them? It would never happen [...]' He said there was never a chance that the army would shoot at the people. 'There were clear instructions from the army. Never shoot at the people. Don't use any live ammunition.'

Later in the year, as tensions in post-Mubarak Cairo escalated, soldiers killed protestors and the army's human-rights record came under sustained and justified pressure. But in the dangerous and unstable last days of Mubarak they showed restraint. The officer offered more cake around and recalled that on the day that Mubarak stepped down the crowd outside the presidential palace grew until it looked as if they might try to break through the fence. One of the officers from the elite Presidential Guard, he said, told his men to take the magazines off their weapons.

'He felt a lot safer when he did that and he kept telling the crowds that he was one of them and he wouldn't do anything [...] If anyone had told them to shoot, of course there was no way they were going to do it. And even if they had opened fire, there were too many people in the crowd. It didn't make sense. They'd use all their ammunition and the people would still have come.'

The day after the army's assurances to the protestors, Hosni Mubarak went on TV and said he would not stand in the presidential elections that were due in September. It appeared to be the start of a quiet departure but, twenty-four hours on, the regime's party, the National Democrats, sent out thousands of thugs to try to break into the square. To the disgust of many of the protestors, the army did not fight for them. It rescued a few injured people from the crush, but at first did nothing to stop running battles surging across the centre of Cairo. The president's men enlisted horsemen and camel-keepers to attack Tahrir Square in a mad cavalry charge. Barricades sprouted around the fringes of the square, improvised from everything from buses and lorries to broken-up pieces of scrap metal and wood. Someone made a catapult, a siege engine for the twenty-first century, to fire bits of the paving stones that had been smashed up by the square's procurers of ammunition. The device had a milk crate wired to its arm to hurl the rubble over the barricades at Mubarak's people, who were handing out beatings, stabbings and worse. The square's defenders managed to snatch some of their attackers, dragging them away for 'questioning' about links with the hated police and intelligence services via a gauntlet of kicks and punches, bleeding heads and noses knocked flat.

I left, as usual, in the early evening to prepare my report for BBC news. Moving through the streets was very difficult. Law and order had broken down in parts of Cairo and every few hundred yards men, many of them armed, had set up roadblocks. Revolutionaries and local vigilantes were fine and usually friendly. What we did not want to do was to run into any of the thugs who were supporting Mubarak. In the morning, at an angry rally of his people before they marched on Tahrir Square to try to break in, the crowd had turned against us. As they pressed forward Raouf bundled us back into his increasingly battered Dodge Durango, hit the central locking and managed to get out as they beat on the windows and spat on the windscreen. In the evening as we left the square a report was circulating that supporters of the regime had beaten a European reporter to death. It turned out to be false but it added to the tension as we drove through deserted, dark streets to get back to the office, not knowing what was round the next bend.

After hours of the usual stress of editing a report and breaking the curfew again to go back through the roadblocks to the roof where we did live broadcasting, I stood on my hotel balcony to try to clear the day out of my head, shivering slightly in the chilly, dank night. Almost no cars were moving during the curfew so Cairo, usually one of the noisiest places in the world, was unnaturally quiet. From Tahrir, perhaps a mile away, the sound of fighting drifted across the Nile. It sounded like the roar of a distant football match, punctuated by gunfire.

Some people did not make it out of the square. Twenty-four hours later, Taher Ahmed was looking for his older brother, Muhammad, who had not come home. He called his phone repeatedly, but when it finally answered a voice he did not recognise answered. They arranged to meet in the square. 'He didn't want to tell me over the phone that Muhammad was dead. But when we met he said, "I have to be honest with you." A doctor gave me the phone and he told me the man who owned it had been shot and was a martyr.' Muhammad had been pushed into an ambulance and raced away to hospital, but no one knew which one. Taher spent the next twelve hours going from hospital to hospital, looking at the living in the wards as well as the dead in the morgues. He found Muhammad's body at the Anglo-American hospital on Zamalek, the island in the Nile that has been Cairo's smartest district since the time of the British.

'They told me that he died before he came to the hospital because he bled so much. He was hit under his chest on the left side near his heart and the bullet exited through his back [...] He was shot by snipers near the museum. Someone else had been shot and he ran to help him. There was another shot and he went down [...] It was very sad because my brother was everything to us. He spent his whole life making us happy, and ignoring himself. He worked and gave us the money, he never said he wanted to get married, he never lived life like most guys in Egypt; he was a really good person. He deserves to be in heaven, to be that brave and to give his life for something he believes in. I'm sure God will give him what he deserves.'

*

Until the revolt Cairo was a place where people could not speak freely to a journalist without risking arrest and a beating. It was intoxicating for the protestors to discover that they could talk, even to a foreign television team. Crossing the square could be very slow, as so many people would stop to ask, usually politely, if they could make their statement about the revolution. Sometimes if we stopped for a break after hours of filming and interviewing, irate protestors would demand to know why the Western media were refusing to cover their revolution. One man, trying to show that his views were important, flashed the keys to his Mercedes as if it was the identity card of a person of substance and standing.

I was in Tahrir Square every day from 28 January, when they captured it, to 11 February, when Mubarak resigned. The atmosphere changed daily, sometimes hourly, and it was the place to take the temperature of the revolution. The sense of unity was remarkable. People took up residence there, under improvised tents, and managed to live in relative harmony. A shared desire to rid themselves of Mubarak defused the kind of conflicts that flare up often in a city with such extremes of wealth and poverty. Women were prominent, which was unusual in as patriarchal and traditional a society as Egypt. Many Egyptian women told me, delighted, that for the first time in their lives they were not subjected to the sexual harassment that can be routine in Cairo, though there were some shocking incidents, including a brutal assault on a friend of mine, the CBS News reporter Lara Logan.

Tahrir sprouted a tent city that started on the grass roundabout in the centre of the square, and spread across towards the Mogamma, the monumental government office that straddles the south side. It is the hub of Egypt's bureaucracy, such an allegory of national decline, decay and inefficiency that it has figured in books and films. In the movie *Terrorism and Kebab* a man gets so frustrated that he ends up grabbing a guard's gun and holding some of the other lost souls in the Mogamma hostage. Just when he seems done for, he slips away from the police, the small man resurgent. The revolt in Tahrir was also about the triumph of individuals, whose will to make change happen was severely tested by violence, a challenge they overcame.

Different groups set up stages with banks of loudspeakers. Some days the square was angry and violent; on others it was relaxed, a political festival with speeches, music and takeaway food. One of the stages belonged to the youth wing of the Muslim Brotherhood, who had good relations with their secular neighbours at that charmed time. Five times a day, long lines of men went through the rituals of Muslim prayer. Many Egyptians are pious, and the prayer did not mean that the Tahrir political festival had become a festival of political Islam. The Muslim Brotherhood was Egypt's best organised and most popular movement, with the strange status of illegal yet tolerated. Since 1928 the Brotherhood had pioneered the idea of political Islam, built its relationship with the people by providing free education and healthcare, and spread its teachings about the need to live every part of life according to the holy Koran right across the Islamic world. Apart from its youth wing, the Brotherhood was an instinctively cautious spectator in Tahrir Square, deliberately not deploying its considerable forces. It did not start the revolution and saw no need to jump on to its bandwagon. The job was being done for them by the huge crowds and by the army's declaration that the protests were legitimate and would be protected, so they could get on with planning the future. Mubarak's rule was weakening. The Brotherhood's time was going to come once the president had gone.

Plenty of beards and hijabs were in Tahrir, but secular young people, the shock troops of the revolution, were setting the pace. They provided energy, ideas and audacity. They were prepared to risk their lives and most of them were young enough still to believe they would not be killed. But shock troops, in politics as in war, have a specific purpose. They are good at carving out a beachhead, using surprise as a weapon against enemies who might have been stronger than them if only there had been time to turn their guns in the right direction. Tahrir's revolutionaries did all of that. A party started across the country when Mubarak resigned, and secular youth celebrated loudest and longest. Even weeks later, some of their leaders were regretting bitterly that they had left the square. It would have been impossible to sustain an occupation of the centre of Cairo – once Mubarak resigned most Egyptians wanted to resume their lives – but without it they lost leverage. Secular liberals began attempting to organise a political movement that could seize the imagination of enough voters to win an election.

But fervour can only take you so far. Once the dictator was removed, the future was not going to be decided by passion. Marking out political territory in a new Egypt was going to need organisation and tenacity and, when it came to elections, networks of followers who made sure that the right messages went to the right people – who then turned up at the polling station. Once the old regime and its political party, the NDP, were removed from the scene, two strong groups were left to fight over the new Egypt: the armed forces and the Islamists. The revolutionaries did not know it as they celebrated their triumph on the night of 11 February, but they were going to get squeezed.

3

COUNTER-REVOLUTION

Green Square, right in the centre of Tripoli, was the parade ground of Colonel Muammar al-Gaddafi's revolution. It was the place where he would stand in one of the exotic uniforms he liked to design himself to review his troops, or harangue his supporters. Its floodlights could turn night to day and while he was in power Green Square crawled with the regime's security policemen. Posses of young loyalists loafed around, a mob in waiting. Libyans who did not like the regime avoided the square. Unfamiliar faces attracted the wrong kind of attention. Foreigners, especially foreigners with TV cameras, were watched constantly. So it was even more remarkable that the old man made his move, on a sunny and cold day at the beginning of March 2011. His message was in a handshake. It lasted about a second. Then, without another sign of recognition, the old man took off, walking down the wide boulevard lined with trees that ran out of the square and along the Mediterranean shore. The message he left behind in the palm of my colleague's hand was a spent bullet casing from an AK-47 assault rifle. Colonel Gaddafi's men were trying to pacify the city, ready to crush or kill anyone who dared to face them on the streets. They were using live ammunition, and the old man was making sure that we knew. I wanted to ask him why he had the bullet casing in his pocket and why he decided to give it to us. Where did he pick it up? Was he carrying it, waiting for a chance to pass it on to someone who might understand its message and act on it? I tried to see where he'd gone but his head had bobbed away into the crowd.

Perhaps he had wanted the bullet casing to be like the black spot that Robert Louis Stevenson's pirates in *Treasure Island* gave to an enemy as a sign that his doom was coming. Maybe the old man hoped that via television we could somehow deliver the blackspot for him to Colonel Gaddafi. Predicting the end of the Gaddafi regime was not so difficult a few months later, when NATO was bombing his forces and when weapons and training were reaching the rebels who had taken up arms in eastern Libya and in the mountains near the border with Tunisia to the West. But only a few weeks after the fall of Hosni Mubarak in Egypt, before first the Arab League and then the United Nations Security Council voted for a no-fly zone, Gaddafi and his sons still had a swagger, which made the old man's action very brave.

Once Mubarak went in Egypt, revolution was looking like an infectious disease. Opponents of authoritarian regimes across the Arab world had drawn the same conclusion. If it could happen in Egypt, the most populous Arab country, America's lynchpin, with its highly developed police state, it could happen anywhere. The model of how to do it had worked in Tunisia and Egypt, and it looked simple. Demonstrators needed to find somewhere central, a square right in the heart of the capital, and occupy it. Not only would it be a defiant dagger in the eye of the regime; it would also be a symbol that the world would not be able to ignore. If popular demonstrations were big enough, weight of numbers alone could overcome the regime's forces. Faced with the defiance of the people, the regimes of Ben Ali and Mubarak had crumbled. Why shouldn't it happen elsewhere?

By the time the old man pressed the bullet casing into the hand of one of the very few foreigners who were left in Tripoli, demonstrations were happening from North Africa to the Gulf, from Algeria through Jordan and Iraq and down to Bahrain and Yemen. The seismic activity touched off by the revolutions even seemed to be spreading beyond the Arab world. In Iran, protestors were back on the streets of Tehran, trying to revive the Green Movement that had been crushed by force after it challenged the elections in 2009. The police in China cracked down on demonstrations that looked to be inspired by Tahrir Square and brought back echoes of Tiananmen Square twenty-two years earlier that made the Communist Party nervous. In Spain, protestors against the austerity measures brought in to deal with its economic crisis set up a camp in one of Madrid's main squares.

The Gaddafis were determined to smash the new model of Arab revolution. The revolutionary cavalcade was going to be stopped in Libya. Colonel Gaddafi, his sons and his other advisers had a simple strategy: use force, because force works. The mistake made by Ben Ali and Mubarak was not using enough of it. They had been half-hearted, blinking in the face of the people's anger. A counter-revolution needed teeth or it was nothing. It would fail. Colonel Gaddafi was not going to make that mistake, and he had a precious advantage. He had seized power in 1969 as a twenty-seven-year-old army officer, and since then had spent his working life eliminating potential opponents and creating a form of government like no other. He called Libya the Jamahiriya of the people, a state of the masses, and wrote up his philosophy in *The Green Book*. In the late 1990s when Libya was under sanctions that banned flights I travelled to Tripoli on the overnight ferry from Malta. Once the ship had slipped out of the Grand Harbour in Valetta the crew prepared the evening's entertainment. Handwritten quotations from *The Green Book* were pinned up around the ship, on the companion ways and in the saloons, next to portraits of the Brother Leader, as Gaddafi liked to be known.

Wage earners are but slaves to the masters who hire them.
Parliament is a misrepresentation of the people.
Plebiscites are a fraud against democracy.
An individual has the right to express himself or herself even if he or she behaves irrationally to demonstrate his or her insanity.

The highlight of the evening was a quiz on *The Green Book* in what might originally have been the bar. An enthusiastic crowd cheered when the contestants came up with the right answers. If anyone needed any last-minute revision, there was a *Green Book* library on the same deck. Any public gathering of Libyans was so riddled with informers that it would not have done to have approached the contest with any sense of irony. It was a pub quiz, without the pub and with only one category of questions – the philosophy of the Brother Leader – and it was not advisable to get these questions wrong.

Gaddafi did away with most conventional institutions of state, claiming that without them the will of the people would be paramount. Revolutionary committees were set up across the country, to create a corps of loyalists who had sworn allegiance to Colonel Gaddafi and his works. It was the closest thing to a ruling party in Libya.[1] Members could get guns, and were a ready-made source of informers and thugs. In her excellent book *Tripoli Witness*, Rana Jawad, the BBC correspondent in Tripoli, recalls how after the first protests started in Benghazi Libyan state television transmitted live images of members of the city's revolutionary committee driving around the city kissing pictures of Colonel Gaddafi. 'In the Old Libya, this kind of broadcast was a clear message from the state, to say, "We are everywhere and we will overshadow you."'[2]

The reality was that his system was an unusual front for a familiar form of government, a dictatorship that concentrated power in the hands of the colonel and the people around him. State institutions that might have been able to take on a political life of their own were eliminated, hollowed out to stop them obstructing the will of the regime and the ruling family – which was very much the same thing. The military was restructured to make sure that another ambitious colonel in the army could not push Gaddafi aside as he had overthrown the king in 1969. It was broken down into autonomous brigades, and Gaddafi put loyalists, and then his sons once they were old enough, in command of the most powerful units. Once the uprising started the role of the army was crucial, as it had been in Tunisia and Egypt. Both had armed forces that regarded themselves as institutions that were part of the DNA of the country, not the backbone of the regime. At key moments not only did they refuse to turn on the people; they also made themselves into a barrier protecting the demonstrators from the regime. In Libya, protestors against Gaddafi had nothing like that. They were on their own.

The uprising against the Gaddafi regime began in Benghazi on 15 February, only four days after the fall of Mubarak. It went almost unnoticed in the outside world. International broadcasters were still preoccupied with Egypt and the rest of their attention was on Bahrain and Yemen, where the revolutionary circus seemed to be heading. By midday on 15 February big crowds had gathered in the capitals of both countries, protesting against the rulers. In Bahrain the police were preparing to storm Pearl Roundabout, which protestors were trying to turn into their version of Tahrir Square. In Yemen, they were trading rocks with supporters of the government. It is not surprising that the first protests in Libya did not force their way into the global news cycle. A lot was happening in other places and, while it was not easy for journalists to get into Bahrain or Yemen, it was not impossible. Libya, to start with, was almost closed. The modern world had been wired for news in the time that Gaddafi was in power, but he had done a better job than most Middle East autocrats to keep his country isolated. The regime did not grant many visas, which made it good at keeping people out. In a perverse way years of international sanctions helped that process, turning the country in on itself literally and metaphorically as at different times commercial air links were cut. What it could not do was stop information getting in. Satellite television was everywhere. And messages started circulating on Facebook and Twitter calling for demonstrations on 17 February. When Mahmoud al-Tarhuni's brother Riad pointed them out to him at their home in Tripoli, he gulped. 'When he showed me the date on the internet, I said they'd kill us if we tried.'

He was not at all sure that the revolutionary magic that worked so well in Tunisia and Egypt would spread to Libya. Like many Libyans, Mahmoud dreamt of an end to the quixotic dictatorship of Muammar al-Gaddafi. He was thirty-seven, and his life had not been easy. It infuriated him that a country with enormous reserves of oil and a huge income from exporting it should contain so many impoverished, badly educated people. Almost everyone in Libya could read, but most people's overall education happened in schools without many resources or properly trained teachers. The teaching of English and other foreign languages was prohibited for a decade in the 1980s. Even after the ban was lifted many teachers had only a sketchy knowledge of the language their students were supposed to be learning. English teachers would often prefer to be interviewed in Arabic.[3] Tarhuni wanted a better life, so, when he managed to get to Malta to work, he learnt English on the street selling soft drinks and then spent five years teaching himself by reading on the internet and writing in chatrooms. But, even though the calls for demonstrations on 17 February made Mahmoud very nervous, he decided he was going to do something.

Benghazi, where the uprising started, was more than 1,000 kilometres from Tripoli, far enough away in the east from the Gaddafi's centre of power in Tripoli for the sheer size of the demonstrations to overwhelm the regime's forces. But the capital was a different matter. The Gaddafis had plenty of guns and trigger fingers, and alliances with tribal leaders who preferred the status quo to sudden, violent change. The regime's resources looked formidable in Tripoli, especially to people who were thinking about challenging them on the streets.

Salem al-Fituri was a neat, self-possessed and well-educated young man in his early twenties, with a good job in Tripoli at the global accounting firm PricewaterhouseCoopers. But within a few weeks he was buying guns and smuggling them to men in his part of

Tripoli who wanted to fight Colonel Gaddafi's forces. Like millions of other young people across the Arab world, he watched the revolutions in Tunisia and Egypt on television, and in the last days before the fall of Hosni Mubarak he became convinced that Libya would be next. Like Mahmoud al-Tarhuni and his brother, he had seen the Facebook page calling for demonstrations on 17 February. He believed that the fall of the rulers of Libya's neighbours had thwarted what would have been a dark alliance to stop the revolutions. After all, the three leaders had a lot in common – years in power sustained by fear not consent. Like President Mubarak, Colonel Gaddafi had been grooming a son, Saif al-Islam al-Gaddafi, as his successor. Fituri, as he always liked to be known, felt that the time was right.

'I'm only twenty-two years old and it's been forty-two years, and nothing good came out of this government. So anyone would come up with that decision unless the person was crazy or something [...] If it had happened in Libya first it would never have succeeded. The other two presidents would stand with Gaddafi, and they'd help him by blocking the borders. It wasn't going to happen here before Egypt and Tunisia.'

Al-Tarhuni and Fituri lived in Tajoura, a breezy piece of the suburban seaside on the edge of Tripoli, sprawling along the Mediterranean. Near the beach big villas stand in groves of palm trees, though the streets get narrower around the Murad Agah Mosque. Tajoura had a reputation as a centre of rebellion long before the uprising got into its stride. Even the mosque was named after an agitator, an Ottoman general who organised local Muslims to rise up and to expel the Christian Knights of St John in the 1600s. Local lore had it that Muammar al-Gaddafi hated Tajoura after local people refused to turn out for triumphal demonstrations supporting him after he seized power in 1969. Many houses relied on wells for their water because they had never been connected to Tripoli's admittedly patchy infrastructure.

When the demonstrations started in Benghazi, Mahmoud al-Tarhuni wanted to do something similar in Tripoli. It wasn't going to be easy.

'From here Benghazi feels further away than Kuwait, and there were many more undercover police in Tripoli.'

The seventeenth did not take off as a date for revolution in Tripoli. The first big demonstrations in the city started in Tajoura on 21 February. Word spread, and people also went on to the streets in Souk al-Joumha and Fashloum – two other rebellious districts. A big crowd of protestors made it to Green Square. The security forces drove them out of the square and broke up the other protests with teargas and live fire, and the first people were killed. But for Mahmoud al-Tarhuni just getting on to the streets felt like a liberation.

'It felt good shouting after forty years. Normally we whispered. After half an hour Gaddafi troops arrived in their Toyota Tundras [...] but we felt good, and that day there was no fear in Tajoura.'

Friday 25 February was going to be the next flashpoint. Mahmoud and his friends went to lie low in a farm, and made banners. A woman friend made twenty-five old-style Libyan red, green and black tricolours, with a white star and a crescent. It was the flag Gaddafi's revolution had replaced with a plain green rectangle, and it became Libya's revolutionary banner. Just as in so many other Arab countries in 2011, the plan was to start after the noon prayer. The prayer was a public assembly that the authorities could not stop, which is why across the region it became a focus for dissenters. On 25 February in Tripoli the prayer, and a defiant sermon, were followed by chanting and marching – and killing. They wanted to emulate the successful protest movements in Tunisia and Egypt, to adopt the new model of Arab rebellion by heading for the centre of the capital and taking over the most strategic and symbolic ground they knew, which was Green Square. It was going to be their Tahrir. The day before was the last one before the regime switched off the SMS text-messaging service. Texting was a good way to organise, but a bad way to keep a secret. Green Square is around eight miles from Tajoura. Judging by video taken on some of the marchers' phones, there were a couple of thousand people present. Fituri and the others had the Cairo example in their minds. If they could set up their own base in the centre of Tripoli, they hoped there would be safety in numbers.

'Well, everyone thought that if we reach the Green Square and a good number, maybe 100,000 or 50,000 were there, we thought that it's not going to be like it is here in Tajoura, like the regime cannot start shooting and kill people [...] We thought like that.'

But around halfway there, at Souk al-Joumha, a centre of anti-Gaddafi activity, they were attacked by the regime's forces.

'They knew we were coming [...] and they were waiting for us. They started to shoot randomly at the beginning and when we pulled back the snipers started to shoot. And many, many people were killed that day [...] hundreds. The estimation was 200–250. But people disappeared that day and we don't know where they are. We didn't find their bodies, they weren't in prison.'

That morning I was on a Libyan aircraft flying to Tripoli. Colonel Gaddafi's crown prince, his most prominent son, Saif al-Islam, had decided to let in foreign journalists. The day before he had telephoned Marie Colvin of the *Sunday Times*, asking her to put together a group to travel in on one of his planes. She asked me if I wanted to come. But Saif's aircraft was stuck in Malta and the visas had been issued, so we travelled on Afriqiyah, a Libyan airline. It had been a little tense as we waited for the plane at London Gatwick airport. The managements of the big British broadcasters had been talking to each other about the dangers that might lie ahead and were making each other more and more nervous. All the journalists waiting for the plane were getting anxious phone calls from managers, which only ratcheted up the tension. We had no idea what to expect. Almost no information had been coming out of Tripoli, except for some blood-curdling reports about demonstrations and people being killed at roadblocks run by mercenaries. One competitor pulled its team off the plane, then changed its mind and tried to get them on board again. I had a phone call from the BBC management to tell me that none of us had to go, that they weren't forcing us, and asking if I was aware of the potential dangers ahead. I resisted the temptation to tell them I had a better idea than they did. I had left some friends and my two young children and their mother skiing in France the night before. I felt guilty enough about that, as well as a little dry-mouthed about what we would find in Tripoli, but I had taken a decision to go, and did not need to share the nerves of the people who were staying behind in the office. It is always good to be part of the first reporting wave into a huge world story, but it is often a leap into the dark. Our managers were not the only ones who were jumpy. I rang a normally amiable senior official at the Foreign Office to see what he knew.

'Can't talk,' he snapped. 'Only priority is getting our people out. They're in real danger. Do you realise how dangerous it's going to be there? Do you know what you're getting into? This is about the most nasty regime around. Got to go.' And he rang off.

I had been an occasional visitor to Tripoli for twenty years and it was always about the hardest place in the Arab world to work, because the authorities imposed so many restrictions. I tried to reassure the managers – and myself – by telling them that it was not in the interests of the regime in general and Saif al-Islam in particular to let anything bad happen to us. The risk would be from the regime's thugs; and, since we were on an official invitation, their masters ought to be able to keep them muzzled around us. The aircraft was reassuring. It was a brand-new airbus (less likely to crash) with green leather seats and a friendly crew. Alcohol was hard to find in Gaddafi's Libya, and judging by the fumes rising from some of the newsmen they had spent the waiting time at Gatwick fortifying themselves against whatever lay ahead. Afriqiyah served juice.

*

The airport in Tripoli was in chaos. It was under siege by thousands of foreigners who wanted to get out. Around a million Egyptians worked in Libya, with around a million more from other Arab countries, Asia, sub-Saharan Africa and Europe. Libya had a small population, and liked hiring foreigners to do everything from the dirty work to the baking of bread to running the oil industry. Eventually the journalists, and their mountainous piles of broadcast gear, were chivvied into a line of minibuses. We were struggling against the flow. No one else was trying to get out of the airport and into Libya. Shooting was happening in the eastern part of Tripoli and some colleagues were getting messages from London telling them that they should not risk leaving the terminal and should not travel into the city. I could not hear any shots, and planes were coming and going. I tried to remind the reporters who were getting micro-managed from a long way off that it was up to them to take the decisions now.

The night was wet and freezing cold. Pathetic lines of huddled, hungry people sat in the rain, surrounded by their luggage, hoping that someone would come to rescue them. Military aircraft – C-130 transports – from Italy and Turkey were sitting on the tarmac, ready for evacuation flights. But there was nothing from Egypt, Ghana, Nigeria, Bangladesh and all the other countries that had most people waiting. Some lucky souls were being issued with high-visibility jackets and led through their crowds by staff from their country's consulates or by officials from their oil companies. They needed the police to open up a path for them into the terminal building. Most people could not get near it.

The building had been overtaken by pandemonium, jammed inside by passengers who could not leave, surrounded outside by several tens of thousands of humans, all with their own tragedies. It was weeks before they could all be evacuated. Eventually the Egyptians organised themselves enough to start flying their citizens out. The Nigerians had to wait longest, begging for help. Some never managed to leave by plane and tried to lie low in Tripoli or to take the road to

Tunisia, which meant braving around thirty extremely nasty road-blocks. For weeks they camped at the airport, utterly destitute, surrounded by human sewage in every likely-looking ditch. Most people I spoke to said they had not been paid, and many said they had no documents because their former employers had not returned their passports. People left behind picked through huge piles of luggage discarded by other migrant workers who were being told they could take one small bag each on to evacuation flights. Some of the world's poorest, who had come to Libya to try to give their lives a sense of hope and possibility, ended up leaving destitute.

The minibuses provided for the journalists edged their way through the crowds of exhausted, frightened people. On the way into the centre of the city I looked for the roadblocks, and the mercenaries who had supposedly been recruited in sub-Saharan Africa. I didn't see one of either that night – but then again we were not driven through the centres of the rebellion in Fashloum, Tajoura and Souk al-Joumha. Later the BBC's Rana Jawad heard of Sudanese soldiers who were promised a Libyan passport as well as money to fight for the regime. The city was still dark and mysterious, in the way that cities in trouble always are when you arrive at a time when every other foreigner is trying to get out. We were delivered to the Rixos hotel, which for the next six months became the outside world's main window into the Gaddafi regime. It was an elegant, low-rise modern building, luxurious and, as the months went by, more and more bizarre. Colonel Gaddafi, perhaps because of his rejection of any kind of colonial legacy, or perhaps because it reflected his own personality, had cultivated a chaotic style of government. The Rixos became a microcosm of the regime, the baby brother of confusion and delay.

In between trying to file for news networks that were ravenous for any detail of what was happening in Gaddafi's Libya, we were welcomed by a man who would not give his name. Twenty-four hours later I found out he was Muhammad Abdullah al-Senussi. His mother was a sister of Gaddafi's wife, which made him the colonel's nephew. His father, also called Abdullah, was Gaddafi's senior enforcer, intelligence chief and closest adviser, about the most feared man in Libya. But, in a burst of modesty, Muhammad Abdullah left us to find out how connected he was. He spoke excellent English and said he had studied in Italy, where he had also, it seemed, learnt his fashion sense. He sat under a glass chandelier in a conference room in the splendour of the Rixos, dressed as a designer urban fighter in a beautifully cut green combat jacket, the kind Italians buy in expensive shops to wear on holiday or for a weekend stroll in the spring. His boots were made of sleek blue suede. Muhammad Abdullah's face, studded with a few days' fierce black stubble, was framed by a black commando-style woollen cap-and-scarf combination that looked cosy enough to be cashmere. Elegant and martial, he channelled the thoughts of his uncle Muammar.

'If someone comes to your house, what do you do? How did the army collapse in Benghazi? Because they didn't like to kill innocent people [. . .] Chaos is everywhere. Now how do we save the people of Libya and their future? It won't be easy or immediate to take the guns back. In the west of Libya we will quietly and calmly ask them to stop shooting. It will take three to six months to get the weapons back. The government is shooting to scare, but the rebels are shooting to kill. In the night they take drugs, then in the morning they go out to cause trouble.'

His talk ranged from apocalyptic to what seemed to be an attempt at reassurance.

'The system has collapsed. The only place now where there is a system is in the middle of the country and in the capital [. . .] Tripoli is quiet but there are some people inside Tripoli causing trouble. They will destroy the oil, the pipeline and the schools. It is very dangerous [. . .] But we have guns and also tanks.'

Muhammad Abdullah al-Senussi was just the warm-up act. The main event was Saif al-Islam himself. That night, 25 February, at the Rixos in Tripoli, Saif was at his most urbane. He was nine months and a

whole world away from the hunted, battered, heavily bearded
man he had become by the time he was captured in the desert in
November, with a hand smashed either by a NATO bomb, as he
apparently claimed, or by his captors as revenge for the way he wagged
his fingers at them in threatening television broadcasts. Three days
after the uprising had started, Saif had said, right index finger pointing and pumping, that Libya was not Tunisia or Egypt. It would be
a civil war, and Libyans would kill each other. If it had been meant
to intimidate the rebels, it didn't work. Their hatred of his hectoring
turned into a morale booster. A fierce speech by Colonel Gaddafi
himself about the same time was also adopted and tamed by the
rebels. He threatened to hunt them down 'inch by inch, house by
house, alleyway by alleyway'. The Libyan Arabic word he used for
alleyway – *zenga* – became a guaranteed way to raise a smile from any
rebel. An Israeli journalist, Noy Alooshe, made it into a YouTube
video, called 'Zenga Zenga', with dance music and a gyrating woman
wearing almost no clothes, and it went viral in the Arab world.
Lampooning Gaddafi was so popular that the video was still down-
loaded by thousands of Arabs even after they found out it had been
made by an Israeli. Alooshe was even asked to do a more Islam-
friendly version, without the woman. Mocking the Gaddafis was a
good way to make them seem vulnerable. After his fall Gaddafi's
threat was turned into a range of fruit drinks called Zenga Zenga,
which an enterprising Lebanese company set about exporting to the
Libyan market.

That first evening Saif strolled through the lobby of the Rixos, wearing a grey sweater from his extensive collection of Italian knitwear, his
balding head barbered trendily short, with a couple of days' worth of
stubble and a broad smile. One of the female producers in the Rixos
called him the forbidden crush. The man who in Arabic had predicted
death and civil war had a very different message in English. Everything
was calm in the capital, Tripoli was safe, people were happy, peace was
coming back to the country. We're united here, he said, against black

forces. You may hear fireworks from time to time in Tripoli, he added with another smile. Please don't believe it's shooting...

But it was shooting, and it became part of the drumbeat of the city – especially at night. Sometimes it was firing in the air. You didn't hear it before the uprising but since then every Libyan I have met with access to firearms likes to shoot at the stars or the moon or the sun, whether they are happy or sad, angry or celebrating. But it became clear that people were firing at each other too. To start with it was one-way traffic, from the regime's forces to the demonstrators. But, as the weeks went by, they managed to get their hands on weapons and started shooting back.

Saif's father did not turn up at the Rixos that night, though he did on other days. Instead he made another speech, every bit as defiant as 'Zenga Zenga' the week before. This time it was from the ramparts of the Red Fort that made up one side of Green Square. The night was cold and, as fashion conscious in his own way as his son, he wore a fur-lined trapper hat, its flaps dangling like Snoopy's ears as he held a microphone and told the big crowd assembled way below him under the Green Square floodlights, 'Here I am among you [...] Dance, sing rejoice.' The east of the country was in the hands of rebels, and there had been serious violence inside the capital, but he was telling his supporters that he was not going anywhere.

'We can crush any enemy. We can crush them with the will of the people. The people are armed and, when necessary, we will open arsenals to arm all the Libyan people and all Libyan tribes.'

In New York, at the United Nations, the entire Libyan delegation defected to the rebels. Later that night at the Security Council the Libyan ambassador, Abdurrahman Shalgham, who only days before had talked of Colonel Gaddafi as his friend, said the audience for the speech in Green Square had been 'children brought from asylums and soldiers dressed as civilians'. Shalgham started his speech by associating Gaddafi with Pol Pot and Hitler, and said, 'Muammar al-Gaddafi and his sons are telling the Libyans – either I rule you or

I kill you.' Shalgham's defection infuriated the regime people I got to know. As we sat and talked, night after night at the Rixos hotel, whenever his name was mentioned they alleged that Shalgham was a drinker and a traitor.

That night cleaning gangs went to work in central Tripoli, dealing with the mess left by the clashes. Algeria Square is in the part of the city that shows the architectural legacy of the Italian colonialists, with limestone porticoes and an elaborate cathedral to make them feel at home. Modern Tripoli is a big sprawling city, with a population of around two million – a third of the entire country. But the white-washed squares and avenues left by the Italians have a distinct Mediterranean charm, and still feel like a medium-size town somewhere south of Rome. By the morning Algeria Square was almost pristine. The only clues about what had been happening there the previous day were empty hoardings with fragments of portraits of the colonel, small pieces of broken glass in cracks on the carefully swept pavements, and a big wooden club, its handle bound with insulating tape, sitting in a rubbish bin. Men drinking espressos in a pavement cafe under the porticoes – the Italians left a coffee-drinking culture behind as well – queued up to pledge allegiance to Muammar, lightly tapping their hearts with a clenched fist as they declared their love for him. After a few minutes what began as a grindingly familiar Libyan ritual became a supposedly spontaneous demonstration praising the leader. Posters appeared, joyful men and women blocked the traffic, and I heard the chant for the very first time that rang in my ears for months: *Allah, Muammar, Libya, wa bas* – God, Muammar and Libya, that's all. Some of the faces in that first demonstration became familiar as they popped up regularly in Green Square, at Gaddafi's speeches, even in outlying towns where fighting was going on, running through their repertoire of chants and frenzied expressions of devotion.

They were caricatures of a paid mob. But Gaddafi did have genuine support in the city. It was impossible to say with any accuracy exactly how much, but it existed. He had been in power so long that there were two, almost three generations who knew no other leader. From birth they absorbed the cult of personality. Mahmoud al-Tarhuni in Tajoura told me after Gaddafi fell how growing up in his Libya meant being isolated from the rest of the planet. When the outside world popped up on television events were always presented through the Brother Leader's eccentric prism. Mahmoud was frustrated that many Libyans swallowed Gaddafi's cult of personality whole.

'It's just that people didn't learn much at school and never knew what happened in the world [...] They'd follow him to get money and a car, and some of the soldiers, if they didn't go to the Gaddafi army, they wouldn't be able to live because they had no education. Gaddafi made bad people believe that we were the best, but it was bullshit. They'd see Gaddafi on television, with his beautiful clothes, and they liked it. Lots of people believed in him.'

After the fall of Gaddafi the BBC *Panorama* programme managed to interview a man who had been a guard at Abu Salim prison. He talked almost longingly of why he had followed Gaddafi, and tortured prisoners on the regime's orders.

'He spoke to the Western world with a lot of courage and strength. He spoke up about Palestine and spoke up about Iraq. You could see a human being, a president and a leader and a Muslim, speaking against those people, against America, and many American presidents, with total honesty and courage. It made you want to support someone like him. And his fiery speeches [...] If he says, "Let's go to Palestine!" you'd want to go to Palestine; you'd follow him to Iraq. The whole world used to watch his speeches and the whole world used to listen to him. He was the only person who, as we say here, speaks his mind. But then he made mistakes.'

At a well-planned 'spontaneous' demonstration against the UN outside its headquarters in Tripoli a man told me in an on-camera interview that he loved Gaddafi so much that he would sacrifice his son for him. A few minutes later, with the camera away filming the tribal drummers who were there too, the man came back to me, wanting to talk some more.

'You know what I just told you about sacrificing my son?'

Yes, I said, all ears because I was expecting that away from the camera he would express hatred for Gaddafi and all his works. The man did not realise I was wearing a radio mic that the cameraman, Rob Magee, could hear in his headphones. Out of the corner of my eye I saw him about ten yards away swing round to focus in on what we both thought was going to be a confession.

'What I said about my son, I really meant. I do love Muammar that much.'

And he went off smiling. I would often get complaints from anti-Gaddafi activists when I reported the fact that some people, for a whole variety of reasons, supported him. A strong majority wanted him out, and some of them were prepared to take up arms to make it happen. But every dictatorship creates a class of people who depend on it to survive, not just because they are implicated in repression but also because it pays their salaries and they cannot imagine another way to live. A big middle ground also existed in Tripoli that did not like Gaddafi but feared violent change too. Once he was gone, they were delighted. But they were not prepared to put their own lives at risk to bring him down.

At the start of the uprising, you did not need to go to Benghazi to meet the regime's opponents. Tajoura was a twenty-minute drive away, where many of the people were prepared to risk themselves, especially in the first three weeks before Gaddafi rebuilt the barrier of fear in the capital. Getting to Tajoura on a Friday was not easy. We were supposed to travel around with a government minder but on trips that might involve rebels we would try to sneak off without him. The minders had a magic piece of paper that they waved to get us through roadblocks. Many of the journalists at the Rixos managed to steal copies of this paper. We decided to try the direct approach, deploying our stolen IDs at the main checkpoint blocking the road into Tajoura. It was manned by some of the biggest, nastiest-looking armed men in uniforms I had ever seen. I sank down into my seat, nervous and muttering an unbeliever's prayer, while their leader puzzled out what was written on the paper. I was encouraged by the way his lips moved when he read. Fortunately he did not get to the bit at the bottom that said it was valid only in the hands of properly identified official from the Ministry of Information. The government crest at the top was enough. He waved us through. Other times, at other roadblocks, they could read faster, got to the bottom of the page, saw that there was no minder, and arrested us.

In Tajoura we cruised the streets until we saw a crowd of people. It was a funeral procession for a man killed by government forces, a chance for opponents of Gaddafi to chant slogans and to feel closer to liberation. The graveyard was on a low hill, with clods of red, sandy earth ready to fill in the graves, clumps of pine trees and a distant minaret that local people said was used as a sniping position by the regime's gunmen. The man being buried was called Abdul Fattah Misraki, and the mourners said he and three others being interred that day had been shot in the head by snipers. They were all talking about the death of a woman too, killed in her kitchen, perhaps by a stray bullet, but one that had been fired with intent. Nearby at the local polyclinic a doctor who would not give his name said the wounded were brought to him rather than to the main infirmary. 'People are afraid to go to public hospitals. They come to my private clinic at night. They're frightened they'll be taken if they go to the hospitals.'

The demonstrators in Tajoura had their own version of Tahrir Square, a traffic intersection with a big roundabout, where they would demonstrate until the riot police came to break it up with teargas if reporters were around, and with live rounds, according to the locals, if they were not. Once the security forces were on the rampage getting out of Tajoura was as hard as getting in. Local people helped, loading us into their cars, finding back ways through lanes and a half-built highway, reversing rapidly when they turned a corner and found a checkpoint, and making sure we jumped out fast on the hard shoulder of road near the Rixos. It was a risk for them, but they were brave, and in forty-two years Colonel Gaddafi's cruelty had left behind big scars, and swathes of unrequited hatred and revenge.

Our first visit was a few days after their attempt to reach Green Square was turned back by the regime's bullets. Once word spread that we were there, people started pressing memory sticks into our hands containing videos they had taken on their phones. These corroborated the accounts local people had been giving, of unarmed civilians being shot, sometimes killed where they had been standing and sometimes dragging themselves away with terrible wounds.

Tajoura was not the only centre of rebellion in Tripoli. Souk al-Joumha was another, and thirty miles to the west there was Zawiya, which in the first month of the uprising was in the hands of rebels. At first the regime let us go there because they said it would prove their point that the uprising was led by a small group of drug-crazed Islamists. Instead it showed that a decent cross-section of the population was against the regime. One man was so amazed to see foreign journalists that he handed one of the BBC team a polite note, which said: 'Why have you been allowed just now to come in?' I wrote in my notebook: 'I've been wondering that myself all day and it's now 3.15 in the afternoon.' It was electrifying to see so much opposition to the colonel so close to the capital, in his own backyard. The central part of the town, around the mosque, was in control of the rebels. Men with guns waited in improvised strongpoints for the next attempt by the regime to take Zawiya back. Crowds marched up and down near the mosque, running through their repertoire of chants.

Gaddafi, go to your death.
The people want the fall of the regime.

Among the men I met – there were almost no women in the crowds – was a sense of anger and frustration at wasted years and wasted lives, talk tumbling out about people who had disappeared into prison and never emerged, of billions of dollars of oil revenue wasted over forty years. 'It's a revolution of honour,' someone said. 'A revolution of sanity.' Zawiya was surrounded by the elite troops of the 32nd Brigade led by Gaddafi's warlike son Khamis. A few weeks later his tanks bashed their way in, but until Gaddafi's fall Zawiya stayed a seething, uneasy place for his security forces.

At night in Tripoli the regime's secret police and paramilitary gunmen would drive slowly around areas they did not trust, sometimes firing at random, sometimes conducting sweeps and raiding houses and arresting any likely-looking suspects. One man keen to talk about what had happened was Muhammad al-Ziani, twenty-four years old, who ended up in the Abu Selim prison after he tried to attack the regime's forces with a primitive bomb. His self-belief kept him going even after he gave himself up to save his family reprisals, and Gaddafi loyalists came to arrest him at his home in Tajoura.

'My heart was beating faster than a cheetah's [...] But they were just so scared. I'm just a normal guy; I don't have a machine gun or anything [...] They don't have something to believe in. They just believe in Gaddafi. It's not something big to defend. This is something that made me step forward for what I'm doing. When we see them moving in the cars and everything, they're always scared, I swear, always scared.'

A BBC Arabic team had a long look at the regime's interrogation centres. Getting arrested is an occupational hazard for foreign correspondents. It happened to me several times in Libya in 2011. But a foreign passport and the name of a big broadcasting organisation like the BBC is usually enough to get you released. Arrest usually means you miss at least half a day's work, and more often than not end the day with half a report to file. But the BBC Arabic team was detained for more than twenty-four hours, in a way that was painful and frightening. It was worse for them because one of them, a journalist called Feras Killani, was Palestinian, without the protection that his two colleagues, Chris Cobb-Smith, who was British, and Göktay Koraltan, who was Turkish, had. Feras, unlike some Palestinians, had never acquired a foreign passport, so he travelled on a laissez-passer issued in Syria, where he had grown up as a refugee. Even though in theory all Arab states support the Palestinian cause, in practice Palestinians often have to deal with suspicion and sometimes with violence from regimes who see them as potential troublemakers, and whose policemen know that Palestinians have no one to intervene on their behalf.

The BBC Arabic team was trying to get to Zawiya before it was retaken. So were most of the other journalists in the Rixos, and most of them were arrested at one time or another. Almost all of them were returned to the hotel, frustrated, their dignity a little dented but otherwise unharmed. But BBC Arabic, and especially Feras, had special treatment. Almost from the start of their detention he was beaten with boots, sticks and knees. Arabic broadcasters had been singled out in the official Libyan media as enemies of the regime. One of the men who was kicking and punching Feras told him he would be punished because he was a spy. When they were transported from one detention centre to another one of his torturers told the driver to kill them if they spoke. Chris was told that if he said one word in English he would be killed. When they reached their destination Feras was masked and beaten again, and was made to kneel as his guards cocked a Kalashnikov in his ear and made as if to kill him. He was kept in a cell overnight with Libyans who had also been tortured, sometimes for days. There was blood on the wall, and Feras tried to assist his cellmates who were handcuffed – a guard had cut his cuffs off. He helped them drink, and even to urinate. The other two were kept in a cell with a man who was so terrified that he prayed all night and kept peeing in his trousers. Chris said the man behaved as if it was the night before his execution.

'He kept making throat-slitting gestures as if he knew he was going to die. They kept coming in, screaming at him, terrorizing him, and the guards were making throat-cutting gestures too.'

The next day all three of them were moved to another detention centre in an overcrowded van with men who had been tortured.

'Everyone was crammed in,' Chris said after he was released. 'Every time you moved someone screamed. There were mashed faces, broken ribs.'

At the next location they were lined up against a wall while a man pointed the barrel of an automatic weapon at each head in turn. When he reached Chris Cobb-Smith he put two shots into the porch of the building a few inches from his ear. By then the officials we dealt with at the Rixos were trying to extract them from Gaddafi's gulag of torture. They realised what was happening was doing the regime no favours. The final bullets were a last warning, long after their identities were established. Back at the hotel Musa Ibrahim, the regime's spokesman, tried to explain it away.

'This isn't right. I'm not looking for excuses, but the atmosphere is very tense. It feels like it's war, as if Britain is coming with its war machine [...] I'm on your side. I'm media too. But there's no established tradition of the media dealing with the military here. This whole thing is completely new to any of our people. They are gobsmacked by the invasion of the media.'

Without a doubt the idea of having journalists operating independently, turning over stones and making themselves a nuisance was new and foreign in Libya. The much more familiar official media had been weighing in against all of us, led by Yousef Shakir, a bearded man with a bad temper who broadcast his nightly talk show from a studio in the basement of the Rixos, where, like a number of other stalwarts of the regime, he had moved with his family. We all assumed that this was because they believed the proximity to the resident foreigners would make them safer from the bombing – an ironic insurance policy for Dr Shakir, the regime's head cheerleader, as most nights he accused us of lying and undermining Libya. He would grumpily line up in the queue for the hotel's lavish buffet alongside the journalists he slammed on television as dishonest, anti-Libyan agents of foreign powers. His incitement did not help matters. But the fundamental issue was that our team had a rare taste of what it was like to be powerless and in the hands of the Libyan intelligence and security services. Gaddafi's men were following standard operating procedures that they had perfected over forty years.

The colonel himself was elusive. Trying to get to him to do an interview was a priority for every journalist in Tripoli. Ever since the regime, on Saif's orders, threw the gates of the Tripoli wide open to reporters, everyone wanted to meet the leader. The BBC tried through our elegant new friend Muhammad Abdullah al-Senussi. But the journalist with the best contacts was Marie Colvin of the *Sunday Times*, who had built up connections with the Gaddafi family over twenty years. In the end she was offered the interview, but they asked her to find an international broadcaster and an American television network. So she chose two friends who fitted the bill: Christiane Amanpour of ABC News, and me.

As with everything in Gaddafi's Libya, the interview was not certain to happen – until it happened, at short notice. Muhammad Abdullah al-Senussi came running up to me as I was leaving my room in the Rixos, for once a little flustered in his designer combat gear.

'Come on, Jeremy, the leader is ready, we must leave now!'

I thought I'd better smarten myself up. TV is a waist-up medium, so I was wearing a decent shirt and jacket with a scruffy pair of jeans. I told him I had a suit in my room. Muhammad Abdullah looked me up and down and after a moment of hesitation decided.

'Don't worry: it's war! Jeans are fine!'

We hurried out in front of the Rixos, where two shining, golden BMWs had been drawn up. Muhammad Abdullah directed the rest of the team into one of them and a minibus. My producer, Cara Swift, joined me in the back of Muhammad's car after she had put her bag in the boot.

'There's a Kalashnikov in there,' she muttered out of the side of her mouth.

The doors shut with solid clunk, a deep and reassuring bass note. The BMW was heavily armoured. Even so, it drew away smoothly and powerfully, very unlike the roaring, grunting armoured Land Rovers I have driven for years in various trouble spots. I found myself stroking the ceiling, which was lined with suede so fine it could have been made into a suit. It reminded me of an interview I did with the former Saudi Arabian oil minister Sheikh Yamani about the notorious terrorist of the 1970s Ilich Ramirez Sanchez, better known as Carlos the Jackal. The sheikh, Carlos and Gaddafi were in their own very distinct ways iconic figures in the seventies.

I had asked the sheikh what the Jackal was like when he held him hostage after he stormed the OPEC conference in Vienna in 1975. He sat back in his armchair on his enormous yacht and recalled, almost wistfully, 'He had a wonderful safari suit. Pierre Cardin. Suede . . .'

Muhammad Abdullah twisted round in his seat, more relaxed now that we were moving, at high speed, through Tripoli. He noticed I had been admiring the car's suede lining.

'Great, isn't it? It's a James Bond car!'

Muhammad Abdullah al-Senussi liked fancy cars. Six months later he was killed in another one, with his cousin Khamis al-Gaddafi, trying to get away from Tripoli after it fell to the rebels. Both, it seems almost certain, died when their convoy was attacked, though no pictures of their bodies ever emerged. For that reason I wonder still whether one of them will reappear. Local rebels found one of my notebooks in the car they claimed had been driven by Khamis. I had lost it somewhere near Misrata a couple of months earlier. My scribbles were in the first part of the book. The rest was used for what a rebel commander near Bani Walid said were Khamis's war plans. He kept it on his desk as a trophy of war.

I expected to be taken to a tent in the desert, or at the very least to one in the grounds of Bab al-Azziziya, Gaddafi's vast walled compound that took up as much space in Tripoli as a good-sized suburb. Instead the BMW hissed to a halt outside the closest thing to cutting edge that Tripoli possessed. It was a modern glass-and-steel Italian restaurant, overlooking Tripoli docks, with a shingle beach of pebbles underneath its transparent plate-glass floor.

Colonel Gaddafi arrived punctually for an Arab authoritarian, behind a pair of aviator sunglasses, dressed in a robe of russet brown with a matching headdress. He was alert, cheerful, reasonably focused and defiant. He picked up themes that his regime had already stressed, and which it never let go until the day it fell. He blamed al-Qaeda for the trouble in the country. Jihadists had come in from outside the country, broken into military bases and seized weapons to terrorise the Libyan people. The weapons had been given to youngsters who had been driven mad by drugs fed to them by al-Qaeda, but now they were laying down their arms as the drugs started to wear off. It was an attempt to press one of the buttons he thought would work in the West. In the 1980s President Ronald Reagan called Colonel Gaddafi the 'mad dog of the Middle East'. But since Libya had agreed to give up its plans to build weapons of mass destruction in 2003, the Gaddafi regime had become a valuable ally for the United States and Britain in their war on terror. Intelligence staff from MI6 had been in Tripoli working with their counterparts in the regime, until the week before I spoke to him. What the colonel still had not properly computed was that no amount of talk about al-Qaeda would help him. The UN Security Council, propelled by Western countries, had unceremoniously put Gaddafi's Libya back into the pariah category a few days before with a strong sanctions resolution. It imposed an arms embargo, froze assets and referred him to the International Criminal Court for crimes against humanity. Gaddafi denied he had any assets to freeze. He said if the British prime minister, David Cameron, could find any money he would split it with him.

'I'm challenging him to show me my bank account in Britain to see if I have any deposits there. I have a tent. I don't like money. That's the challenge and I'll put two fingers in their eyes if they can find anything.'

Since sharing an embrace with Tony Blair when he visited Libya as prime minister in 2004, Colonel Gaddafi had developed a special relationship with Western countries who wanted contracts and intelligence. Now, in a matter of weeks, he had been dumped. It wasn't, he said, as if he had an official position.

'Of course it's a betrayal. They have no morals. If they want me to step down what do I step down from? I'm not a monarch or a king.'

I pointed out that he represented Libya around the world.

'It's honorary; it's nothing to do with exercising power or authority. Who has the power in Britain? David Cameron or Queen Elizabeth?'

He did not have a formal position – it was part of the fiction that his Jamahiriya was the state of the masses – but everyone knew who was in charge. And over the years he had acquired a few other handles as well as the relatively modest one of Brother Leader. They included Leader of the Revolution, the Supreme Guide and the King of African Kings. The man with the titles told me I didn't understand how things worked in Libya. By then I had irritated Colonel Gaddafi enough for him to switch into English. He must have wanted to make his points very clear because Arabic-first was part of his philosophy. He made sure Libya made no concessions to non-Arabic speakers, even banning English from road signs. But the young Muammar al-Gaddafi had received military training in Britain, and he fell back on the language of a country he had condemned many times as a colonialist oppressor.

'You don't understand the system here, no, no, no. Don't say, "I understand." You don't understand. And the world don't understand the system here [...] The authority of the people [...] You don't understand it.'

'But how do the people here show their authority then – because some who've gone out on to the streets to protest say that your people have shot at them?'

'No demonstrations at all in the streets. Did you see demonstrations?'

'Yes. I saw some today. I saw some in Zawiya yesterday . . .'

'Are they supporting us? They're not against us.'

'Some were against you and some were for you.'

'No, no one against us. Against me for what? Because I am not the president. They love me. All my people with me. They love me all. They will die to protect me, my people.'

In the end there were Libyans who died to protect him. But there were many more who were prepared to give their lives to destroy the colonel and the Jamahiriya. A couple of years earlier, in 2009, I was in New York City when Colonel Gaddafi made a speech at the United Nations. He delivered it at more or less the high point of his rapprochement with the Western world. He had even been at the G8 summit in Italy that summer. A lot of the press coverage of his first visit to America focused on his staff's efforts to find a place to pitch his tent. It was at an estate owned by the flamboyant property tycoon Donald Trump for a while, but everywhere Colonel Gaddafi and his retinue went the neighbours complained. It looked as if Ronald Reagan's mad dog, who loved trying to chew up the parts of the world that disagreed with him, had been defanged. He had been so neutered that he was having disputes with suburbanites who didn't want him in their back yards. He had gone from being the ogre to providing material for light-hearted reports from the local television stations who sent their news helicopters into the New Jersey sky to track down the colonel, the tent and his female bodyguards.

The UN speech was a stream of consciousness, which rambled on long after the time limits that the General Assembly suggests and most foreign leaders observe. He was not like that on his home turf, not in the desert, where he always said he felt best, but in the trendy-looking restaurant overlooking Tripoli's port. He answered the questions that were asked of him, and there seemed no doubt that for the colonel and his supporters his replies seemed entirely logical. The reason for that is easy to see. Colonel Gaddafi, by 2011, was one of the longest-serving leaders in the world, in power since he led a coup in 1969, when he was in his late twenties. The regime's television channels liked to remind the people of that in some of their promos, emphasizing his experience, and his place at the top table. They would play photo albums and video of his early meetings with allies, presidents like Josip Broz Tito of Yugoslavia and Gamal Abdul Nasser of Egypt, major world figures of the fifties and sixties. The colonel had been in power for almost all his adult life. All political leaders live in a bubble. Gaddafi's was more hermetically sealed than most. After all those years there were plenty of yes-men around him. When he told me that his people loved him, and would die to protect him, it sounded as if it was the main assumption of his unusual life.

For a man under pressure, Colonel Gaddafi seemed very relaxed. Perhaps he felt more comfortable back in his old role as the West's bogeyman in the Middle East than he did embracing Tony Blair and Silvio Berlusconi and the other leaders who, for a brief moment, saw Libya as a new, benign, even pro-Western frontier in the Arab world. The interview, the last he ever gave, happened before the UN Security Council opened the way for the NATO bombing campaign. His troops were pushing back hard against the rebels in the east, and advancing down the coastal highway to Benghazi. Yes, there was trouble, but he must have thought that he, Gaddafi, Brother Leader, King of African Kings, Libya's old fox, was dealing with it. He was going to show his weak neighbours – Tunisia's president, Zine al-Abidine Ben Ali, by then exiled in Saudi Arabia, and Hosni Mubarak in Egypt, under virtual house arrest at his compound in Sharm al-Sheikh – how to deal with a rebellion. The colonel seemed happy to talk all night. We cut the interview short after an hour because deadlines were pressing. When Gaddafi left the restaurant, I thought I saw a spring in his step.

4

BULLETPROOF DOVES OF PEACE

A warning came from the bible, via Twitter, as we drove towards the Syrian border. *Watch out*, it said. *Saul went blind on the road to Damascus*. Banks of snow had been ploughed into piles on either side of the modern Damascus highway, which starts from Beirut on the Mediterranean coast and goes on up over the Lebanon Mountains to Syria. Just ahead, laid out down below like a tablecloth covered in goodies, was the Bekaa Valley and beyond, across the border and past the Anti-Lebanon Mountains, was Damascus. The Bekaa is long, lush and flat and watered by two mountain ranges, which makes it a great place for farmers to raise cash crops. Rustling plantations of leafy marijuana were the favourite during the lawless days of the civil war, and the Lebanese government still struggles to break the local clans' attachment to growing the lucrative weed. The Bekaa is also excellent for grapes, which makes it the centre of Lebanese winemaking. Some people whisper that certain impressive wineries were built as laundries for drug money. The valley, though, is usually in the news because of its time in the Middle East's crucible, most recently as one of Israel's big targets in the 2006 war with Hezbollah, the Lebanese militia that is also the most prominent Shia political and social movement.

But down below the snow line the Bekaa was benign that day, familiar and safe compared to whatever was waiting on the other side of the border. I tweeted that I was pleased to be getting into Syria after

waiting ten months for a visa. Someone who must have been a sup-
porter of President Assad buzzed back straight away, asking grimly,
'Let's see how you repay the Syrian people for making you wait so
long.'

We had a bit longer to wait. It took three hours to pass the tests set
up at the border by bureaucrats, officials and the mukhabarat. The
Syrian passport officer behind the window had the nervous attention
to detail that comes only to people unfortunate enough to be minor
functionaries in nasty regimes. He looked longingly at his colleagues
who were sipping coffee, puffing their cigarettes and dealing with
uncontroversial truck drivers. Checking foreign journalists, taking the
responsibility for letting them in, was the morning's short straw. First,
he scrutinized minutely each page of every passport for any suggestion of an Israeli stamp. Syrian visa-application forms have a box
asking if you have been in occupied Palestine. They will not use the
word Israel. Proof, in the form of an entry stamp to the Zionist fragment – another well-loved Middle Eastern synonym for Israel – is
enough for a uniformed visa official to turn you back. Foreign correspondents in the Middle East get over the problem by carrying two
passports, one for Israel, one for the rest. Pulling out the wrong passport is always the big fear. Once he found that our visas were not
forgeries the hapless border guard (and I was feeling sorry for him
by now) made phone calls to check that we really did have permission
to be in Syria before another forensic examination of the passports,
just in case.

Outside, in a customs area that was like a deep freeze, an agent
from the mukhabarat, sucking on cigarettes, went through every
item in every one of the BBC's considerable pile of boxes and bags.
TV crews do not travel light. The search said everything about the
paranoia of the Assad regime. The smallest pouch was opened and
examined. The agent was no low-grade thug from the border either.
He was a big city boy whom we had been told to transport down
from Damascus to do the search, with an expensive sheepskin jacket,

blow-dried hair, thorough, professional and deeply unfriendly. The wind whipping in off the snowy mountains bored its way through my thick down jacket, but the secret agent smoked more cigarettes and doggedly ploughed on. Anything that looked as if it could be left for activists to send pictures out of Syria was confiscated. It showed how much the endless video stream of atrocities pumping out on to the internet every day was hurting them. The man from mukhabarat found Cara's camera with the magic letters GPS on it. It was confiscated too, in case it could somehow aid the enemy. It was all signed for and given back when we left, but I could hear the sound of stable doors slamming long after the horse had gone. President Assad's heavies, like their colleagues across the Arab world, were finding it hard to adapt to a world where information could not be blocked. The old methods – intimidation, violence and killing – were perfected in an era when regimes could work in secret, without being bothered by squeamish outsiders. Hundreds of hours of video of demonstrators being attacked were getting on to the internet every week. But a man from Syria's feared State Security apparatus was reduced to confiscating Cara's camera, and her holiday snaps, to try to save the state from more harm.

Someone had pinned a poster up next to the visa window. It showed a dove of peace, surrounded by guns, each labelled with the name of a foreign news broadcaster. One gun belonged to the BBC. The dove was surrounded, and under fire. But the bullets were bouncing off its feathers, which were bulletproof because they were the colours of the official Syrian flag – white, red, and black – with two green stars. By the beginning of 2012 Syria was turning very violent, and the bullets were not bouncing off. Too many were finding a target. The UN gave up counting the dead when its tally reached 5,400. The fog of war was descending too fast to get reliable numbers. By the Summer, anti-Assad activists were claiming around 20,000 dead. President Bashar al-Assad and the people around him appeared to have absorbed and acted on the dictator's lesson from the fall of the regimes in Tunisia and Egypt – which was that force works, if only you use enough of it. They said their soldiers' actions were a legitimate response to terrorists who were trying to destroy the country on the orders of foreign conspirators. But the evidence was very strong that civilians were dying in big numbers, that the regime had from the very beginning of the uprising been ordering its men to open fire on unarmed demonstrators.

President Assad had, at first, believed that Syria was immune to the virus of change that was racing through the Arab world at the beginning of 2011.[1] While tens of thousands of protestors were occupying Tahrir Square in Cairo to try to overthrow Hosni Mubarak the president gave an interview to the *Wall Street Journal*. As usual, he radiated the inner belief that drives him, that directly contradicts the gawky and nervous image he had when he inherited the job in 2000 on the death of his all-powerful father, Hafez al-Assad. The first President Assad was an air-force general who had been part of a series of military juntas after the Arab nationalist Ba'ath Party came to power in a military coup in 1963, and then seized the presidency in 1970. Bashar's self-confidence – the kind you get if you grow up in a family that believes it is destined to rule – is useful for a leader if it goes with good judgement and a certain mental flexibility. But if your views do not reflect reality, the best advice usually is to adapt or abandon them. After the *Wall Street Journal* interview the second President Assad, with characteristic stubbornness, stuck to his particular view of the world even as it was splattered with blood. Perhaps he believed he was a Syrian Churchill, battling in his nation's finest hour.

Bashar, a doctor by training who studied ophthalmology at the Western Eye Hospital in London, chose some medical metaphors. He compared political stagnation in the Middle East to a pool of polluted water full of microbes, 'a kind of disease'. The wrong diagnosis, he argued, would have been to assume that Syria would have gone down with a bad case of fever. The West wanted Syria to get ill, and had certainly been trying to lower its resistance. Unlike Egypt, with its powerful and generous American friends, Syria suffered from Western sanctions. It was 'under embargo by most countries'. That meant 'we do not have many of the basic needs for the people. Despite all that, the people do not go into an uprising.' His triumphant, complacent conclusion was that Syria under the Assad family had developed immunity to the consequences of the Middle Eastern disease. It had earned its vaccination against revolution because he had refused to play the game of compromise with the West and with Israel. Syria had belief. It had a cause in a part of the world where ideology mattered. The people and the leadership were one because President Assad was on the same wavelength. Perhaps Dr Assad thought he had some evidence for this diagnosis. On 5 February 2011 calls for protests in Syria to mirror the turmoil in Cairo had been ignored.

What happened during the next year showed that the president was fooling himself. Less than a month after a textbook display of hubris in front of the reporter from the *Wall Street Journal*, he had the beginnings of an uprising on his hands. His reaction, and that of his regime, to peaceful protests transformed events that could have been containable into an armed insurrection. As president, the responsibility lies with Bashar al-Assad. Even so, a year on, it was still possible to find Syrians who were opposed to the regime who still had a germ of hope that Bashar might change.

That was because Bashar al-Assad, as he claimed, had been on the same wavelength as many of his people – or was at least closer to it than most Arab leaders. Some Syrians always opposed his authoritarian regime, but others had liked the way he stood up to the West and its friends. He came to power promising that Syria would be different under his leadership. In his father's final years, Syria was in an economic time-warp. Mobile phones were available only to the trusted elite; internet access was very limited, though satellite broadcasting swept into Syria in the nineties as it did across the Arab world, with dishes sprouting on every roof. Bashar al-Assad allowed the people to have phones and computers if they could afford them, though there were still many restrictions on what they could see easily online. When Facebook started it was blocked, though it was easy for Syrians who wanted to use it to find a way through the barrier through proxy servers. Had Assad delivered on the political reform that he had spent ten wasted years promising, a combination of real change and his obdurate resistance to Western pressure might even have been a vote-winner – had he ever dared to hold a free election. Even without that, by the beginning of 2011 President Assad had more legitimacy than most other Arab presidents. The awkward heir had brought in enough economic reform to make some of his fellow Syrians believe that he would do more politically if he had the chance. His support of the Palestinians, and of Hassan Nasrallah, the leader of Hezbollah, was popular. Nasrallah was the rock star of Arab politics after his men fought Israel to a standstill in the 2006 war, infuriating Sunni despots from the Gulf to Cairo who raged at their people for cheering a Shia upstart. President Assad enjoyed plenty of reflected glory.

Western powers were always conscious of Syria's pivotal position in the Middle East. It borders Jordan, Israel, Lebanon, Turkey and Iraq. Most of the Middle East's fault lines – of war, politics, religion and sectarianism – run through Damascus or very close to it. Hafez al-Assad became a master intriguer who could ride the region's turbulence and sometimes direct it. He built a strategic alliance with Iran, and made Lebanon into his fiefdom. After he died, Tony Blair, then Britain's prime minister, made a premature attempt to move Bashar into the Western camp, inviting him on a state visit to London. On Blair's return trip to Damascus weeks after the 9/11 attacks in 2001, President Assad lambasted him with a public lecture about Western double standards, condemning the bombing of Afghan civilians, praising Palestinians as freedom fighters and slamming Israelis as state terrorists. It was a shrewd and popular move by Assad: he said nothing that Syrians and other Arabs were not saying every day, but they would never hear these things from pro-Western leaders like Hosni Mubarak. Blair's public embarrassment and private anger was a good price to pay for scoring points in the Arab world. Bashar's father had brought him up to believe that Syria was too important to be ignored. The likes of Blair would always come back.

Bashar worried that after the invasion of Iraq by the United States and its allies in 2003 his Syria would be the next country on the agenda for regime change. Bashar emphasised his Arab-nationalist credentials by welcoming the hundreds of thousands of refugees who crossed the border into Syria as the sectarian killing in Iraq worsened. The frontier runs through a gritty, flat desert, where the wind howls during the winter storms. One dark, wet and brutally cold day late in 2005 I watched processions of Iraqis in cars loaded up with children and possessions inching past potholes full of liquid mud to enter Syria. All of them told tales of terror and random death. Bashar al-Assad allowed them in, offering sanctuary to so many that sections of Damascus felt like parts of Baghdad, with pavements and shops full of people with Iraqi accents. A bus service to Baghdad still ran, and sometimes would arrive in Damascus with exhausted, relieved passengers and bullet holes in the windows. But at the same time that Bashar opened Syria's doors to refugees from the violence in Iraq, he deepened it by allowing jihadist fighters to cross in the opposite direction, moving through Syria to get into Iraq. The intention was to create more problems for the American occupiers. He could hit back at his enemies in the West by pushing them deeper into the morass they had created by invading.

At the same time, he tried to strengthen his position to the West by tightening Syrian control of Lebanon. Since his father's time, holding Lebanon was considered vital for the strength and success of the Assad regime. It gave Damascus a range of Middle Eastern levers to pull, all connected to the region's fault lines, and it was a source of wealth. For years there had been allegations of Syrians plundering

Lebanon, treating it as a private bank account. Even Beirut's famous Casino du Liban had to pay a rake-off to Syrian agents.[2] For Bashar, demonstrating that he was his father's son meant showing Rafik Hariri, the Lebanese prime minister, who was boss. Hariri was a business tycoon, a billionaire who had made his fortune in construction in Saudi Arabia and had presided over the rebuilding of Beirut after the end of the civil war. Hariri stayed close to his Saudi patrons, had many Western allies and a close personal friendship with the French president, Jacques Chirac. The Hariris' base in Paris was a house that once belonged to Gustav Eiffel, the man who built the tower. Hariri was rich and well-connected and the Syrians feared he could offer Lebanon a way out of their domination. According to Nicholas Blanford, one of the best foreign correspondents in Beirut, Hariri was so agitated after being browbeaten and accused of being an American agent by Bashar and his proconsuls in Lebanon that he had a nosebleed. In August 2004 Bashar decided to extend the term of the Lebanese president, who was his puppet. When Hariri protested he is said to have threatened to 'break Lebanon on your head and the head of Chirac'. On St Valentine's Day the following February Hariri was assassinated in a massive bomb attack on his motorcade in central Beirut that killed twenty-two others and wounded more than 220. In the teeth of outrage in Lebanon and among Hariri's many allies abroad, Syria was forced to end its military occupation, and for a while was back to being a pariah. A UN-led investigation into the death of Hariri alleged links between the killing and the presidential palace in Damascus. In the end senior members of Hezbollah, the paramilitary Lebanese Shia movement, were indicted for the killing. The allegation begged the question of why Hezbollah would have wanted to do it, and whether it happened on the orders of its main patrons, Iran and Syria. Since Hezbollah has not, at the time of writing, given up the indicted men for trial, the truth might take many more years to emerge.

*

Despite all the condemnation Syria received from the West around the time that Rafik Hariri was killed, Syria was too important to be ignored and the West came back, as Hafez al-Assad had predicted it would. Bashar's Syria was seen once again as a key to calming the Middle East and reviving some sort of peace process between Israel and the Palestinians. In 2006 James Baker, the former American secretary of state, and Lee Hamilton, a veteran US Congressman, recommended in a much ballyhooed and controversial report that the United States could 'flip' President Assad on to the Western side. Flipping Assad would be part of a comprehensive peace plan that would transform the terms of trade in the Middle East. The report never became official US policy, but to proponents of realpolitik in America's foreign relations it was influential and logical. Assad's history did not matter; nor did the actions of his regime or the allegations of involvement of his regime with Hariri's assassination. Bashar was being seen, like his father, as a crucial figure, a man who could not be ignored. In 2008 the president of France, Nicolas Sarkozy, wooed him with a visit to Damascus. It went so well that Assad was invited to the Bastille Day parade in Paris. The Sarkozys hosted the Assads at the Élysée Palace. The two presidents' glamorous wives shone brightly alongside them.

When he was faced with an uprising, weeks after he said it could never happen, President Assad seemed to assume that Syria was too strategically important for the West to freeze out his regime. Just after his interview with the *Wall Street Journal*, in which he insisted that Syria would not succumb to the Arab virus of rebellion, *Vogue* published a gushing profile of his wife, Asma, that called her 'a rose in the desert [...] the freshest and most magnetic of first ladies' and admired her choice of Christian Louboutin shoes by sighing that she cut 'a determined swathe through space with a flash of red soles'. The Assads appeared to be set fair. His insistence that he was talking to the West only on his terms, along with his talk of reform, had helped earn him genuine legitimacy among many (though not all) Syrians. He told me once that he saw himself as a bridge between East and West, an ally of Iran who could also be friendly with the US and Europe while continuing to support the favourite Arab cause of Palestinian liberation. In other words he could have his cake and eat it. He seemed to calculate that his position at home, and his blossoming friendships in Europe, if not the United States, would survive setting his men on demonstrators. He was wrong.

The first big protests were in Dera'a, a medium-sized town at the centre of a province of the same name in southern Syria, along the border with Jordan. On the walls of their school a group of fifteen boys wrote 'the people want to bring down the regime', the biggest slogan of the Arab year. They were arrested, beaten and tortured while they were in prison. Some had fingernails pulled out. After prayers on Friday 18 March the tribes in Dera'a marched to protest about what had happened. The regime hit back hard, killing five demonstrators. Very quickly the regime and its sympathisers had their explanations ready. Suspicious and subversive outsiders were to blame, including Palestinian jihadists. Others implicated were the Syrian official media's favourite rogue's gallery – the Muslim Brotherhood and the followers of the president's uncle Rifaat al-Assad and the former vice-president Abdul Halim Khaddam, who were both exiles who had split with the regime. The police, the official press insisted, had been ordered to contain the trouble without using firearms, and the people of Dera'a were united in condemning what had happened.[3] All that contradicted many reports coming out on the internet saying that thousands of locals had marched peacefully through the town. By the twenty-third, after five days of protests and the start of what would become routine killing by the regime's forces, local people had set up an improvised clinic in the Omari Mosque, where the protests had begun. In clips of the wobbly amateur video that was beginning to come out of Syria by then, volunteers padded around in their socks tending to the wounded between oxygen cylinders and plasma bags set up inside the mosque's stone arches.

Evidence piled up about what the regime was doing. Much of it came from deserters from the military who had escaped over the border to Lebanon, full of disgust at what they had seen happening and in some cases had done themselves. One deserter said he got out after his unit was ordered to shoot at protesters. He said he saw one officer kill two men who were bystanders, not even demonstrators.

'They'd say, "We are going to hunt birds." They consider protesters to be like birds that have to be hunted. I think this word is enough to you to understand what is going on on the ground there. I gave orders to my soldiers not to shoot there for a long time and my soldiers agreed with this and they didn't shoot on people. I said to them clearly, "If anyone shoots a bullet I will shoot him." But finally the higher commanders discovered me. They investigated me: "Why do you give such orders to your soldiers?" Then I get orders that you should go to this place to support the security forces by yourself. And stand in this place. These orders were very clear to me. If I didn't shoot on people I thought that I would be shot there, I will be terminated. That day I left the army. After, I get arrested and I escaped from the unit, stayed hidden in the near city for a while, then I ran across the country till I reach here. I didn't imagine that I would reach here alive because I didn't know the way.'[4]

Human Rights Watch interviewed other defectors who had fled the country.[5] Some of them had been in Dera'a. Their identities were disguised. One who was named as 'Amjad', from the 35th Special Forces Regiment, said that he was ordered to shoot at demonstrators on 25 April, when about forty protestors were killed.

'The commander of our regiment, Brigadier General Ramadan, usually stayed behind the lines. But this time he stood in front of the whole brigade. He said, "Use heavy shooting. Nobody will ask you to explain." Normally we are supposed to save bullets, but this time he said, "Use as many bullets as you want." And when somebody asked what we were supposed to shoot at, he said, "At anything in front of you."'

Human Rights Watch found a man who had been in the town with air-force intelligence, who they named 'Mansour'. He said his commander, Colonel Qusay Mihoub, ordered them to use live ammunition.

'Our orders were to make the demonstrators retreat by all possible means, including by shooting at them. It was a broad order that shooting was allowed. When officers were present, they would decide when and whom to shoot. If somebody carried a microphone or a sign, or if demonstrators refused to retreat, we would shoot. We were ordered to fire directly at protesters many times. We had Kalashnikovs and machine guns, and there were snipers on the roofs.'

By the time I reached Dera'a with my BBC colleagues in January 2012, around ten months into the uprising, it felt as if it had been under occupation for a long time.

Five army roadblocks checked traffic coming into Dera'a on the main road from Damascus. Unexpected visitors were not welcome. Inside the town there were more roadblocks, sandbagged military positions and plenty of armed men, occupiers in their own country. It reminded me of a Palestinian town on the West Bank, Nablus perhaps, at the height of an uprising against the Israelis. President Assad had convinced himself that his people loved and respected him because of his refusal to stop denouncing Israel's occupation of Syria's Golan Heights and Palestinian land in Jerusalem and the West Bank. But in Dera'a he had created his own occupation: of Syrians. The people in the streets had the sullen, guarded air that people have when they know a wrong step can land them in jail or worse. I asked one man what he thought about the president. 'I won't comment,' he said, eyeing the regime security men who had accompanied our busload of journalists into Dera'a, 'because I'd have to tell a lie.'

We headed for the Omari Mosque. The Syrians felt confident enough to send the BBC team in a minibus, without a minder, followed by a carload of State Security men from the mukhabarat. The mosque is a four-square, long-slung stone building, looking strong enough to be a fortress. It was in the hands of the army. Soldiers in combat gear peered from behind sandbag walls. Truckloads more of them were positioned around the back of the mosque. The Omari Mosque was a symbol of who held Dera'a, and the governor and his bosses in Damascus had decided that symbols mattered. The soldiers were on alert, not taking chances, staying behind their sandbags or close to them. I guessed from that they feared local people also believed in the power of symbols and were waiting for a chance to get the building back.

Then there were some shouts. A couple of hundred yards away, up a street that wound up a small hill, about half a dozen young men were calling out and gesturing. They wanted us to walk up to them. I had a look at the men from mukhabarat, squeezing out of their car with the usual black leather jackets, cigarettes and firearms. This was going to be a test.

I assumed that the men from the mukhabarat would follow us, or stop us, but we had to try to get up the hill to the young men, who were still waving. Syria is usually considered to have an even tighter police state than Libya's during the time of Muammar al-Gaddafi. That meant it didn't look good. On bad days in Tripoli in 2011 we would be followed if we left the hotel to buy some supplies in the shops down the road. They had their reasons – foreign journalists often pretended to go shopping as an excuse to break away from the minders – but passers-by foolish enough to exchange even a few pleasantries with foreigners risked being interrogated on the spot and if they were unlucky were paid a visit from Gaddafi's mukhabarat. I didn't look back as we walked towards the young men, but I was expecting to hear shouts, or footsteps, or even the sound of a weapon being cocked, the secret policeman's equivalent of a shepherd whistling to his dogs. But there was nothing. They didn't follow and we walked up to the group of young men – or boys, to be more accurate, no more than teenagers. They were jumpy, adrenaline pumping, shouting all at once, and full of defiance. I realised that we might be the first foreigners to have reached them in almost a year of protest and killing. They wanted to tell their stories. Some of them covered their faces when they saw the camera, but others did not bother. (When the pictures were broadcast, we decided to conceal their identities for them by superimposing blobs on their faces.) One of the older ones, no more than eighteen or so, emerged as a spokesman.

'This is a street of martyrs. Eighteen have been killed in this street alone in the last ten months.' Eighteen might not sound like much in the context of all of Syria's bloodshed but it was a small street, made up of a handful of buildings. More young men emerged from their houses. They lived in a town but it was still a traditional, tribal society. The women stayed indoors, but I could see them peeping out from upstairs windows. A girl of about twelve emerged from a doorway, smiling in a shy way and carrying a blown-up photograph, mounted in a gilt frame, of a plump, innocent-looking boy not much older than her.

'That's her brother,' the self-appointed spokesman said. 'They killed him last year.'

The girl did not seem to be connecting too strongly with what was happening or with the growing crowd of young men milling around the strangers who had arrived from the outside world, so far away from the small and concentrated corner of hell in which they had been living. That road near the Omari Mosque had been at the centre of the violence and upheaval for almost ten months and it must have marked her. She just kept smiling, and holding her brother's portrait across her chest. I looked back down the hill towards the mosque. The soldiers were behind their sandbags, but the secret policemen had disappeared. It looked calm down there, but I was starting to get worried about the safety of the crowd. Some of them had been pointing across the valley to what looked like a military position about 500 yards away, where they said snipers positioned themselves to shoot at them. They would have to be good shots, I thought, but it wasn't impossible.

'The Assad gangs are killing us, and the army, and the mukhabarat,' one of the others said. 'They'll break into our houses and arrest us after you've gone.'

I thought of the pictures that I had seen on the internet – so many of them that they had become a badly focused, jerky blur in my mind – that came from Dera'a and its surroundings. Or were said to come from Dera'a, anyway. The outside world had become too reliant on those shaky images, mainly filmed on mobile phones and then uploaded to the internet. It was often impossible to work out where they were from, and when they were filmed. As the operation became more slick, some of the amateur cameramen took to holding pieces of paper with the place and the date in front of the lens, or shouting out the details so they would be picked up by the microphone. By the time that the regime was besieging the Babr Amr district of Homs, Syria's third biggest city, a month after I was in Dera'a, an amateur cameraman filmed shells smashing into a burning mosque while shouting, 'God is great' and calling for help to Muslims around the world. The pain and exhaustion of the siege was in his voice, which would go up to a squeak every few words. Sometimes it was clear what was happening. The cold-blooded, murderous intent of the security forces in some of images that came out of Syria was chilling. Early on, an anti-Assad demonstration was broken up when men in plain clothes who had driven up to it in a car produced guns and started to shoot into the crowd at point-blank range. And the pictures often showed remarkable displays of solidarity, men taking terrible risks to rescue the wounded or to drag bodies in off the streets.

I didn't want our little video sequence to turn into another disaster movie from Syria, or to put them in any more danger – which was probably an absurd notion, because they had been in danger for almost a year. How could we make it worse? This was no time to find out. Besides, we had a strong story. As we left them they were chanting, 'Bashar, we want to hang you.' On the way back down the hill a female member of our team hid the memory card with the pictures on. Many of our strongest images of the Arab uprisings spent time next to the skin of female colleagues. Since the police and mukhabarat never had female officers with them, it was always a good idea to give anything that needed to be hidden to a woman – the hope being that men would not search a woman in a foreign news team. With us, it worked. Other women who were dragged off to cells and police stations had horrendous experiences.

I was still bemused that the mukhabarat had let us walk off to see the protestors. What was even more remarkable was that the only secret policeman still waiting when we reached the Omari Mosque was smiling. The others were back in the car, smoking. It was a cold day. He gestured, like a kind host, towards the minibus. There wasn't one question; no anger and shouting, as there might have been in Libya, and no attempt to get hold of our material. I did not want to make things worse by asking, but could not work out whether they knew the people in the street, and would get them later, or whether that group of secret policemen could stomach no more violence and had effectively defected to the other side. In Cairo a few weeks later the Arab League met and decided to step up their aid to the opposition. With them there was a representative of the Syrian National Council, the fractious body that was trying – and failing – to unite the opposition. He claimed that the regime was being eaten from inside by disloyalty in the intelligence services that amounted to defection. Hundreds of people, he said, were being picked up by the mukhabarat. But instead of being interrogated, intimidated and perhaps tortured, they were being released un-harmed after twenty-four hours in custody. Perhaps it was happening that day in Dera'a. Weeks later, though, in Homs and elsewhere, the regime still had plenty of men to make arrests and pull triggers. Even if some security men were sick of what they had to do, many were not.

*

The combination of violence, tension and the secretive and paranoid nature of the regime created excellent conditions for rumour-mongering. About half an hour after we left the Omari Mosque a rumour started circulating among the Ministry of Information minders that the BBC had an undercover team (as well as us) in Dera'a because the secret team had been seen meeting protestors. It was nonsense, of course, but the first assumption was that it was true – yet more proof of the conspiracy.

A broad boulevard runs through the centre of Dera'a, past the administrative headquarters where the governor was waiting in his office. The side of the boulevard closest to the building, a big office block, was closed to traffic. Soldiers had set up roadblocks at either end, and more soldiers were posted on the gates of the HQ. They were all in combat gear. It was the Assad regime's outpost in hostile territory. Before the Arab uprisings started it was hard to see visual evidence of the distance between the regimes and the people. But in Dera'a it was all laid out.

In his office the governor, Muhammad Khaled al-Hannous, a man in his sixties, sat smiling and cracking jokes as if it was a cafe and he was the popular guy in the village. He was a retired general who came from Hama but spent much of his military career in Dera'a province, and who was given the job when his predecessor was fired after the first demonstrations. His military career meant he knew the city and the region, and its tribes. It could have been a shrewd appointment, but his orders were to pacify Dera'a – and its people did not want to be pacified.

Under a bust of Hafez al-Assad, the governor denied that Dera'a was a town under occupation. Like President Bashar, he blamed a foreign conspiracy for any trouble in the town, orchestrated by the United States, Israel, Britain and France. Another factor was to blame – drugs.

'I'm not saying they're all our supporters out there,' he said. 'There are protestors and there are armed people [...] and there are those who kill for money [...] They use drugs.'

I couldn't believe my ears. I asked him if he realised that Colonel
Gaddafi had explained away protests in Libya in exactly the same way.
The governor gave his best, seen-it-all, grandfatherly smile.

'I won't talk about Gaddafi. We're in Dera'a.'

Governor Hannous sat surrounded by portraits of the Assad
dynasty. The most looming presence was the patriarch, Hafez al-
Assad, unsmiling, still a formidable memory more than a decade after
his death. His chosen heir, Basel, charismatic, an army officer with a
reputation as a ladies' man, was pictured dressed as a magnificently
military equestrian and mounted on a white charger. Basel was killed
in 1994 when he took his Mercedes instead of his horse down the
Damascus airport road in thick fog and drove it, the regime said, into
a roundabout. In another frame next to him was Bashar, a man with
none of Basel's swagger, who found himself the crown prince after his
brother's death.

By the time the governor met the press in his office in January
2012 the nature of the conflict in Syria was changing. What had
started as a series of peaceful demonstrations was becoming a fully
fledged armed insurgency. Since it took the regime so long to give me
a visa I was not able to see those first demonstrations for myself. But
there is a big – and I think convincing – body of evidence that the first
marches were peaceful. Not only that, but peaceful marches continued throughout that first summer even though people went on to
streets with the certain knowledge that the security forces would open
fire. It takes a lot of courage and determination to demonstrate when
you know you might die. That fact alone must have been deeply
depressing for the president and his regime. They were trying, and
failing, to reinstate the barrier of fear that every authoritarian ruler
needs. I have no doubt that those opponents of the regime who had
weapons and were prepared to use them shot back whenever they
could. But there is no evidence to back up the regime's claim that
from the very start it was facing an organised, armed conspiracy. It
took until the summer of 2011 for Colonel Riad al-Asaad, who had

defected to the opposition, to announce in Turkey that he was leading a group called the Free Syria Army, often known simply as the
Free Army. It took months more for them to move beyond being just
groups of local men who had taken up arms. It was not until May or
June 2012 that evidence began to emerge of coordinated and successful attacks by the Free Army on government positions.

In other words, the slide into civil war was not inevitable. At the
very beginning Bashar al-Assad could have dealt with the protests in
a way that might even have calmed the country and strengthened his
regime by making it more legitimate. If he was as serious about
reform as he had claimed, he had a chance to show it when finally he
spoke to the Syrian people about what was happening in Dera'a. An
announcement came that he would break his public silence about the
demonstrations in Dera'a in a speech to the parliament. For a few
days at the end of March in the run-up to the speech it looked as if
he might be prepared, at long last, to step away from his father's iron
legacy. Tantalizingly one of the family's longest-serving advisers,
Farouk al-Sharaa, hinted that the response to the protests would be
the reforms Assad had been promising but not producing for more
than a decade. Al-Sharaa, who had spent twenty-two years as foreign
minister under both Assad presidents before being made vice-
president, said the speech would contain decisions that would 'please
the people'.[6] But then the speech was postponed by a couple of days,
which might have been a sign that the most important voices in the
regime, the president and members of his extended family, could not
agree about what it should contain.

Bashar al-Assad spoke in the end to the Syrian parliament on
30 March 2011. It is an obedient body whose members gave him
repeated standing ovations, chanting their adoration, occasionally
interrupting to praise his wisdom and bravery. Assad smiled indul-
gently as men much older than him outdid each other with flattery.
One told him that leading the Arab world was not enough, as he
should be the leader of the entire world. As usual he did not stick to

a set text, lecturing the parliament and the watching world. Instead of announcing that the time had, finally, come for the reforms that he had been promising since he came into his inheritance, he explained that Syria was fighting for its life. It was threatened by sedition, by traitors who were in the pay of foreign conspirators who wanted to destroy the country. The usual nods to reform were there. It was still his objective; but he wasn't going to do it under fire, in the heat of the moment. The MPs cheered and chanted. Outside the parliament, those who had already rejected the regime and all it represented were not surprised. The veteran dissident Haitham Maleh, who spent eight years in the regime's jails, told me that he did not believe a word the president said.

'He didn't say anything new. All his speech was a repeat from the past [...] This is a bad regime. They rule the country by fear.'[7]

In Jordan, just over the border from Dera'a, a man who said he had fled with his family after he saw security forces shoot dead a fourteen-year-old boy carrying an olive branch was watching the speech on television with disgust.

'These are dogs, cheering every time he opens his mouth.'[8]

Some of the officials who had been hoping that he would lift the emergency law that had been in force since the Ba'ath Party seized power in 1963 were deeply depressed.

One told me: 'He's got to get rid of the old guard, or the ship is going to sink. This isn't Egypt. Syria doesn't have a political system, it has a family system, and the Assads don't have a long history of making concessions. The more you corner the regime, the more stubborn it will be. But if he doesn't respond he's going to lose what's left of the regime's legitimacy and popularity. I believe in the survival instincts of Assad. It's not too late. The Syrian people are very emotional and he can change their mood. There's a new Syria, whether we like it or not. They can't reinstate the barrier of fear. Either the president will ride the wave of reform – and pretend it's his agenda – or get swept away by the tide.'

Others who had hoped Assad would break with the past claimed a year later, looking back with dismay at the blood that had been spilt, that it was not the speech that Assad had planned to make.[9] A Syrian diplomat insisted that Assad had wanted to announce that he was lifting the emergency law, claiming it was in his speech until the morning it was delivered. 'But five hours before the speech he was told that if you give them more they'll ask for more. They won't be satisfied. You'll go the way of Ben Ali and Mubarak.' The diplomat also said that Assad had wanted to go to Dera'a, to meet families of the dead and local leaders to attempt to calm the trouble, but was persuaded that that was a bad idea. Dera'a is a tribal society and that approach might even have worked. President Assad senior was adept at making alliances with tribal leaders. He was a believer in the stick, and used it without compunction, but he also understood the need for carrots.

It is impossible to say what went on in the internal debates inside Syria's highest decision-making body, which is the Assad family itself. Perhaps the president did want to go to Dera'a. Perhaps he was persuaded it was a bad idea. Perhaps he did consider stepping away from his family's tradition of responding to challenges to their rule with violence. They looked at what happened in Tunisia and Egypt, and they saw that Colonel Gaddafi in Libya had knocked his rebels back by not hesitating to use deadly force. It was clear that there was a mood for change in the region, and whatever the president said Syria was not immune. The emergency law was lifted in April, but with so many conditions that nothing was different. Demonstrations still needed permission, and the interior minister, Muhammad Ibrahim al-Shaar, even told people 'to refrain from taking part in all marches, demonstrations or sit-ins under any banner whatsoever'. If they did, 'the laws in force in Syria will be applied in the interest of the safety of the people and the stability of the country'.

The acid test was the fact that the security services in Syria were still above the law. The killing went on. There is no guarantee that Assad could have headed off the protests by offering reform, and by punishing the men who decided to arrest the teenagers who were imprisoned and tortured for protesting. But it might have worked, might have spared Syrians from what was coming and might even have preserved the Assad regime. The President claimed, wrongly, that he was facing an armed insurgency from the start. Instead, the regime's own reaction made its nightmare come true. Violence begat violence, and a year on from the speech to the parliament the insurgency was getting more organised and there were signs that jihadists, sympathisers with al-Qaeda, were arriving to take up the fight against the regime.

After he made his speech in Damascus on 30 March 2011, Bashar al-Assad left the parliament building past crowds of his supporters who had been installed behind police lines, cheering, chanting and pumping their fists as he beamed and waved on his way to his limousine. The president looked delighted with his day's work. In fact he had made the biggest strategic blunder of his life. He had blown his only real chance to defuse the crisis.

5

TRIPOLI UNDER THE BOMBS

At the interview with Colonel Gaddafi I made a new friend. He was a Libyan diplomat, a senior adviser to the colonel, who had worked with him for many years. He is still in Tripoli, so I will call him Muhammad. He had a lugubrious expression most of the time, broken up with sudden laughter and some sharp humour. A few days after the interview, on 2 March, the colonel made a public appearance at a conference centre on the same campus as the Rixos hotel, arriving at the head of a long competitive motorcade which, as usual, was made up of fast cars and 4×4s full of armed men, jockeying for position in the convoy to get closer to their leader, but in slow motion as he was trundling along in a green single-seater golf buggy. I reckoned piloting his electric kart was less a statement of his commitment to the environment than it was about his security. The foreign media had been brought in for his speech and he did not want to look even slightly threatened by the international coalition that was building up against him. As we waited for Gaddafi's triumphant, bizarre entrance, I saw Muhammad in a crowd of officials. He waved and came over. Like the colonel himself, he was shocked by the speed with which Libya had gone from being an ally in the war on terror to a pariah.

'I don't understand why two friendly countries suddenly have to have a crisis like this. It seems it was planned for many years. What's the point of having diplomatic relations and cooperation with MI5 and MI6 against terrorism? The leader uses the word betrayed, and it's *betrayal*. Remember what he said when you met him. It's like the woman who burns down the tent to kill the mouse.'

He smiled, then amazement and disbelief flooded back, and tears welled up in his eyes, and he found another metaphor.

'The way they've treated Libya. It's like a man who has a pretty wife, who's a good mother, then he divorces her, and everyone asks, "Why did he do that?" I worked always on getting closer to the West. I am so personally disappointed and let down.'

I got to know Muhammad well in the months I spent in Gaddafi's Libya. He often talked about what he believed was the involvement of al-Qaeda in the uprising, which was a universal theme among those who were close to the leadership. A gory video of dead Libyans, mainly with their throats cut, had been broadcast repeatedly on the regime's television channels. He gave me a DVD of the pictures.

'It's ten to fifteen Libyans killed the Taliban way. They've had a kangaroo trial. They're using typical al-Qaeda methods. I'm telling you, if you hit a camel he doesn't forget: he kills you when he gets the chance a year later. Al-Qaeda's the same. The West will regret it if their plot against the leader results in al-Qaeda coming to the country.'

He broke off because Colonel Gaddafi was arriving to make his speech to supporters who had been bussed in, who whipped themselves into paroxysms of delight and adulation, standing on their chairs, kissing posters of their leader while he drank the reception in from the podium, smiling, sometimes acknowledging them with his favourite slow-speed bent-arm fist pump. His claque stood to attention, some saluting, as the national anthem, 'Allahu Akbar' played. It was based on a song that was a hit in Egypt when its leader Gamal Abdul Nasser defied Britain, France and Israel during the Suez war in 1956. Nasser, the prophet of Pan-Arabism, was still alive when Gaddafi took power thirteen years later, and Muhammad explained that the song was adopted as a sign of respect to the senior Arab leader and his creed of Arab nationalism. It was easy to sing, with much repetition of the phrase 'Allahu Akbar' ('God is greatest'), and mixed with lyrics that could have come from one of Gaddafi's speeches.

> God is greatest! God is greatest!
> And God is greatest above plots of the aggressors,
> And God is the best helper of the oppressed.
> With faith and with weapons I shall defend my country,
> And the light of truth will shine in my hand.
> Say with me! Say with me!
> God, God, God is greatest!
> God is above any attacker.

That day Gaddafi's speech lasted for more than two hours. It was to mark the anniversary of the introduction of Libya's political system in 1977. It had no formal president or parliament in the conventional sense, which was why the colonel continued to say he had no post from which to resign. He reprised all his favourite themes. Foreign conspirators wanted Libya's oil, and to re-colonise the country. Libyans would fight to the last drop of their blood to resist it. It was abrasive, familiar stuff which made exhausting listening. Even his loudest supporters, young men who had swayed and chanted like a football crowd, were not producing the same volume of noise after the first sixty minutes. Muhammad too was getting worn down by Colonel Gaddafi's remorseless, relentless, repetitive rhetoric. He had heard it all before.

'I warn you,' he muttered in the seat next to me. 'The West should think twice before deciding to cause trouble to this regime. The threat from al-Qaeda is not imaginary. I'm getting hungry. The buffet in the Rixos is open. I'm going to eat.' And he slipped away.

*

But Western countries, led by Britain and France, were thinking very seriously about intervening in Libya. In London, on the day I interviewed Colonel Gaddafi, David Cameron was at the dispatch box in the House of Commons defending his suggestion of a no-fly zone over Libya in the face of some weary scepticism, most significantly from the US defence secretary, Robert Gates. The United States, Britain and their Western allies had been struggling since the start of the year to catch up with the changes in the Arab world. They had been caught short, and were trying to find policies and responses that worked. The crises in Tunisia and Egypt had left them behind and they were not used to accepting that they were behind the curve. Some rapid rethinking had to be done. Decisions were taken, in the words of one recently retired senior US diplomat, at 'warp speed'. It had taken the United States just over a week to break off its thirty-year relationship with Hosni Mubarak. Now they had to decide how to respond to Gaddafi and Libya's would-be revolutionaries.

The Libyan crisis broke days after the fall of Mubarak, which had followed seamlessly from the fall of Ben Ali in Tunisia. Bahrain and Yemen were also getting wrapped up in trouble. It was an onslaught from a region that months before had seemed barely more than politically moribund. One Western diplomat said: 'The system was under great stress. We were juggling a perfect storm of crises. And we made the classic mistake of fighting the last war. We assumed that the Middle Eastern dominoes were falling very fast. We thought it would be like 1989 in Europe.' The strain showed. William Hague, Britain's foreign secretary, said on 21 February that he had information that Colonel Gaddafi was on a plane to Venezuela. One of his most senior advisers had asked him not to make the announcement, which was based on information from an air-charter company and intelligence that turned out to be wrong, but he went ahead with it, feeling the pressure to generate diplomatic momentum at an EU foreign-ministers meeting about Libya. The assumption was that Gaddafi would go as quickly as Ben Ali and Mubarak, and had the politician's desire to get on top of a crisis which had been moving far too fast to catch and gather.

Two events changed everything, and in the end sealed Gaddafi's doom. First of all the Arab League voted on 12 March to ask the UN Security Council to impose a no-fly zone. Colonel Gaddafi had made many enemies over the years in the Arab world. He had even tried to arrange the assassination of Saudi Arabia's King Abdullah when the monarch-to-be was still crown prince. Two respected members of the Arab leaders' club, Mubarak and Ben Ali, had gone. The other members were wondering who was going to be next. They could feel – and see on television – the forces at work; they could hear the chants about the downfall of the regimes, and they needed to show their people that they were not circling the wagons but were responding to legitimate grievances. When it came to the vote, Colonel Gaddafi had no friends left at the Arab League to defend him. Even Libya's own delegation defected to the opposition, along with their colleagues at the United Nations in New York.

The second decisive factor was the rapid advance of Gaddafi's forces as they stormed along the road east from Tripoli towards Benghazi, recapturing some of the huge swathes of land that had been seized by the rebels. Libya is a big country, but most of the towns lie along the coast, linked by a single highway. We would sit in Tripoli watching news reports of the largely untrained rebel fighters hurtling up and down the coast road in pickup trucks, with plenty of fighting spirit but little idea of how to harness it. Against them were professional soldiers, armed with tanks and heavy artillery. Gaddafi's brigades were no match for a Western army, but with their heavy weapons they brushed aside the untrained volunteers and advanced rapidly towards Benghazi. In Tripoli, the regime started to relax. But as his troops pushed through Ras Lanuf and Brega and on to Ajdabiya, the last rebel stronghold before Benghazi, Gaddafi renewed his threats to the people of the city. The mantra was by then well known. His men would go house to house, alley to alley, to crush the rats. Schoolchildren fixed brightly coloured posters of rats in traps, their class artwork, to the railings outside the Rixos. The head of the rebel National Transitional Council, Mustafa Abdul Jalil, warned that half a million people would die if Benghazi was recaptured by the regime.

In London, Paris and Washington the genocidal ghosts of the 1990s – of Bosnia and Rwanda, Sarajevo, Srebrenica and Kigali – had risen and were stalking the corridors. The talk of a massacre in Benghazi was not dismissed as an empty threat. At the White House Samantha Power, one of President Obama's most influential advisers on national security, was arguing for action. During the Bosnian war she had been a journalist, basing herself in Sarajevo. Back then, she was always articulate and determined. After the war she became an academic and wrote a highly influential book about America's response to genocide. In it she describes her struggle to interest her editors in the first reports of the genocidal killings of Bosnian Muslims by Serbs in Srebrenica in July 1995. At the time, Power had not realised how bad it would get.

'It never dawned on me that General Mladic [the military commander of the Bosnian Serbs, by 2011 on trial for genocide] would or could systematically execute every last Muslim man and boy in his custody [...] I was haunted by the murder of Srebrenica's Muslim men and boys, my own failure to sound a proper early warning, and the outside world's refusal to intervene even once the men's peril had become obvious.'[1]

Her response to Gaddafi's threats was to take them seriously. Back in Tripoli Muhammad said that was not what had been intended, and pooh-poohed them. 'When the leader talked about rats he meant al-Qaeda elements. He didn't mean literally house to house.'

Samantha Power had an ally in Susan Rice, the US ambassador to the United Nations who had been an adviser on Africa to President Clinton when the Americans did nothing to stop the genocide in

Rwanda. The two women, deeply troubled by the failures of the 1990s, won over Hillary Clinton, the US secretary of state, who had been in the White House as first lady while her husband, Bill Clinton, wrestled with the dilemmas of responding to late-twentieth-century genocide. In London, William Hague's special adviser, Arminka Helic, a Bosnian who had come to Britain in 1992 as a refugee from the war, argued the case for intervention. A headline in the *Independent* pulled her up. It said: 'Gaddafi Orders Shoot to Kill'.

'I said, "This is a war crime. Are we going to do nothing?" I said to the boss that we needed a menu of options and the most obvious was the International Criminal Court. We need to send a warning not just to him – he's a gonner – but to peel off those around him who are less certain about Gaddafi cause.' On her side was Ed Llewellyn, Prime Minister Cameron's chief of staff. He had worked in Bosnia as an aide to the High Representative, Paddy Ashdown, who had campaigned for international intervention during the Bosnian war. When Ashdown was leader of the Liberal Democrats in Britain during the war in Bosnia, he would often pop up in Sarajevo – sometimes literally from the tunnel the Bosnians had built underneath the airport to help them evade the Serb siege. The failures of the 1990s, and the lessons to be drawn from them, were being re-examined on both sides of the Atlantic.

The shame and the impotence of those years left a mark. One was a strengthened aspiration that it is wrong – and even politically costly – for a powerful state with a belief in the rights of humankind to watch killing when it could be stopped. The desire to avoid another Bosnia or Rwanda was a powerful motivator among people who were in the position to make a difference in 2011 when they had been only horrified spectators in the 1990s. They knew they would have to tread carefully. Western military intervention in the Arab world was deeply controversial, contaminated by the catastrophic consequences of the invasion of Iraq in 2003, and seen as a cynical and hypocritical return to imperialism by many people around the world. But after Bosnia and Rwanda Western countries no longer wanted to stand and stare.

With Colonel Gaddafi's troops advancing on Benghazi, time felt very short. Decisions were taken very fast. 'You had to ride the wave,' one official recalled. 'We were responding, not strategising. We went from saying that we'll never intervene to bombing in only six days.' Another said, 'We didn't have the luxury they had in the 1990s of having time to react to events. We had to think really fast about how to deal with it. Would we allow it to happen like it happened in Bosnia – cities falling, siege, shelling, militias and mopping up?' NATO's senior political forum, the North Atlantic Council, discussed the Libyan crisis for the first time on 25 February, the day before the UN Security Council passed Resolution 1970 imposing sanctions on the regime in Tripoli. No discussion about the no-fly zone as a serious prospect was held before the second week of March. On the fourteenth the Foreign Office in London was still saying that the idea would not work. Officials who had been formed – and seared – by the invasion of Iraq in 2003, rather than the Balkans in the 1990s, argued for caution. The British military, stung from a round of big cuts in defence spending and fighting a war in Afghanistan, did not want any more commitments. Senior officers reminded the prime minister, with a certain relish, how much more feasible the operation would have been with the aircraft carrier he had just scrapped. At first the foreign secretary, William Hague, was in the lessons of Iraq camp, rather than the legacy of Bosnia. But then Power, Rice and Clinton won the argument in Washington. President Obama decided to back the idea of a no-fly zone. The weight of the United States, along with the political force of the Arab League's call for intervention, was irresistible.

Insiders at the Foreign Office said the crucial meetings dealt with the need to stabilise Libya because of the impact that protracted bloodshed and disorder might have on hopes for democracy in its neighbours Tunisia and Egypt. They were also deeply apprehensive about the prospect of thousands of Libyan refugees landing on the Italian island of Lampedusa, which is closer to North Africa than it is to Sicily, or even on the northern shores of the Mediterranean. The sources said there was no discussion about securing Libyan oil, or protecting the big commercial interests Britain had in Libya, especially BP's huge contract. But it is hard to believe that oil reserves were not part of the calculations that were being made in London, Paris and Washington. If they were not, they should have been.

The pictures and news reports coming out of Libya were by then a highly influential factor, according to some of the people involved in the discussions. They were setting the agenda of politicians and officials, putting them under pressure to move fast to keep up. Many of the pictures were generated by the Libyan people themselves, who were using their phones to film what they were seeing then uploading their videos to the internet. Individuals put testimony about what was happening, and their fears, on to social media. It was another sign of the way that the world had changed and speeded up. It would have been much harder for Western governments to sit on their hands, as they did during most of the Bosnian war from 1992 to 1995 and during the Rwandan genocide in 1994, if there had been pictures arriving in near-real time of the killing from places professional journalists could not reach. In her book Samantha Power observes that once the killing started in Rwanda 'it is shocking to note that during the entire three months of the genocide, Clinton never assembled his top policy advisers to discuss the killings [...] Rwanda generated no sense of urgency and could safely be avoided by Clinton at no political cost.'[2] Power's own arguments about the need not to ignore what was happening in Libya, in the face of initial scepticism in the Obama White House, were reinforced by the video that flooded the internet.

Once the rebels had captured eastern Libya, the frontier with Egypt opened and professional broadcasters with cameras and satellite dishes were able to pour in towards Benghazi without visas. They reported the joy when the regime's men had gone, the exhilarating advance through the desert in a cavalry charge of Toyota pickups, and then the fear of a massacre as people in Benghazi listened to Gaddafi's speeches and saw the casualties coming back from the front. The fact that so much reporting was coming out of the rebellious east forced the regime to let journalists into Tripoli. By accepting a visa, journalists were trading freedom for the chance to peep into the dark kingdom. Regimes like Colonel Gaddafi's give journalists visas only when they think they can control the message that comes out. Saif al-Islam, Gaddafi's son and heir, who had been as comfortable in well-heeled parts of London as in his family's palaces in Tripoli, certainly believed he could get the Gaddafi view to drown out the others.

We try, always, to prove them wrong. By the time I had clocked up my first month at the Rixos hotel in Tripoli, it was feeling quite like the al-Rashid hotel in Baghdad in the time of Saddam Hussein. Minders patrolled the marble lobby, and were supposed to accompany us everywhere. Armed guards were on the main gate, ostensibly to secure the hotel, but when there was violence in the city – especially on Fridays – their job was to keep newsmen and women on campus, controllable in our five-star cage. But enough reporters and crews were able to get out to report the unrest by using the rat-like cunning that our predecessor Nicholas Tomalin, killed on the Golan Heights in the 1973 Yom Kippur War, once said was a must for every journalist.

Back in the Foreign Office in London William Hague was advised that it might be time for another go at what they were calling "humanitarian intervention" that Tony Blair championed in Sierra Leone and Kosovo when he was prime minister. The consequences of the invasion of Iraq were a dreadful lesson, but cheerleaders for intervention in Libya argued that the problem with Iraq was the failure to get a clear UN resolution authorising action. Responding to Libya would need unarguable international legality and legitimacy, and the focus moved to the UN in New York. Britain played a big role in drafting Resolution 1973, which the Security Council passed on 17 March. It used strong language to condemn the actions of the Gaddafi regime, said that the systematic attacks that were taking place against civilians could amount to crimes against humanity, and authorized member states 'to take all necessary measures [...] to protect civilians and civilian populated areas under threat of attack in the Libyan Arab Jamahiriya, including Benghazi, while excluding a foreign occupation force of any form on any part of Libyan territory [...]' The specific prohibition of an occupation was designed to reassure all those who feared another Iraq-style invasion, but the key phrase was 'all necessary measures'. It meant that the resolution could be backed by military force as long as it did not lead to an occupation.

In Tripoli my friend Muhammad in Gaddafi's office was still hoping for negotiation. The African Union, among others, was trying to push a peace plan. He believed the colonel could be persuaded to step down, given time, persuasion and careful talking. He gripped my wrist as he made his point.

'Look, my friend, negotiating with the leader is like making love to a beautiful woman.' I asked him how. 'If you want her, you don't just say, "Come to bed." You ask her if she wants a cup of coffee. It's the same with Gaddafi. If you want to make a deal with him, you don't tell him what to do. You just say, "Let's talk ..."'

But when it came to Gaddafi leaving the country, even Muhammad's optimism ran out. Throughout 2011 I found that Libyans could agree on only one point, which was that Gaddafi would not go into exile and was determined to die in Libya. No Libyan I spoke to disagreed – from Gaddafi himself, to his son Saif and his closest advisers right through to enemies of the regime, including secular intellectuals, revolutionary fighters and Islamists who had been tortured in his jails.

*

I flew out of Libya for a break a few days before the no-fly zone was declared. The airport was still surrounded by foreign workers, mainly black Africans and Egyptians, who had been camping there for a month in terrible squalor. Once the no-fly zone started the only route in and out was by road. Libya was back in isolation, under UN sanctions, as it had been in the nineties after the Lockerbie attack. So when I returned a few weeks later there were no more Gaddafi-green seats in business class on Afriqiyah Airlines. Instead there was a hard journey overland from Tunisia. The island of Djerba, about a two-hour drive from the border, had the nearest airport, so it became the jumping-off point. Djerba is usually a place Europeans go to for keenly priced Mediterranean sun and sand. The hotels there soon had two tribes: package tourists from France and Germany; and journalists, aid workers, human-rights investigators and all the others who drift towards warzones. The tribes eyed each other warily. Tourists stared at the camp-followers of war, and their piles of television gear, flak jackets, cases of water and fuel. The people on their way to Libya looked just as suspiciously at the tourists checking in, enjoying their welcome drinks, heading for the beach, the spa or the bar. Twenty years earlier I would have felt much cooler than them. But the wars in between had given me a good idea of what lay ahead, and I thought how much fun my children could have on the beach, and small pangs of loneliness and curiosity about a different kind of life jabbed my stomach. Some real warriors were in the hotel, too, amiable ones in the desert-pattern camouflaged flight suits of the Qatari Air Force. Their C-130 transports, also in desert colours, sat on the tarmac at Djerba airport, not far from the tourists' budget airliners with web addresses painted on their fuselages. Qatar had started to arm Libyan rebels and, though the cheery Qatari flight crew – a number of whom were Europeans – would not say what they were carrying, I could not see any other reason why they would be there if not to bring in weapons.

Crossing some frontiers in the Middle East takes a drive through no-man's land between the border crossings. It is just a step between

Tunisia and Libya, through a low blue barrier fence. On the Libyan side about a dozen men lounged around a sentry box, leaning on their side of the barrier, cradling their Kalashnikovs, staring into Tunisia. One of them, a little older, more important – a man the younger guys deferred to – carried a nickel-plated Kalashnikov with a deeply polished wooden stock. Maybe it was some kind of badge of office. Only the customs man had a formal uniform: a white shirt, a greasy peaked cap and an uneasy smile for his new, hard-faced helpers. The others were dressed in assorted green fatigues, and the ones around the man with the nickel gun had the ubiquitous black leather jackets that the mukhabarat across the Arab world love to wear.

On the Tunisian side the border guards suggested politely in French that it was a good idea to be careful in Libya, trying not to make eye contact with the baleful-looking gang of gunmen eyeballing the foreigners who were about to surrender themselves by crossing the blue fence and handing over their passports. Plenty of Tunisians were grumbling about the fact that their lives had not changed enough since their revolution, but they were heading for elections and a new constitution and every Tunisian knew how lucky they were compared to the neighbours in Libya. While Libya was tortured by civil war, one of the biggest issues in Tunisia was whether its citizens should try to do more for the economy by working in the afternoons in the coming summer. Traditionally they could knock off at one o'clock to get to the beach. In revolutionary Tunisia they could also make political jokes about Arab leaders, which in Tripoli would have led to betrayal by one of the regime's stooges and a painful encounter with the intelligence services. One of Tunisia's top radio shows was a satirical phone-in, which was making Wassim Herissi, who did all the voices, into a star. His impersonation of Colonel Gaddafi, a regular caller, was spookily like the Libyan leader's high-decibel rasp. On the show he plunged straight into the row about summer afternoons off.

'It's a good idea,' said Wassim's colonel. 'In the afternoon there will be no NATO, and no International Criminal Court. I'll be able to swim in the sea and dance with the people, because [*switching to English*] they love me, they love me all.'

I liked the last bit about the people loving him, which was becoming a catchphrase, as it came from the answer Colonel Gaddafi had given, in English, to one of my questions at the end of February. On Wassim's show his fictional Gaddafi often argued about who was most popular with Tunisia's former president Ben Ali, who had chosen a comfortable exile over his own personal Götterdämmerung. After one of his broadcasts Wassim told me that Tunisians were lucky.

'We had a clean revolution. The former president turned out to be a coward. He just ran away. Not like the others – like the poor Libyans, or in Syria – but it lit the fuse to all the other revolutions.'

The campaign against the corruption of the Ben Ali era had not reached the border. The Tunisian side of the crossing was an unpleasant place to spend any time. Unfriendly, often aggressive touts offering to change money or provide drivers were everywhere. When we brought in our own, trusted driver from Djerba they surrounded his 4x4 and refused to let him out because we were not using one of them. The soldiers who were supposed to be securing the area just watched the standoff. The local drivers and touts must have been paying off the soldiers because they let the local mob walk past their sentries into the customs area, which Tunisia, like most countries, democratic or not, usually kept secure. Our row with them ended only when an officer who was prised out of the headquarters building realised that holding foreign broadcasters to ransom did not show the new Tunisia in its best light. The Libyan side was much worse, a mess of half-finished buildings, potholed roads, dust, blowing litter, guns and confusion. So all that summer it was a strange relief to find the man who had been sent from Tripoli to meet us, to escort us back to the Rixos, to its rules, sudden bus trips to bombsites in the early hours and strange encounters at its extensive, lavish buffet. The journey there, after every bag and box had been searched for undocumented satellite gear and booze, was usually one of the most dangerous parts of the trip. The drivers liked to go as fast as they could, keeping at least half their minds on making phone calls, lighting the next cigarette, fumbling for another CD of Gaddafi anthems. The music blared the whole way, sampling his speeches, celebrating his greatness and generosity.

It was always tempting to close your eyes and wait for oblivion – preferably sleep rather than death in a head-on collision – but I tried to stay awake because the route into Tripoli always offered some clues that the regime might not have wanted foreign reporters to pick up. You could tell which towns that sprawled along the coastal highway had offered resistance to Gaddafi's counter-revolution by the amount of damage they had suffered. The first big town was Zuwara, which was badly battered. Gaddafi's son Saadi had wanted to make it into Dubai-on-the-Mediterranean, with turquoise sea and long, unspoilt beaches and dunes to pull in the tourists. He had even summoned well-known architects to discuss spectacular signature buildings that never left the drawing board. When the uprising started the people took over the town. Zuwara's population was mainly Amazigh, usually known around the world as Berbers, an ethnic group that was in North Africa before the Arab invasion in the seventh century. The fact that they are not Arabs is an important part of their identity. The evidence left by the damage showed that subduing them had taken a lot of force. Buildings along the main street had gaping holes of a size usually produced by a tank shell. Honeycombs of holes framed windows that had been blasted by hundreds of bullets. Buildings were burnt out. Most telling of all, the place was almost a ghost town, always quiet, with very few open shops and empty streets even when the less-damaged towns either side were busy. The Amazigh-Berber fighters were not beaten. They had just pulled back inland to their stronghold in the Nafusa Mountains, still fighting, and preparing for what became a decisive contribution to the downfall of Gaddafi later in the year. In Tripoli we would sometimes see videos from the mountains that had surfaced on YouTube. One chilling clip showed rebel fighters, apparently Amazigh, searching the bodies of a detachment of Gaddafi troops they had just ambushed and killed. They moved around the corpses lying in pools of blood in a way that looked casual, almost routine, and which marked them out as dangerous enemies. As they went through the blood-stained pockets of their victims, they claimed the men were mercenaries from Algeria, Chad and Mali.

Just after the regime had recaptured Zuwara at the beginning of March, I had the bad luck to be part of a group of journalists being driven through the town. Progress was grindingly slow as several hundred supporters of the regime surrounded the bus, firing in the air and chanting, to make the point that they were now in control. When the bus finally broke through their cordon the same demonstrators loaded themselves and their families into cars and pickups, and chased us through the night for at least fifty miles, managing a few times to outflank the bus and stop it again for more staged demonstrations, more shooting in the air, more kissing of Gaddafi posters, and more endless chanting of *Allah, Muammar, Libya, wa bas.* Very young children were bouncing around in the backs of pickups, or leaning out of car windows as they manoeuvred close to the bus at seventy miles an hour and more, punching small fists into the air to the rhythm of the chant. Inside their parents grinned and egged them on. I prayed that no one crashed or fell out. Apart from the obvious tragedy of another avoidable death, I guessed we would somehow get blamed. The hysteria in the regime's supporters was the sort that could easily turn ugly. They must have been doing it to order. Libya produced huge amounts of oil but did not have the capacity to refine enough to satisfy domestic demand for fuel. The petrol queues were getting longer and longer as sanctions cut off imports. Sometimes the lines outside filling stations went on for a mile or more, hundreds of useless cars with empty tanks left by their owners to secure a place in case petrol actually was delivered. No one was going to squander precious fuel to chase a busload of tired, hungry and irritable journalists unless they had been told to do it and had their tanks filled in return.

One of the main refineries was in Zawiya, on the highway between Zuwara and Tripoli. This was another town that had been taken over by rebels until they were pushed out in a fierce onslaught before the no-fly zone had been declared. When I was there one man came up, grey, middle-aged and pinched by life – and rejoicing in his moment of freedom.

'I am happy because for the first time we can express ourselves freely. It doesn't matter about the police, about the surroundings, or the siege. We can speak freely, we can utter, we can allow the world to hear our needs and demands.'

I saw him again a few weeks later, after Zawiya had been retaken by the regime, during a visit to the oil refinery. He had quietly gone back to work. He recognised me, and I wondered if he had suffered as a result of giving us an interview. I tried, probably not subtly enough, to say hello, and he blanked me. I couldn't blame him. But then, five minutes later, he came up to me, said loudly, 'I'll show you where the toilets are,' and led me down a corridor away from the journalists and their minders. In the bathroom he started whispering furiously. 'I'm sorry, I can't talk. We are all so very frightened. There is nothing I can say.' Then he walked out. As he went through the door and back into the corridor, there was the sound of a flush and a man emerged from one of the cubicles. He looked just as alarmed, and hurried out without speaking.

It felt strangely comforting to re-enter the mad world of the Rixos hotel. In the chaos and violence of Libya it was familiar and relatively safe. The minders greeted Cara and me like long-lost friends. Musa Ibrahim, the government spokesman, was particularly welcoming. I liked Musa, even though I knew that he and his assistants were spying on us constantly. The hotel had an excellent wireless-internet system, which meant that we could stay in touch with the rest of the world – but also that the regime could access our messages. I had no doubt that Musa was reading my emails, but I didn't see that as a reason to be surly with him. It was part of the rules of the game. Getting information and the chances to go to places and see things depended on keeping him friendly. He was enjoying the exposure he was getting on television around the world. 'I'm famous now, Jeremy,' he said triumphantly, not exactly joking. 'You need to get me on *Hard Talk*.' He was talking about the BBC programme that features an extended interview. When he appeared on the programme later in the year he looked delighted. 'I can't believe it. A year ago I was a student getting pissed in London. And now I'm going on *Hard Talk*!' He was an effective spokesman, articulate, confident and extremely fluent in English. He presented himself as a veteran of the political game but the reality was that he was a novice who had come back from Britain at the request of Saif al-Islam as part of his plan to modernise Libya. Part of Musa stayed the wide-eyed student, amazed he had found himself with the grown-ups and with people listening to his opinions and writing them down. The night we interviewed Colonel Gaddafi I bumped into him as we got back to the hotel. He tried to choke me off for not turning up to the news conference he had arranged with the deputy foreign minister. When I told him that I had just spent an hour with the colonel his mouth gaped in amazement. 'Respect!' he said, high-fived me, and went off to spread the word. I felt for a long time that Musa was not a bad man, that had he been born somewhere else he would not have ended up defending one of the most notorious regimes in the world. When rumours occasionally circulated that he had defected I was never surprised. But he never did. I realised when I saw the difference in tone between his statements in English and the rip-roaring rhetoric he used in Arabic that he had two skins: one acquired during his years in London and one he had from growing up in Libya. Musa used to say with some pride that he was the first member of his family not to have been born in a tent. He had his chances to get out as the curtain came down on the Gaddafi years but he chose not to take them. He gave the impression of having come back to Libya almost by chance, but at Gaddafi's end he stayed loyal. In the last few days his German wife, Julia, and their baby son left the country and he went into hiding, sending out strident and defiant messages in support of the dead regime. Someone filmed wine bottles in their suite, which was next door to where I stayed in one of my trips there. When I saw the pictures on the internet I wasn't surprised. Musa was a secular Arab, of a kind that is losing power across the Middle East. I wished he had offered me a glass. Occasionally I get Facebook messages from him, always amiable, and for a while there were rumours that he was involved in a new pro-Gaddafi movement. He must be waiting somewhere for his life's second act.

Most evenings, and sometimes during the day as well, great thunderclaps from NATO bombs would shake the hotel. Once the bombing started it became even clearer that Britain, France and the United States wanted Colonel Gaddafi overthrown. One Western official said to me: 'A peace conference in Malta would be a defeat for us. It's not going to happen.' The operative words in Resolution 1973, that member states could use 'all necessary measures' to protect civilians, were interpreted as a charter for regime change, with the argument that civilians in Libya would always be in danger while Colonel Gaddafi stayed in office. It allowed the United States, Britain and France to press ahead with the plan to introduce a no-fly zone, which meant military action against the Gaddafi regime. Even a year later one of the Western diplomats involved with the resolution said he was 'astonished' that the Russians had allowed them to use the phrase. 'We would have settled for much less,' he said with a broad grin. It turned a little rueful, as we were speaking not long after

Russia blocked action against Syria in the Security Council. The Russian foreign minister, Sergei Lavrov, had been ambassador at the UN when the Security Council passed a resolution on Kosovo in 1999 that looked in retrospect like a victory for a Western agenda. Resolution 1973 seemed, in the words of one Western official, 'to have made a fool of him again on Libya [...] he wouldn't let it happen again on Syria.'

Russia soon realised its mistake. The Kremlin was exasperated and enraged that Resolution 1973 was going to be used as a lever to get Gaddafi out. It was not because they had any great love for Gaddafi, but because Western countries appeared to have scored a victory at their expense. On 17 June they sent a special envoy, Mikhail Margelov, to Tripoli. Viktor, the Russian consul general in Tripoli, picked me up at the Rixos to drive to the Russian Embassy to meet him. Viktor ignored the armed guards on the gates of the hotel and they ignored him, which was a relief. They took too close an interest in the rest of us. Viktor drove aggressively out into the traffic in his scruffy white Nissan, and his frustrations with both Libya and Western diplomacy came tumbling out.

'I've been in Libya five years. It's not easy. No films, theatre, not much to do. Just eat.'

'No drink?'

'No!'

Viktor's smoking matched his driving. He sucked on his cigarettes as if the filter was an enemy. I asked him if Gaddafi would be able to hang on. The bombing was putting his regime under a lot of pressure.

'I think he wants to die here.'

'Of old age or because someone shoots him?'

He shrugged and worked the horn, driving jerkily, trying to pilot a way through the traffic. The petrol shortage had thinned the roads out but cars still clogged the main highways in the centre of Tripoli.

'People are tired. Tired from the bombing and double tired from not sleeping.'

He stopped at the lights. They went to green and he moved forward. But the traffic that should have stopped did not. Exasperated, Viktor honked the horn a few times more and pushed on through the chaos.

'It is our light and they move. That's Libya. Look, in the last years Gaddafi has done so much for his country. New roads everywhere. Everyone with the chance to have a satellite dish for TV. There's more democracy here than there was in Iraq, or Iran or some of the other countries I have been.'

What about jailing people for disagreeing with the regime?

'Yes but that happens in Saudi Arabia and Bahrain too. Maybe more people in jail there, we just don't know. So why do this against Gaddafi? And as for saying that he gives Viagra so his men can do rapes . . . It's bullshit. You don't have to give young soldiers Viagra. And anyway, in the five years I have been here I have always seen Libyans being very kind to the ladies.'

Viktor went silent and swerved through more traffic. At the embassy he ushered me out of the bright Mediterranean light and into a little bit of Russia, or at least Russia as I remembered it in the last years of the Soviet Union. Beyond a small hall was a big oblong room, dingy, beige and at one end dominated by the pool table where a couple of embassy staff were immersed in a game. It was more like a common room than an embassy salon. Wood panelling came halfway up the walls. It was decorated with two oil paintings, both of snowy forests of silver birch and pines, and some dying flower arrangements in straw baskets. Viktor disappeared and I passed the time by speaking to a Russian reporter with heels so high I wondered how she could walk. She used to distract the cameramen positioned on the roof of the Rixos for the bangs, crashes and billowing smoke of another NATO strike by sunbathing in a small bikini.

The room smacked of the dingy death of the Soviet Union, and Moscow's decline in the Middle East compared to the time from the 1950s to the 1970s when it was a real rival to the Americans in one of the Cold War's most important battlegrounds. But Mikhail Margelov, who arrived with his entourage of diplomats, political advisers and Moscow journalists about half an hour later, walked and talked with the confidence of Putin's new Russia, which wanted to get back from the margins to the centre of events. The Russian envoy said his message was that Colonel Gaddafi should leave power, because he had lost legitimacy when his regime started killing civilians. But he warned there should be a deal, because a violent end to Gaddafi's rule could mean a violent future for Libya.

'The military operation, the way it's being conducted, is the worse-case scenario – the longer the bloodshed, the longer bombs fall, the more difficult it is to reconcile the nation. There are no military solutions to a political crisis.'

Margelov was impressive. He was fluent in Arabic and English and gave every sign of knowing what he was talking about. But he had an impossible job trying to navigate between the Libyan opposition – he had already been to Benghazi – the West and the Gaddafi regime. All attempts at mediation (the African Union was still trying too) during what was becoming the death agony of the Gaddafi regime foundered on the same point: the future of the colonel. Margelov was trying to find a way for him to leave power and to stay in the country with the consent of the rebels and under the protection of his tribe. He thought he had a window to make something happen before the International Criminal Court indicted the colonel and Saif for crimes against humanity.

'The clock is ticking [. . .] but we have a lot of cookies on the table, quite a nice variety. We can choose.'

From the beginning of the crisis the regime had sent out constant messages, public and private, to London, Washington and Paris that it wanted to talk. The reply was always the same: we'll talk, but only when Gaddafi goes. Most importantly, the rebels did not just want him out of the country. Plenty of them wanted him dead. Tripoli offered ceasefires, but they had the precondition that Colonel Gaddafi would stay on as leader so were – correctly – seen by his enemies as attempts to play for time and to preserve the regime. Whenever Gaddafi's people talked about negotiations and a ceasefire I remembered what the colonel himself told me: that he would die in Libya. In the end the Russians had no answer to the juggernaut launched against Gaddafi by France, Britain and America and their wealthy allies in Qatar. But Russia learnt a lesson, which had serious consequences seven months later when the crisis in Syria reached the United Nations Security Council. The Russians, helped by China, blocked attempts to get a resolution condemning the actions of President Assad's regime through the Security Council. Even when the Arab League – more divided about Syria than it had been about Libya – added its voice, nothing changed. It was more than sour grapes about being out-manoeuvred on Resolution 1973 calling for 'all necessary measures' to be used to protect civilians in Libya. It was a statement that Russia and China had their own agenda in the Middle East. Russia wanted to rebuild its position as a great power, and exploit any commercial opportunities that came along as a result. The Russians also believed that the vacuum left by the removal of the regime would, in the longer term, mean instability and even the break-up of the country. The Chinese had a tactical alliance with Russia in the security council and were also applying the formulation in the Middle East that had worked so well in Africa south of the Sahara. Their favourite way to project power is to do deals, securing the raw materials needed for their economy at home and not worrying too much about traditional measures of their national machismo.

After the meeting with Margelov a couple of other Russian diplomats present were keen to talk. They were feeling the strain, fastening on alarming reports that may have been rumours or might have been true.

'I've heard that forty-five people have been killed in petrol queues in Tripoli,' one of them said. 'They've got a big law-and-order problem, and the population's under a lot of stress.' His colleague, who said he lived close to the home of Gaddafi's daughter Aisha, was hollow-eyed.

'Last night I hardly slept, only a few hours. All night there were people around Aisha's house chanting, "*Allah, Muammar, Libya, wa bas.*" And firing in the air. Then at five the bombing came.'

The diplomats were trying as hard as they could to work out what was happening in the sprawling city, just as the journalists were in the Rixos. Back at the hotel I wrote a few notes in my diary.

17 June 2011

Evening at the Rixos. Sitting on balcony reading *Matterhorn*, a monumental novel about the Vietnam War, waiting to do a live for the Ten. Crackles of sporadic gunfire. Soft evening light. Mystery about what's going on out in the city. Every night there's gunfire. Is it defiant shooting in the air? Is it to intimidate – Gaddafi's people firing randomly at houses – that's what they told us in Tajoura. Doesn't sound like an exchange. Sometimes you hear the deeper, flatter bass of triple A. That's usually accompanied by a jet engine. Last night I slept through the big attack. Woken only by rattling windows for a very few seconds. Cara recorded it. She keeps her recorder going all night. There was a scream or a whoosh before the explosions. Six of them all told, rapid succession. Whole thing was over in seconds.

Sometimes distant regular shelling or explosions is strangely restful when you're used to it. I used to find it a natural part of the night in Sarajevo. If it's hitting someone else, it's not so worrying.

Continuing mystery about who supports Gaddafi and who doesn't. Tripoli strangely normal-looking though it can't be. It gets bombed almost every day.

David Hirst, a veteran correspondent for the *Guardian*, came up with a crucial bit of advice for foreign journalists in Gaddafi's Libya: don't get on the bus. Musa and his minders liked to lay on bus tours that were often giant exercises in time-wasting and attempted manipulation of the truth. If Musa was the good cop, then the bad cop was one of his assistants – an obstructive middle-aged woman who some journalists dubbed Rosa Klebb, after the Bond villain who could make poison-tipped knives shoot out of her stout shoes. But the morning after I managed to sleep through the bombing there was a bus trip to a bombsite, and some of Tripoli's mysteries revealed themselves despite the minders. The trip was to al-Fatah University, about ten miles away. I'd been there a couple of times before, once to a pro-Gaddafi rally in one of the lecture theatres, when it turned out that the people chanting his name were not students. We journalists had been bussed in. So had they.

This time a bite had been taken out of a three-storey classroom block. Whatever hit it was very directed. Classes a few doors along the same corridor were not badly damaged, though the roof had gone from the section that had been hit. It was the exam season. Students were sitting around in the shade of trees, chatting to their friends and pretending to revise. The sexes did not mix. The girls wore head-scarves and many of them were wearing abayas that touched the ground. The Libyans had told us about the visit the night before. If they wanted to fabricate anything, they would have had time.

In June the miasma of fear was hanging very heavy in Tripoli. One of the university lecturers came up to talk. He had done his PhD in Britain and liked the BBC. Someone was with him, a colleague who took his hand and held one his fingers in the way that Arab men quite often do. I sensed he had something he wanted to say. When his colleague was distracted for a moment and moved away, I asked him about the city and Gaddafi.

'Everyone is against Gaddafi.' He was nervous and glanced back down the smashed-up corridor in the classroom block. 'Eyes are everywhere.' His colleague came back and took his hand again so the lecturer changed the subject, insisted on telling him loudly in Arabic exactly what we were saying and what I was asking. He did not translate the interesting part of the conversation.

Outside the damaged building a young woman with a headscarf started talking to Cara.

'You believe this crap? It couldn't be the NATO, it couldn't. And I'm sure about it 100 per cent. Because they [the regime] want to say to the other people that the NATO attacked civilians.' She made no attempt to whisper, or be discreet, and said her name was Nada. She spoke loudly, in good English. A friend told her to keep her voice down. Nada was certain that NATO would not have bombed the building. Cara asked him if she thought Gaddafi should go.

'We don't like him, we don't need him. You can ask anyone. We don't believe this crap. I'm studying here in this college and I believe it's a huge lie [...] Believe us, we hate him, and we don't want him here. Believe us.' I told Nada I tried not to believe anything people told me in Tripoli. A few months earlier our minibus had been sitting in traffic when a man in the next lane, also jammed, leant out of his window and offered some advice: 'Don't believe anything.' When Rob Magee, the BBC cameraman, raised his lens and asked if he cared to repeat what he had said, the man drove off, looking relieved that the lights had changed.

Nada did not stop talking, overflowing with things to say now she had her first chance to speak to outsiders who could pass her views on. It was a big risk, and her friends, who had been smiling slightly and looking on from a safe distance, were getting agitated. A young man came up to her, with the pretext of giving her a dog-eared photocopy of a couple of chapters from one of their set books. He muttered a warning that she was being watched. We exchanged numbers. I asked her if she was scared talking to us.

'No I'm not scared about anything. I'm not scared.' And she smiled and walked away.

Cara went after her, to see if Nada was being followed. She was. A man in a suit tailed her though the campus, issuing instructions on his phone as he walked. Three others joined him. Cara phoned to warn her that she was being watched. A little later Nada managed quick call. She said was being held in a room at the university. Two men had been taking turns to interrogate her, asking what she had told us, whether she had been filmed or recorded, and demanding to know why we had swapped phone numbers. One she said was nasty, and the other seemed kind. It was good cop, bad cop again, and worrying. We try to protect interviewees. But Nada was unrepentant, thanked Cara for giving her voice a chance to be heard. I met her again after Gaddafi's fall. She had managed to talk her way out of trouble. The secret police contented themselves with trying, unsuccessfully, to frighten her.

Another source of information was our young, extremely cool and composed friend in Tajoura, Salem al-Fituri. Cara kept in contact with him via Skype, and arranged for a clandestine meeting where he could pass on information. A few hundred yards from the hotel gates was a small suburban shopping centre. Journalists were allowed to go there without minders if they could persuade Musa Ibrahim and his cohorts that they were shopping and not up to mischief, which included talking to people. Many people used 'trips to the shops' as a way of slipping away and getting lost for a few hours. Another favourite way of going AWOL was for journalists, often deeply irreligious ones, to claim that they had to go to one of Tripoli's Christian churches to worship. Cara and Fituri agreed to meet in a certain shop, checked they weren't being followed, and without speaking brushed past each other inside. Fituri expertly palmed her a memory stick and went off without either of them speaking. When Cara got it back to the Rixos we found it included video of police cars on fire in Tajoura, and the aftermath of a killing by regime forces in a house in Souk al-Joumha. Some rebel fighters had been ambushed in the house, and at the start of the video some of them were still alive, groaning in pools of blood. One of Gaddafi's men casually went from room to room filming them where they fell. By the end of the video they were all dead. The memory stick also included a document Fituri had called 'facts to know'. It ended with a chilling paragraph.

> In Tajoura you will find nobody on the streets after sunset, it's like a ghost town at night, there is only security forces hanging around the town and opening fire randomly, and they sing, get drunk and dance as their leader told them to do. People never sleep at night, they call us rats and they write it on walls, it's become an unsafe place to live in.

Months into the uprising, the rebels in the east and would-be urban guerrillas in Tripoli were still struggling to organise themselves and to learn how to fight in a disciplined and effective way. But they had an air force, courtesy of NATO, that destroyed scores of tanks and artillery weapons. The bombing campaign made it possible for the rebels to win the war. On the rare occasions the regime took us closer to the rebel enclave in Misrata, a port city west of the capital where rebels were fighting hard, the bus would sometimes, without comment from the minders, drive past burnt-out hulks of Libyan armour. NATO said after the war that it destroyed more than 5,900 military targets in around 9,700 strike sorties. Three countries did around 70 per cent of the raids. France flew the most, followed by Britain and the United States. After the first series of raids, the Americans, not wanting to take the lead in another war after the ones in Afghanistan and Iraq, insisted that NATO take military command and Britain and France take the political lead. Intelligence and air support still came from the Americans, as well as weapons and bombing raids, without any one of which the mission would not have been feasible. Taking a step back was the right thing for them to do as far as domestic politics were concerned. That did not mean ditching their position as leader of the Western world, so from the back seat the Americans kept up a flow of advice to their designated drivers. The rest of the strikes were split between Denmark, Norway, Italy, Belgium and Canada. The UAE, Jordan and Qatar also provided aircraft for patrols, not bombing. The Arab contingents allowed NATO to claim that it was an international operation and not one simply mounted by the West's military alliance, the most powerful in the world. It would never have happened without the request from the Arab League. But had NATO, and particularly Britain and France, pushed for action the Arab League's statement would have stayed words on the page. There would have been no planes in the sky.

It was also clear that civilian casualties would be deeply damaging for NATO members, whose mandate from the UN was to protect civilians. Apart from that, the laws of war, which are in a series of treaties signed by NATO countries among many others, forbid deliberate attacks on civilians. Attacks on military targets have to use proportionate force, and must not cause disproportionate suffering to civilians. Assessing what is proportionate and what isn't is always difficult and controversial. NATO's view is that it 'conducted the campaign for Libya with unprecedented care and precision and to a standard exceeding that required by international humanitarian law. The mission was fully consistent with the United Nations mandate and saved countless lives.'[3]

Waging war without spilling blood, sometimes the blood of the people who the bombs are supposed to protect, just is not possible. The speed of the response to what was happening in Libya, accelerated even more by hourly news reports, meant that NATO had taken on an open-ended military commitment with no clear-off ramp if Gaddafi did not fall fast and hard. A year later a senior diplomat at NATO commented in a private meeting that 'NATO had a good war. It's tempting to think that war is always like that. But we were very lucky.'[4] By 'lucky' the diplomat meant that the anti-Gaddafi forces had won a campaign that had been started in a frantic hurry, and looked for a time to have become a stalemate when the disorganised rebel forces failed to follow up the bombing raids.

More civilians died than NATO was prepared to acknowledge, according to a report released by the UN in March 2012. It concluded that the NATO campaign had been 'highly precise'. But it also found that at twenty sites it visited sixty civilians had died and fifty were wounded. One raid alone killed thirty-four civilians.[5] The *New York Times* investigated the NATO bombing campaign, visiting more than 150 targets at more than twenty-five sites across the country. It concluded that NATO had been unwilling to acknowledge that it had killed civilians. I knew from other wars, other cities I had been in while they were being bombed, that modern weapons guided by lasers and satellites were extremely accurate. But I also knew that weapons were only as good as the target information programmed into them, and that they could also malfunction.

I saw it for myself, once again, in the early hours of 19 June. NATO hit a family house in Souk al-Joumha in Tripoli at around 1.15 in the morning. Quite quickly NATO admitted they had carried out the attack, blaming a malfunctioning weapons system. The Tannoy in the Rixos hotel crackled into action: 'All journalists. There has been a raid. We will take you.' Ironically Souk al-Joumha was one of the main centres of rebellion against Gaddafi in the capital, but it was also not far from the main air base in Tajoura. The home of the al-Gherari family had the front ripped off it, and part of it had collapsed. While I was watching rescuers digging through the rubble, a man came up to me and said everyone hated the regime, and that he classified the casualties as victims of friendly fire. I was expecting the usual pro-Gaddafi demonstration. Several hundred men had gathered in the darkness of the early hours. But there was no chanting, no noticeable anger, just some quiet talk. A desire not to provoke them might have been why the regime was unusually restrained and made no attempt to bus its cheerleaders into Souk al-Joumha. I wrote these notes when I went back to the Rixos.

Body in ambulance under a blanket as we arrived there. Unseemly behaviour by camera crews as they rushed the ambulance, fighting each other to get a view. When back door was jammed with cameras, some went through the front doors. Libyans didn't mind.

In the ruins ... desperate efforts – almost frenzied – to dig out family. Cry went up that they had found a baby. It wasn't a baby – but the body of the children's mother. They passed a stretcher in from the ambulance, the kind that also has drop down wheels. Couldn't be wheeled of course because everyone trying to clamber over mounds of rubble ... When they found the body struggled with it along through gap along the side of the house. Like lots of homes of ordinary people it was half-finished. Concrete floors, rough walls of breezeblocks. But they lived there and compared to plenty in the Middle East they were lucky. Until the NATO strike. Apparently the father worked for the government according to neighbours. Had a car outside. No limo but decent. Crushed by pieces of the house.

The men bringing out the body were neighbours. About six of them held the stretcher high in the air above their heads to get it over the wobbling and precarious pieces of rubble. A bulldozer was tearing at the concrete from close by which made it even less stable. I squeezed back into the side of the wall to let it through. Ian Druce next to me was filming. We both it transpired later had the same thought. They're going to drop her on us. I could see some of her hair poking out of the top of the blanket they'd used to cover her.

We asked the minders to take us to the Tripoli Central Hospital to find the wounded and the dead. The bodies had been deposited in a room just off the casualty department. Some of the cameramen and photographers piled in, all elbows and shoves, to get their shots. We held back until the feeding frenzy was over. The bodies were not going anywhere. In the room on a trolley was the dead woman who had been pulled out of the rubble while we were there in Souk al-Joumha. To preserve her modesty, even in death she was still wrapped in the blanket. They exposed her head, charcoal grey with dust and small flakes of pulverised concrete. Her name was Karima Ali Musbah al-Gherari, and she had been thirty. Her daughter Jomana, who was seven months old, lay on another trolley next to the body of Karima's husband, Faraj, who was forty-seven. The girl and her father, lying side by side on trolleys, looked almost as if they were asleep, except they were too still and dusty. The man was lying in his boxer shorts, and didn't seem to have a mark on him. The baby had a cut on her head, but it did not look fatal. I wondered if they were both killed by the blast. Shockwaves create an overpressure that ruptures organs inside the body causing death by internal bleeding. The child's nappy was covered in the same kind of concrete and cement dust as my shoes and jeans. It was in her ears and on her face. The sight of the nappy made me think of her mother getting her ready for bed.

By the door on a stretcher was another man, fully clothed, under a blue cloth. When I made it into the room I thought he was alive. His mouth was open slightly and he seemed to move. I wondered why the nurse standing next to him was not taking more care of her patient. He had a cut and a bruise on his face. Then I realised he was dead too, and if he seemed to move it must have been because some over-eager journalist had nudged his stretcher in the fight to get to the baby.

Across the way was the casualty area where they were working on the badly wounded arm of an unconscious man. The Libyan media machine had made crude and unsuccessful attempts already to try to persuade journalists they were seeing civilian victims of bombing. My BBC colleague Wyre Davies was taken to a hospital and shown a wounded child, supposedly hurt in a raid. But while he was there

someone passed him a piece of paper saying that she had been injured
in a road accident. Later he saw a man who had been introduced at
the hospital as her uncle at a bombsite, where he admitted he worked
for the government. But this time no choreography was necessary.
They had rushed us to the wrecked house, and to the hospital. Even
before NATO admitted it was their bomb, I knew it was an authentic
raid. I had seen enough of them to know when they were real and
when they were imagined. The doctors and nurses were angry that
news teams were invading their treatment room. Crossly, they pulled
the curtains shut around the beds. They could not ban journalists
because the regime wanted it all filmed. But they were not extras in
some kind of illusion. They were dealing with real casualties from a
real airstrike. Another small child, also wearing a nappy and lying very
still, was wheeled down the corridor. The child looked no more than
eighteen months old, if that, but later I discovered that he was a two-
year-old called Khaled Abdullah. He was rushed into the treatment
room and the curtains were yanked shut. Lenses were still poked into
the gaps between them. The news business does not have its finest
moments at times like this. A couple of minutes later the child was
pushed into the room with the other bodies. It had not taken more
than a quick examination to establish that he was dead. Hamza, a
Libyan diplomat who was the assistant to the deputy foreign minister,
the regime's most senior spokesman, was at the hospital. He told me
afterwards how he tried the kiss of life on the child even after the doctors told him it was too late. I didn't know whether to believe him, but
he had eight children of his own, and the next evening at the Rixos
Hamza was still red-eyed, unshaven, clutching one of his sons. When
I went looking for him after the fall of Gaddafi, one of his former colleagues at the Foreign Ministry told me cheerfully: 'Hamza? He was
one of the rats. He's run away!'

On 20 June there was another big raid, on the home of Lt-Gen al-
Khuwaylidi al-Humaydi, who had been part of the military junta led

by Gaddafi that overthrew the king in 1969 and was for many years after that head of Military Intelligence. He was part of Gaddafi's innermost circle, though his family claimed that he had retired. NATO described the raid as 'a precision strike on a legitimate military target – a command-and-control node which was directly involved in coordinating systematic attacks on the Libyan people.'[6] A NATO general was quoted as saying that the strike meant the regime's forces would find it much harder to 'carry on their barbaric assault against the Libyan people'. The building they hit, in a village called Surman, not far from the Mediterranean coast west of Tripoli, was at the centre of a country estate, with gazelles and ostriches in the garden and a children's zoo with rabbits and ducks. The target was the main house, a big concrete structure, and it was flattened. Men were digging through the rubble when we arrived. I could not see any evidence in the wreckage of the kind of communications equipment that a command-and-control centre would have needed, though down the drive and across the road was a post office and a building next to an un-camouflaged communications tower, which had also been bombed. The house could have been used for meetings of senior leaders, given that Humaydi was one of Gaddafi's oldest friends and allies. My hunch was that NATO had intelligence that the colonel was there, and had ordered a big raid to try to kill him. The workmen stopped to shout with grief and anger when one of them found a gnarled piece of bone and flesh. It might have been part of a chest.

The dead and injured were a few miles away, in the hospital in Sobrata, a seaside town that is famous for Roman remains as stunning as any in Rome. It was a beautiful Mediterranean afternoon, with a light salty breeze blowing across the car park as I trudged in – a little reluctantly as I was expecting a gruesome display of body parts. It was a relief when they seemed to be directing the media into a ward, rather than the mortuary. But inside the ward was a hellish scene. The beds were still made up with white sheets, as if they were ready

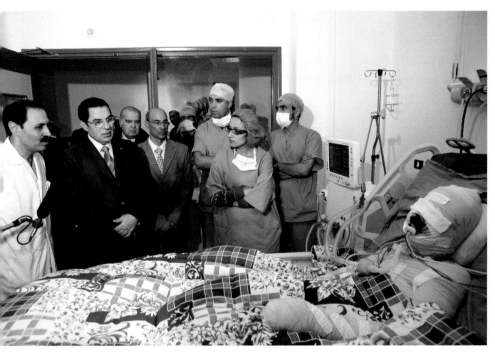

en Ali visits Muhammad Bouazizi as he was dying in hospital after his terrible act of lf-immolation. Many Tunisians thought it was a last attempt by the perpetrator to ke advantage of the victim.

The people got the fall of the regime. Tunisians celebrate their revolution, January 2011.

Tripoli, March 2004. Tony Blair welcomes Colonel Muammar al-Gaddafi in from the cold. Downing Street suggested they met in the Colonel's tent.

What goes up must come down. The daily, deafening ritual in Green Square, Tripoli, during the last months of the Gaddafi regime.

Interviewing Colonel Gaddafi in an Italian restaurant in Tripoli, with Christiane Amanpour on the left and Marie Colvin on the right. Marie was killed in Syria a year later.

Another generation learning what to think. Schoolchildren in a pro-regime protest outside the UN building in Tripoli.

Before the storm. With President Bashar al-Assad in Damascus in 2010. Six months after the uprisings started, just after the President said that Syria would be immune.

President Hosni Mubarak, Arab best friend of the Americans and their allies. Before he was unseated an influential Israeli, only half joking, told me that the first thing his country's top diplomats did every morning was to pray for Mubarak's health and long life.

Battle of the Bridges, Cairo, January 2011. The regime's police losing control of the Qasr al-Nil crossing over the Nile, opening the way for revolutionaries to take control of Tahrir Square.

Battle of the Camels, Cairo, February 2011. Mubarak's cavalry tried a bizarre charge against the revolutionaries during one of the most violent days in Tahrir Square.

Night fighting in Tahrir. The revolutionaries' barricades are on the right. The end of the Mubarak regime turbo-charged uprisings elsewhere in the region.

Piece to camera at the barricades in Tahrir Square. Ian Druce filming, Jeannie Assad watching for stones coming from the Mubarak side. Behind her is Chris Cobb-Smith, one of the BBC's excellent safety advisors.

to help the wounded rest and recover; but, instead of the living, dead bodies and fragments of bodies had been laid out on them, one to a bed or sometimes just a rough assembly of a human in several fragments. I went in there to try to count the dead, but it was impossible to be certain – the total was either side of a dozen – because some of the corpses were in pieces. A dead man lay on one bed, a big hole in his forehead. A nurse sat cradling the body of a boy, who looked as if he had been two or three years old. A man held up a blackened torso, with a child's arm still attached. The bodies did not smell, though the weather was warm, and they still oozed blood and fluids, so I believed the doctors when they said these people were killed that morning. And I had seen the way the bombs had pulverised the buildings. In a report issued almost a year later Human Rights Watch said that thirteen people had died, including five children.[7] The dead included three of Humaydi's grandchildren and his daughter-in-law, who had been pregnant.

Surman was flooded with uniformed soldiers for the funeral two days later, in a field opposite the village mosque. Many mourners were expected – too many for the mosque to hold – but some of the local men gathered on a terrace outside the mosque waiting for al-Khuwaylidi al-Humaydi. A man with a green scarf and a laminated photo of Muammar al-Gaddafi on a green ribbon around his neck positioned himself in front of the camera. In a fine voice, lingering on the last syllable, he shouted, 'Libyaaaaaaaa ...' holding the note a long time. Then he started the chant, the only one possible for someone like him: *Allah, Muammar, Libya, wa bas.* His voice echoed round the terrace but no one joined in. Sirens screamed in the distance and then were louder and closer. It was a motorcade of ambulances, every light flashing, surrounded by police cars blaring their way through the traffic.

Humaydi arrived with his retinue. He was skinny, used to being in charge, dressed in white robes with a few days' grey stubble. He pointed a lot, issuing orders, and people obeyed him – as the local chief and as a man who had been at Gaddafi's side for more than forty years. The ambulances were lined up with the tailgates open. In the back of each was a coffin covered in a green flag, except for the one that was carrying the bodies of the two children of Humaydi's son Khaled. Their shrouds were fresh and clean, newly wrapped, but blood and fluid from the bodies inside was coming through in places. Khaled was standing next to his father. He was a handsome man in his thirties, with aviator sunglasses, a white T-shirt and jeans. His black hair was thinning but was still cut quite long, smart in an Italian-playboy kind of way. He looked like any man whose whole family had been killed. The old man paid his respects at the tailgates of all the ambulances. But the son, distraught, stayed with his children. He picked up each body and sat cuddling it. Their photos, of pretty and privileged kids playing in a sunny garden, were in the back of the ambulances with them. I could see the picture hooks on the back. They had been taken off someone's wall.

The grandfather made an angry speech that was translated even more loudly and angrily by Yousef Shakir, the regime's best-known television personality. On his show broadcast from the Rixos the night that Humaydi's house was destroyed, he laid into Mustafa Abdul Jalil, the leader of the rebel National Transitional Council who had defected from the regime, where he had been a highly placed minister, just as the uprising began.

'You lowly Abdul Jalil. You used to eat in those houses. You unfaithful traitor,' Shakir said. 'To hell with traitors, agents, bastards.' His video report showed him at the bombsite, walking through the rubble criticizing NATO and the NTC before breaking out in tears as he picked up photographs of the family. 'I was having lunch here last week,' he said.

Shakir's first incarnation in the early eighties had been as a self-styled opponent of Gaddafi, telling American TV reporters that he and his family were getting death threats in the post. He had since become one of the faces of the war. A few days earlier, in Green

Square, during one of the highly ritualistic demonstrations of support for Gaddafi, he stopped the traffic, riding round on the top of a 4×4 surrounded by armed bodyguards. They were about the only ones of several thousand armed men in the square who were not shooting in the air. He waved to the faithful, like a victorious sportsman, or a politician who has won an election, or a war.

In Surman, in the big field across the road from the mosque, the coffins were lined up facing a couple of thousand men in lines facing Mecca, ready to pray. Khaled carried his dead children, holding them close, one after another, and laid them on a low platform next to the coffin of his wife and unborn child. Many men in the crowd were crying. The preacher told the crowd that NATO's game was clear. It did not want to protect civilians, but to kill innocents and occupy the country. Flies buzzed around the shrouded bodies of the children. Their portraits were held high by their father and their grandfather and other family members. The photographer had done a nice job. The portraits were relaxed. The kids were having fun. They took the coffins back to the ambulances. Khaled yelled out in English when he saw the TV cameras: 'They're not an army, they're my kids. They're my kids.'

Gaddafi spoke that night on the radio, condemning the bombing and the death of his friend's family and trying to extract every ounce of propaganda value out of the latest tragedy of a war that he could have stopped by stepping down. I listened to it in a lounge that led into the garden of the hotel. As I was recording a piece about the bombing and the speech I noticed a man eyeing me from a nearby sofa as if he was going to burst. It was obvious he was going to interrupt and when he did he delivered a passionate diatribe. People in the West didn't understand the country. Libyans could sort the crisis out between themselves if only they were left alone. He railed about the hypocrisy of the West and its habit of bombing Arabs. Countries in the NATO alliance were also uncomfortable about the deaths. That same day, the Italian foreign minister, Franco Frattini, had warned that 'the risk of killing civilians cannot be run'.[8] NATO tried hard not to do that during its bombing campaign. But, as Human Rights Watch and many others pointed out, it did not try hard enough to investigate what happened to those it did kill. NATO and the leaders of its member states who took part in the Libya operation should not be frightened of the truth. The accuracy of modern weapons means that they can do devastating damage with a fraction of the casualties that the same raids would have caused at the time of Vietnam. But it is wrong to imply, as Western politicians sometimes do, that war can be almost bloodless. It is never like that.

6

GOD AND POLITICS

Algiers can be a sad place, but there is something irresistible about it too. More than one million Algerians died in the savage war to dislodge the French, who were forced out in 1962. They left behind a beautiful city, with a grand waterfront and white-painted buildings that saunter down to the Mediterranean and gleam in the light from the sea. Their windows are tall and narrow, with blue slatted shutters. Some people hang blue-and-white awnings over the balconies to keep the sun out and they billow in the wind that comes off the bay in the afternoons. The city's most recent sadness came after the Algerian military tried to crush political Islam in 1992. Keeping Islam out of politics was an article of faith, an essential law, for secular, authoritarian Arab rulers at the end of the twentieth century. The military intervened to cancel an election that Islamists had won, and touched off a decade of civil war and slaughter. The lesson for the new generation of Arab leaders, as well as the old ones doing all they can to keep power is clear. Defying the will of the people can be dangerous, even if you do not like the way they have voted.

The only way to get a reporting visa in those years was to accept security offered by the regime. It meant visiting the medieval Casbah, just behind Algiers' sweeping waterfront, with a dozen plainclothes armed policemen, and going to the countryside to inspect the aftermath of massacres with a platoon of gendarmes. Our convoys would move fast down empty, straight roads lined with trees, through villages with small town halls and deserted, shady public gardens with gritty paths, the kind the French like to use for *boules de pétanque*. The regime blamed jihadist groups for the killing, but the army and its surrogates were also accused of massacres, supposedly to blacken the name of the opponents. The military intervention and the denial of democracy were criticised around the world but there were never any sanctions. The French made sure that the International Monetary Fund lent money to the Algerian junta. In a classic display of its behaviour in the Arab world before 2011, the West acquiesced, with heavy sighs, mutterings about human rights and then a tacit acceptance of the actions of the authorities – or '*Le Pouvoir*', as the Algerians called them. A price had to be paid to stop the march of political Islam. Algeria was too close to Europe. It was a major oil and gas producer. The city and the *bled*, the countryside, were frightened places, emptying early as people went home to lock themselves in for the dark night.

Algiers kept its secular ideology. Once after an evening drinking the thick local red wine I went out to a nightclub. Our taxi raced through the streets, able to ignore the curfew thanks to the police bodyguards whose cars made our little outing into a motorcade. In a bar where women danced and men mostly stared I drank beer with the chief bodyguard and listened to a lecture about the dangers of religious extremism. On Fridays police and intelligence would surround mosques in the most troubled parts of the city. Once I escaped the security and sat with a Syrian cameraman in Bab al-Oued, a quarter of Algiers next to the Casbah that had seen plenty of violence. Once it was home to poor French Algerians, the *pieds noirs*, some of whom fought French soldiers after President Charles de Gaulle (as they believed) betrayed them by accepting the inevitability of Algerian independence. By the 1990s the local men with guns were armed Islamists and, of course, the representatives of *Le Pouvoir*. Small strong coffees throbbed and steamed out of a ramshackle 1940s hand-pumped espresso machine as we waited for an auspicious moment to start filming the men who were walking to pray between lines of riot police armed with clubs. We thought we were being low key but the moment the cameraman opened the boot of the taxi to get out his gear a dozen plainclothes intelligence men materialised, evil stubby submachine guns poking out of their leather jackets and pointing at our chests, shouting in local Arabic that my Syrian colleague struggled to understand. I tried to calm them in French on the way to an uncomfortable few hours in a police station listening to a violent interrogation a few offices away. When the chief leather jacket let us go he poked me in the shoulder and said, '*Écoute toi...* That was the first time and the last time. Get out of here and don't come back.'

The events in Algeria were a terrible warning about the consequences of denying the will of the people. The boundaries between confronting political Islam and fighting jihadist killers became blurred, at a time when the spectrum of political Islam was constantly evolving and broadening. By the beginning of this century it went from non-violent gradualists in the Muslim Brotherhood, who believed that Islam was the only answer they needed but were prepared to inch along a parliamentary road to get to where they wanted to be, to radical jihadists and their fellow travellers in al-Qaeda and its affiliates. Some kinds of political Islam were acceptable in the West. The Islamists in Saudi Arabia and the wealthy states of the Gulf were Western allies because they kept the oil flowing, made huge investments in their Western friends' economies and granted them lucrative contracts. Some of the richest were for weapons to use against the common enemy, al-Qaeda and its offshoots and affiliates, and to keep in reserve with an eye to the Islamic Republic of Iran.

The problem after the 9/11 attacks was that the Americans, the British, the French and their Arab allies often disregarded distinctions between different groups' philosophies. Violence created violence. Iraq, after the American-led invasion in 2003, developed an al-Qaeda problem where none had existed before, as jihadists infiltrated the country to fight the Americans and to kill Muslims they regarded as apostates. Cracking down on Islamists had the added bonus of strengthening the regimes' ties with the West, which could mean more military aid. Arab authoritarians deployed the full power of the state. Hosni Mubarak in Egypt was particularly zealous. His regime had to deal with attacks on Egyptian civilians and foreign tourists, most notoriously a massacre in Luxor in 1997 that killed sixty people. But the sweeps conducted by his forces also rounded up members of the Muslim Brotherhood who were horrified by the jihadists' killing sprees. Severe action against jihadists who believed they had a religious justification for killing fellow Muslims as well as non-believers was popular. Al-Qaeda was not in the business of making friends. But locking up the friendly and familiar local Islamists who provided healthcare and hand-outs, and who seemed to be the only authority figures on the side of the people, was something else. They went in and out of prison, not least because their popularity and stamina made them the most realistic alternative to authoritarian Arab leaders.

On a quiet street near the water on Roda, one of Cairo's islands in the Nile, I picked my way around a pile of horse dung outside an unassuming apartment building. A man in a workshop on the next corner had his radio tuned to readings from the Koran. The fine tenor coming from the loudspeaker competed with a couple of white songbirds in a cage, and down the street the horse that had left its calling card clopped its cart and driver away into the distance. Through a dusty door and up a few scruffy, narrow flights of steps was a very ordinary, fairly cramped flat. It was nine months on from the fall of President Mubarak, and the apartment had become the headquarters of Freedom and Justice, the Muslim Brotherhood's political party. Egypt was about to have parliamentary elections, and the Brotherhood was heading for victory.

In Mubarak's time the Muslim Brotherhood had an uneasy existence. It was officially banned but unofficially tolerated because its deep roots in Egyptian society would have made outright prohibition impossible. Muslim Brotherhood members were allowed to sit, nominally as independents, in Mubarak's rubber stamp parliament. At the same time its activists and leaders were often arrested and jailed. Despite that, the regime never managed to undermine its position as the most significant social and political movement in Egypt. The Brothers moved out of the Roda flat to new headquarters after Mubarak fell, which was a sign of their organisational strength, financial clout and new swagger. The Brotherhood's skill at organizing itself gave it a crucial advantage over its secular rivals. At a time when the new liberal parties that were the natural home of the secular Tahrir revolutionaries were getting bogged down in factional infighting, the Brotherhood was already settled into a magnificent, freshly painted office block, adorned with its symbol of the Koran flanked by two curved swords. It was a revelation after the pokey, shabby offices in that corner of Roda. Shiny, expensive cars belonging to some of the businessmen who funded the Brotherhood – and its property portfolio – were lined up outside the building. Inside, under golden chandeliers, elderly veterans of the Brotherhood's struggles talked discreetly on ornate sofas and armchairs. Among them, holding court, was a former leader who, his admirers whispered, had spent thirty years in jail.

The Arab uprisings reinvented politics. The people wanted their will to be paramount. They wanted the fall of the regimes. When it came to voting, the first beneficiary was political Islam. For many Muslims, it felt natural, not even slightly alien, to vote for an Islamist party. Recent history was on the side of the Islamists. On the rare occasions that Arabs had the chance to vote in a free election a majority had tended to choose Islamist parties. Not all of the voters were Muslims. Supporting the Islamists was a good way of protesting. Even though inaccurate polls said something else, I had an inkling that Hamas would win the Palestinian elections in 2006 – which were declared fair by the

European Union – after a visit to the bar of the British-owned, Swiss-run and Palestinian-staffed American Colony hotel in the Israeli-occupied east of Jerusalem. That night Christian Palestinians drinking whisky in the Colony bar were saying that they would vote Hamas, because all the other politicians were either corrupt, discredited or both.

Political Islamists spoke to potential voters in a way that they could understand, and they represented the biggest possible break with what had gone before. In Tunisia in October 2011, a month before Egyptians were due to vote, an Islamist party called Ennahda won a democratic election. That was not in the script for the secular revolutionaries who had driven the protests in January and February in Cairo and Tunis, and for Westerners who dreamt that a new Middle East that felt much more like Europe would somehow blossom within months. When the uprising in Tunisia reached the capital, became world news and was quickly – and a little glibly – dubbed the Arab Spring, the men and women in the streets demonstrating for change did not look nearly as frightening as Europeans and Americans might have feared. Tunisia is the most industrialised country in its continent after South Africa, and the protestors were reassuringly familiar types for Western television viewers. Most of the men did not have beards. Most of the women were not wearing headscarves. Their slogans did not blame the West for the problems in their lives, as had so many demonstrations in Arab countries since colonial times. Instead they called for change at home that was hard to argue about: freedom, justice, dignity, a chance to share the country's wealth and an end to corruption. The fact that it felt so secular on the streets was a surprise to many people in the Middle East and elsewhere who had been following political Islam for decades. Ever since the 1980s it had been the most dynamic political movement in the region. Most people expected that change, when it finally came, would be pushed forward by Islamists. Secular nationalists had been given their chance and had failed.

But in Tunisia and Egypt the secularists who drove the demonstrations forward could not seize the initiative once they had

achieved their objective of unseating the ruler. They could not compete with Islamists who had spent years establishing their own
networks, and with some deep-seated attitudes. By 2011, the way that
political Islamists had entrenched themselves had been reflecting
and helping to create social change for a generation or more. You
can see it on television. Zap through the dozens of channels that are
available every night and the changes are plain. Or take a look at
YouTube. Somewhere there will be a rerun of old concerts by the
great Egyptian diva Umm Kulthum, standing in front of an orches-
tra dressed in bow ties and dinner jackets, performing songs that are
still loved by millions of Arabs. In the black-and-white 1960s, television directors liked showing long cutaways of the audience cheering
their idol. Men and women are often smoking, a habit Salafists try
to ban. The sexes are sitting together, with the women wearing
Western dresses, usually with teased and set hair with very few headscarves in sight. Keep zapping through the channels and there will
be Egyptian films from the same period, in which the men drink
whisky and the women wear miniskirts. Then find a modern soap
opera. The women conduct their domestic dramas in their homes,
very often wearing hijab, and the men sit together in cafes and
offices without a woman in sight.

On the eve of the uprisings the Pew Research Center took a
snapshot of a range of countries with a Muslim majority in a poll that
was released in December 2010.[1] Polls conducted in an autocracy are
not infallible, but Pew's results were still an interesting pointer to
attitudes. The poll said 95 per cent of Egyptians wanted Islam to play
a big role in politics. It showed strong support in Egypt for traditional
views of crime and punishment in the 90 per cent of the population
that is Muslim. Eight in ten Egyptians wanted adulterers to be stoned,
77 per cent thought thieves and robbers should face whippings and
having a hand cut off; 86 per cent believed that leaving the Muslim
religion should be punishable by death. But there was a twist, which
secular people in the Arab Middle East, and most Europeans and

Americans, would see as a direct contradiction. Another Pew poll in Egypt in May 2012, after the Muslim Brothers and their more conservative Islamist cousins, the Salafists, had won the parliamentary elections, showed two thirds of Egyptians thought democracy was the best form of government.[2] About the same number believed that Islam should have a big role in political life, with Saudi Arabia, rather than Turkey, the preferred model. Secular Arabs, on the other hand, believed that Islamism and democracy could never mix. The liberals and secularists still struggled to organise themselves even eight months later, when the Egyptian military gave them a second chance by declaring the parliamentary election invalid and calling a new one. The mainstream political Islamists' most serious rivals were not secular liberals but the more austere Salafists. They are religious revivalists who want to recreate the piety of the first followers of the Prophet Muhammad. Until politics started to bubble through during the Arab uprisings, Salafists tended to concentrate on religious and charitable work. But they sensed an opportunity in Egypt and elsewhere and plunged into politics, skilfully using their local networks, as their rivals in the Muslim Brotherhood had done, to build vote-winning machines.

At the old apartment in Roda the Brotherhood's Freedom and Justice Party preferred not to focus on whether or not severe punishments were acceptable and necessary. They pandered to the deep conservatism in many Egyptians. Muhammad Morsi, who became the Muslim Brotherhood's first president, showed signs of wanting to decriminalise female genital mutilation, which was banned but often carried out. But the Brothers would also talk all day about what they called democracy with an Islamic flavour, a concept that drew a hollow laugh from Arab secularists. When I arrived the apartment door was half open, and al-Jazeera was blaring out. Men in suits bustled around, trying to win the election, insisting that they were committed to democracy and would always respect the rights of others to disagree with them. Most of them had the round calloused bruise in the centre of their foreheads that many pious Egyptian men get from rubbing their heads on the ground during the five daily prayers to show how seriously they take their duties before God. Essam al-Erian, one of the Brotherhood's senior leaders, came out smiling and talking about the birth pangs of Egyptian democracy.

'Egypt is now in a bottleneck ... It's non-stop. The Arab Spring is going to continue. Arabs can convince the whole world that they are ready for democracy, that their civilization, their culture, is compatible with democratic principles and that it is the time to accept this Arab Spring and accept the results of the democratic process.'

Plenty of secular Egyptians who had been in Tahrir Square to unseat Hosni Mubarak did not believe a word that Erian and his colleagues were saying. They dreaded political Islam; they feared the potential power of the Muslim Brotherhood and believed that its talk about democracy was a sham, designed to ease it into a position where it could transform Egypt into an Islamic state complete with a full range of judicial punishments entirely in accordance with Sharia law. They believed that the Muslim Brotherhood and its offshoots across the region were choosing to play down its austere ideology with a false conversion to democracy. When the time was right, secularists warned, the real Islamists would surface, spitting venom at everyone who did not knuckle down to what they were told. Islamists who declared they wanted democracy had a serious credibility problem among many of those who had marched against Ben Ali and Mubarak. When Ennahda in Tunisia even said that it was not necessary to enshrine Sharia law in the new constitution, foreigners who wanted the revolution to produce a stable, open society were relieved. I asked one Western ambassador in the region whether he believed Islamists who were standing in elections when they talked about believing in democracy.

'You know, I do. I believe them. I had some of them round here and gave them a real grilling. I think they're telling the truth about accepting the will of the people. Apart from anything else they have to, as if they don't the people who have been in uprisings are just not prepared to take it.'

But those who were not Islamists in Tunisia, Egypt, Morocco and every other Arab country were deeply suspicious, and simply did not believe what they were hearing. In Tunisia very few minds on the secular side of politics were changed when Rachid Ghannouchi, the leader of Ennahda, said he supported Tunisia's liberal human-rights statute, the Code of Personal Status, and that Ennahda would not try to stop tourists wearing very little and drinking what they liked when they were on the beach.

Until people had a chance to vote, secular Arabs used to claim that support for Islamists was overstated. Election results showed that it was not. The reason was that in Egypt and across the region Islamists were respected and well-organised, and worked efficiently and quickly to turn movements that had been semi-underground into electoral machines suffused with Islam and led by men (always men) who had paid their dues. They had been thrown into prison, and sometimes tortured. Rachid Ghannouchi emerged from prison into twenty-two years of exile in London. Millions of people trusted Islamists. It would have been a surprise if they had not won in the places where they were able to stand. Islamists dominated the first wave of parliamentary elections. In Morocco King Muhammad IV remained the man in charge, with the final say on defence, security and religion. But, to blunt a protest movement that might even have swept the monarchy away, the king had brought in rapid constitutional reforms. One of them was a law that said the government was to be formed by the strongest party in elections, not the one the king preferred. When Morocco's Islamist Justice and Development Party won most seats in the November 2011 election, King Muhammad kept his promise. Like Ennahda, the party avoided focusing too hard on bikinis, beer and headscarves – both to placate secularists and because Morocco, like Tunisia, needed the money foreign tourists spent. In Algeria, still recovering from the civil war, there were claims that only electoral fraud blocked another Islamist victory. Throughout the region, moderate Islamist parties kept saying that they would work within a democratic system.

The Muslim Brotherhood has been the driving force behind political Islam for decades. It was founded in Egypt by Hassan al-Banna in 1928, and spread fast through Sudan, Syria, Lebanon, Palestine and beyond.[3] The Brotherhood's offshoots dominate Islamic politics throughout the Sunni Muslim world. It had its roots in ideas first put forward by nineteenth-century reformist thinkers, which al-Banna developed into the first manifesto for political Islam, calling for Islam to be part of every facet of life. The Brotherhood would educate and care for the people, lead the fight against colonialism, and eventually set up an Islamic state. By the 1940s some members of the movement turned to violence, assassinating public officials and politicians in Egypt. When it opposed Egypt's president, Gamal Abdel Nasser, he fought back with executions, imprisonment and torture.

Activists, often in their prison cells, debated the Muslim Brotherhood's gradualist approach for years. The movement split. Some offshoots went deeper into violence, and formed groups that eventually evolved into al-Qaeda. They were inspired by the writings of a leading member of the Brotherhood called Sayyid Qutb, who was executed in one of Nasser's prisons in 1966. The core of the movement stayed with the original strategy, believing that if they worked with the people, educating them, offering them medical care, supporting them at every stage of their lives, a new Islamist state would emerge by consent. Then in 1981 Anwar al-Sadat, Nasser's successor as president, was assassinated by soldiers who were members of one of the violent offshoots of the Brotherhood.

Sadat was killed at the annual parade to mark what Egypt declared was its victory over Israel in the 1973 war (Israelis do not agree they lost). Questions about whether one faction or another supported violence did not matter a jot to Hosni Mubarak, who was wounded in the attack, blood splattering his dress uniform. As Egypt's new president, he launched a wholesale campaign of arrest and interrogation against supporters of political Islam. Essam al-Erian, then a young activist, was among those rounded up.

'Of course, after the assassination of Sadat we were exposed to big torture to link us with the assassination [...] but I've never been scared. We studied that under dictatorship you were exposed to arrest, so we were ready. As young men arrest was the usual thing in your life.'

'Were you kept with political prisoners?'

'Yes, all the time with the Muslim Brothers. They split us away from the criminals [...] I think this was a good experience for us, to know each other, to live together, to tolerate each other. We had our differences with some of the other groups. But I think this is an era we would like not to see repeated in Egypt's future at all!'

And he laughed loudly. He said that prison time did not make them heroes, but that was a little disingenuous, because part of his political self-confidence was built on the knowledge that their supporters admired the sacrifices they had made for their beliefs, and deepened their conviction that these were serious men, with ideas that could not be shaken. Erian said that their sentences gave the leadership of the Brotherhood a special bond. 'Even when Nasser was killing some of our leaders, he could not kill our beliefs.'

The meeting in the flat was the first time I had interviewed Essam al-Erian since 27 January, the day before protestors captured Tahrir Square. I tried to ring him after they forced their way into the square, to check out the Brotherhood's view, but his phone was off. He had been arrested before dawn and was back in jail. By Sunday the thirtieth he was out again. The police had withdrawn from the streets and the families of some of the prisoners came to break open the jail.

'It was the shortest sentence ever, about sixty hours [...] They brought all the tools [and the guards] faced them all night from inside the prison and then they gave up because they could have been killed. And then it was easy to break the doors of the prison to take the people out [...] and we know of course that many prisons were broken.'

He said with another shout of laugher that the political prisoners followed the criminals out through broken doors and holes in the walls.

'We called our relatives also. They came to get us because all the country was in chaos and we could have been killed in the streets. I came straight to this office to work, not to my family. We felt during that day and night that the country was in revolution.'

Erian took his duty to spread the word about the importance of religion very seriously. He had reacted with a slightly shocked look when I said I wasn't religious, and had a quiet word about it to my Egyptian colleague, Angy Ghannam, as the BBC team was leaving his offices. Angy has liberal political views along with a strong Muslim faith, and wears a headscarf. He asked her to make a big effort to explain to me what religion, in this case Islam, meant, and to explain that she was making her own choices, including her decision to wear the hijab. She passed on Erian's message when we were going back down the stairs.

'He said, "Look, Angy, you're free, you're working, and you're veiled – what's the problem? Talk to that man and explain religion to him. they don't understand."'

It is true that Europeans who come from societies that are essentially secular can find it hard to grasp the degree to which religion defines lives in the Islamic world. The USA is a much more religious society than Western Europe, but that rarely generates much empathy for countries that worship the same God through a different set of beliefs. For millions of voters and would-be voters in the Middle East and North Africa it does not seem at all strange to elect parties whose policies are shaped by their religious beliefs. In Libya after Gaddafi's fall it felt very natural for the men who rallied in the centre of Tripoli to precede a political rally with one of the five daily prayers. One of them told me with horror that Gaddafi was Godless. 'When we broke into Bab al-Azziziya [his enormous, sprawling walled compound in Tripoli] we didn't find a single mosque. Not one!' Opponents of Gaddafi and other Arab despots would congregate in mosques, often listening to highly political sermons that would fire up the faithful to go out afterwards to demonstrate. On the day he declared national liberation complete, the leader of Libya's National Transitional Council, Mustafa Abdul Jalil, also proclaimed that Sharia law would be the 'basic source' for legislation. The tens of thousands in the crowd that day in Benghazi cheered, even though most of them could not hear properly as the sound system could not compete with their noisy enthusiasm. The idea, once they realised what he had said, was uncontroversial for all but a handful of Libyans, many of whom had Western educations. That night they celebrated the future in Benghazi and across Libya with bursts of anti-aircraft fire that lit up the sky and battered the eardrums.

Even though the Brotherhood in Egypt was hard at work preparing for the future when the demonstrations against Mubarak were happening, it was instinctively cautious after so many years trying to operate within a system in which it was officially illegal. It stayed in the background, essentially as an observer, which infuriated activists in the Brotherhood's youth wing who were in the square. They argued bitterly with the older leadership that they wanted to be part of modern Egypt, that they agreed with the secular protestors about toppling the regime if not about what would follow it; they believed that for the Brotherhood to be credible it had to be part of what was happening. In Tahrir mass prayers were held every day. I had to keep explaining to BBC editors who assumed that meant the Muslim Brotherhood was in charge that it was perfectly possible for someone who planned to vote for a secular party also to have a strong faith in God. Belief in democracy did not automatically equal being secular.

And being secular most definitely did not mean an automatic love of democracy and freedom, as some of the hard-faced men under generals' hats proved every day.

But all the while Essam al-Erian and the future President Muhammad Morsi as well as the rest of the Brotherhood's leadership bided their time, making only low-key appearances in the square, staying in their offices to prepare for life after Mubarak. The pattern was repeated elsewhere in the region: Islamists did not want to appear to be stealing the limelight from secular groups who were driving the protests, or to give regimes an excuse to use violence against them, to rally support in the West by claiming they were acting against dangerous fundamentalists. That changed in the run-up to the parliamentary election in November, which was all about seizing the limelight and keeping it. After Mubarak fell, secular revolutionaries distracted themselves with forming parties, debating strategies and a failed campaign to get more time to organise themselves before elections. The Islamists worked hard and well to overhaul their networks and to massage their core supporters. A few weeks before the parliamentary elections the Brotherhood and the Salafi al-Nour Party competed to distribute tons of free meat to families who could not afford to buy it for the traditionally carnivorous Eid al-Adha holiday. The Islamists said it was an extension of the charitable work they had been doing for years. Secular liberals and leftists complained the meat was a bribe. They might have been better off trying to match it, but to do that they would have needed funds and organisation. They complained again that the Brotherhood was campaigning illegally when Egyptian parliamentary elections started in November 2011. Activists from the Brotherhood, dressed as usual in suits, usually worn without ties, set up laptops, powered by car batteries or a cable run into the homes of sympathisers, which they used to collate their lists of who had voted and direct their supporters to the right polling station if they were in the wrong place. This was the kind of organisation that is basic in elections in Europe and the United States. In Egypt, secular parties claimed – unsuccessfully – that it was cheating. They had nothing to rival it. And the people were keen to vote. Six months later I asked one woman who stood patiently in the queue during the presidential elections how long she had been waiting to cast her ballot. 'About thirty years,' she replied with a laugh. The woman next to her was just as cheerful. She said she was worried about the election.

'Why?' I asked, sensing the discordant note that journalists like.

'Because this time we don't know who's going to win!' Against that sort of mood, complaints from badly organised liberals about electoral irregularities seemed to millions to be not much more than sour grapes.

Increasingly, political Islamists across the region were able to operate openly, to organise and to win elections, because of the new freedoms. But there was a flip side to the death of the police state. Law and order collapsed in Egypt, and frayed badly in many parts of Tunisia. Hard-line Tunisian Salafists conducted violent demonstrations, attacking shops that sold alcohol and galleries that showed paintings they believed insulted their religion. One spelt the word 'God' with lines of ants. Another showed a naked woman. The Islamist-led government in Tunis condemned all extremism, secular or Salafi. In Libya armed militias, rather than the flimsy central government, enforced law and order, and often led the way in undermining it. In Egypt trouble between Muslims and the 10 per cent of the population who were Coptic Christians came surging to the surface. Christians were treated as second-class citizens and faced discrimination in the jobs market; permits to build churches took years to get. The Mubarak regime manipulated sectarian tension for its own ends, but generally kept a lid on it. Its American allies did not like Christians being hurt, and violence on the streets was not the best way to control a society. But, without the police state to put the brakes on, dozens died in communal violence.

Some of the worst was in a teeming, overcrowded slum called Imbaba, which is as big as a good-sized town. Poor Christians lived alongside poor Muslims in parts of it. The road into Imbaba was chaotic and crowded, with heaps of uncollected garbage where pavements should have been. Sheep, goats and chickens picked about in the piles, scrawny animals nuzzling filthy bags for something worth eating. Space was so limited that someone had squeezed a children's playground into the narrow strip of concrete that ran down the middle of the main street. The trampoline was the most popular item. Luckily for the children, because cars and donkey carts were passing within a few feet, it had netting strung up around it. Health and safety is usually not a priority in Egypt. The street was half dug up and half mended, with clouds of dust from the dried earth in the patched-up potholes and badly filled trenches blowing with the garbage in the wind. Either side of the street stood hulking concrete and brick tenements separated by narrow alleys that were steep canyons of laundry, each one stretching for fifty to a hundred yards. The alleys were wide enough only for carts, the occasional small van or auto-rickshaws, tuk-tuks that are rarely seen in the boulevards of central Cairo. All of Cairo's street life was there. There were cafes where men smoked shisha, inhaling sweet tobacco deeply through bubbling, murky nicotine-tainted water. Women and children bought carrot and fruit juice from stalls, fruit and vegetable sellers spilled across the pavements, bakers' boys on bicycles balanced trays of flatbread on their heads, nimbly doing their deliveries in traffic that was either choked or crazed. If human energy could be connected to the national grid the voltage on Cairo's streets would power half the city.

But on a morning in May 2011 hundreds of soldiers in combat gear were enforcing a zone of calm in Imbaba, throwing up a perimeter in the streets where, in riots between Christians and Muslims, twelve had been killed and more than 200 wounded. The soldiers cordoned around churches that had been attacked, forming long lines with their Kalashnikovs, sand-coloured uniforms and armoured vehicles. More army trucks with several thousand rein-forcements on board were waiting in the streets nearby. The police force in Imbaba, as in most of Cairo, had never been revived prop-erly after the fall of Mubarak. The army was not taking any chances, but it felt as if the stable door was slamming much too late. The vio-lence started after rumours that a Muslim man had come to the area to find his wife, a convert from Christianity, who was supposedly being held against her will in a church. No real evidence emerged that the story was true, but it did not matter. Anger simmers con-stantly in places like Imbaba among tens of thousands of poor people, especially the young, whose lives seem to them to be blighted with no chance of improvement.

Christian youths mobilised after they heard that Salafis were threatening their churches. For the Copts on the streets of Imbaba, Salafist was a highly pejorative, catch-all term for militant Islamists who they saw as a threat to their existence in Egypt. The communal tensions were magnified by poverty. Young unemployed Muslim and Christian men, living in cramped apartments with their fami-lies, too poor to get married in a society that did not take single men seriously, had plenty of time to brood about their enemies. The violence, when it happened, was very real. A Muslim man in his sixties called Fouad Muhammad Hassaneid was standing near the Azra Mariam church, horrified by what had happened. He said rumours had been flying that mosque had been set on fire by Christians.

'I heard an explosion, saw three young men with jeans and T-shirts. Not Salafists, not bearded. The three had Molotovs, which they tried to get into the church through the cross-shaped stone windows. They were shooting at the church windows to try to make a hole to insert the Molotovs.'

Inside Azra Mariam the story was different. Another sixtyish man called Malek, who said he was one of the church guards – caretaker would be a better word, as he did not look the fiercest of men – said he had been inside when the Salafists broke into the church. He claimed that he had been forced to recite the Shehada, the Muslim declaration of faith, at knifepoint.

'Then more Salafists entered the church. They pushed me to the ground. They cut the throat of Salah, who was the other guard.'

The clean-up was still going on, with a strong smell of burning and wet ash. The baptismal room on the ground floor, where they said Salah was killed, was gutted, with a charred and blackened font. A woman was mopping water from the floor. A middle-aged couple brushed past on their way out, both weeping. In the main church on the first floor four heavily bearded Coptic priests were sitting together on a pew, staring at the fire damage. One of them, Father Sarabamon, seemed to be the most senior and did the talking. I asked him if he feared it would happen again. He said God would protect them.

'We are Christians. We love everyone.'

'Do they love you?'

'We wished they loved us.' And then he gave a hollow laugh. 'You have your answer.'

My Egyptian producer, Angy, who Erian from the Muslim Brotherhood had asked to teach me about religion, broke down in tears at the sight of the church and of the heartbroken members of the congregation, mainly middle-aged and elderly couples who were commiserating with the priest, kissing his hand and holding it to their foreheads. A sympathetic priest took Angy off to another pew, sat her down and spoke to her in a quiet voice while she recovered herself. Like most Egyptians, she was appalled by sectarian tensions and the collapse of law and order since the revolution. More and more people blamed Field Marshal Tantawi, the head of the ruling military council. Christians staged a sit-in outside Maspero, the main state television building, on the Nile Corniche, a short walk from Tahrir Square. As usual the slogans told the story. They yelled that Tantawi had a cell waiting at Tora prison, the jail where many of Mubarak's main lieutenants, including his sons, were being held.

'Tantawi, you're not with the oppressed, but with the oppressor … You're an agent of the old regime.' Throughout the summer the violence continued spasmodically. In October twenty-four people died and hundreds were wounded in clashes between the security forces and Christian demonstrators outside Maspero. Some demonstrators were killed when army vehicles drove into the crowd.

The lack of law and order was one of the biggest challenges facing the new governments. The desire for a strong hand to restore calm almost delivered the Egyptian presidency to Ahmed Shafiq, Mubarak's last prime minister and a retired general who lost only narrowly to Muhammad Morsi of the Brotherhood. Everyone had a story about the disruption and fear that the absence of police created. A diplomat in Cairo told me about how the motorcade of William Hague, Britain's foreign secretary, was held up when an irate motorist kicked over a police motorbike that was trying to block a slip road on to a highway. A businessman talked about how he was suffering lost productivity in his factory because his staff were too scared to walk to work as they were being mugged on the way. Raouf, the BBC's driver, said his neighbourhood had been in chaos after a row between a butcher and a customer escalated. The customer returned with a couple of carloads of armed men, wrecked the shop and vandalised the neighbours' parked cars.

The rapidly evolving new Arab democracies did not grant a honeymoon period to their new governments. Western politicians generally get some time while the electorate, pleased to have dispensed with the other lot, gives the new people the benefit of the doubt. Ennahdha in Tunisia and the Muslim Brotherhood in Egypt found that the appetite for change was so strong that the electorate was impatient. That was one reason why the Brotherhood in Egypt fought so hard against the decision by judges appointed in the Mubarak era to overturn the results of the first parliamentary election. They were not confident they would do as well next time round.

In Libya, the most religious society in North Africa, where the vast majority did not need the Muslim Brotherhood to tell them Islam was the answer, overtly Islamist parties lost out in the July 2012 elections to the National Forces Alliance. Its leader, Mahmoud Jebril more than anything else was seen as a politician who could get things done. Militias who had led the fighting in the civil war were still the most potent force in the country. Benghazi was unstable and at times deadly, and in the Sahara there were serious clashes between warring tribes. Voters decided that Mr Jebril was the best man to deal with security, and to revive the economy. He had been educated in America, was one of the political leaders of the rebels in 2011 and had shown some honesty and foresight by warning about the dangers of unrestrained militia power before the fall of the old regime. Libya's religious parties, including ones that had sprung from the Muslim Brotherhood, the Salafists and the Libyan Islamic Fighting Group did not have the social and political infrastructure that Islamists had in Tunisia and Egypt. But they were also hurt by Colonel Gaddafi's habit of building Islamist rhetoric into his homespun, brutal ideology. It made Libyans suspicious of anyone who told them how to live, including Islamists. Rana Jawad, the BBC's Libya correspondent was astonished at how many new voters were offended by even the existence of religious parties. '"We're all Muslims here! Who do they think they are preaching to? They're not more religious than us!"' was a common reaction.[4]

The victory of the Alliance, which was careful to define itself as liberal, rather than secular, did not make Libya any less pious. Jebril, like the leaders of the religious parties, promised that Sharia would be the basis for Libya's laws. The National Transitional Council, which led the revolt against Colonel Gaddafi, handed power over to the elected assembly in a ceremony that was presented by a Libyan woman who did not wear a headscarf. The last act of the outgoing head of the NTC,

Mustapha Abdul Jalil, was to ask her to leave the platform. A nervous looking man took over to present the second half of the ceremony.

The Libyan election results were a strong sign that while political Islam would have a big role, even a dominant one, in a new world of voting, politicians who defined themselves by their religious beliefs rather than their ability to run their countries and tackle their problems did not have a god-given right to office. In countries struggling to become democracies, where voters also felt that the Islamic nature of their societies was secure, competence mattered.

Dr Nada Mahmoud, a young and pious dentist working at a Muslim Brotherhood clinic in a poor part of Cairo still thought her employers did good work helping the poor, but she was already losing faith in their ability to deal with the country's problems.

'I can't be sure; a lot of things have changed. We saw them in parliament and not all the people like what they're doing right now. We don't think they're as effective as they should be.'

'Does that mean that after years of impunity for authoritarian rulers across the region the new politics is going to be different?'

'They are taking the responsibility. They wanted it, they have to pay for it; they have to face the consequences. People know exactly what they want and they're not stopping until they get it. They want to live well. They want good health and good education. They want to be treated as human beings – that's the main thing. They want dignity.'

'You're religious. Do you always want a religious political leader?'

'We have religion anyway. We carry it in our hearts. We don't need people to tell us what God wants. We know what he wants. It's in one book and not so hard to find out. We want politicians, whoever they are, to do their job and it doesn't have anything to do with religion.'

'So it's all about results?'

'No doubt. Some people think that the people here aren't smart enough to take their own decisions. But the Muslim Brotherhood have been providing services for such a long time in the street with the people so they knew them [...] Democracy is very important. I hope they don't disappoint us, we have expectations [...] I support anyone who makes this country better. I don't care who they are. Just make this country better.'

'So you wouldn't just vote for an Islamist?'

'Not these days. I study politics hard. I go on the internet. I read every bit of information I find to know who I'm going to elect. It doesn't have anything to do with religion. I hope it's the same for the patients. They don't have the internet but they talk to each other a lot and rely on the services the politicians offer more than me. I have a completely different life.'

Her last comment showed the size of the gap in the new Arab democracies between educated people and the rest of the population. It is particularly wide in Egypt because of the way that state schools were starved of investment and direction in the Mubarak years. That matters, since Egypt, because of its size and cultural weight, sets the tone for the region.

In the end the biggest guarantee that the old cliché about Islamist parties allowing one person, one vote, one time will not come true is the engrained habit of protest among the people. Across the region, they have realised the power they have when they get on to the streets. I met a musician called Adam al-Elfy who was in a band called Cairokee, which became famous singing to protestors in Tahrir Square. Adam was a secular young man, disappointed that the liberals who led the revolution had not been able to organise themselves to win an election. He was hoping they would do better next time. He was also certain that there was going to be a next time and that Egypt and its Arab neighbours were having real revolutions, even though they were incomplete.

'Of course I've got some worries, like any Egyptian. But I feel good about one thing. We took the first step. We don't fear anyone now; if there's anything we want to change we know how to change it. The first four years will be hard and bumpy but we can always do something about it.'

'What if after four years the president of Egypt or another country says that there are so many problems he has to postpone the elections?'

'That's not going to happen again, no way. It would be another revolution, I guess.'

'You mean you know the way back to Tahrir Square?'

'Yes, it's ten minutes from here. It's not far away. We're changed forever. People woke up and we won't be fooled anymore. People know they have rights now. That's the only thing I'm not worried about.'

7

PUT ON YOUR UNIFORM, BASHAR

You could see how tough life was getting, the bite of the winter and the strain of fighting the rebellion was visible on the faces of the people of District 86 in Damascus. District 86 is poor, tough and overcrowded, with roughly built concrete apartment buildings, rutted roads and the sort of faces that get lined and tired long before they should. Many of the men in District 86 are lucky enough to have a job working for the Syrian government's security services. They are not the chiefs who sit in offices and give the orders. They are the ones who carry the guns and pull the triggers. In the lines of people waiting for minibus taxis were men in their twenties and thirties wearing camouflage fatigues and carrying Kalashnikovs, heading back and forward to their jobs fighting for Assad's Syria. Some of the local men with guns did not wear uniforms. Syrians with me said that they were part of the Shabiha, the militia that does much of the regime's dirty work. Some men were grouped around the gas burner at a coffee stall. Its operator was friendly enough, offering coffee and refusing to take any money. It was another bitterly cold day. A few women hurried past with their shopping, but most of the people on the streets were men. Many women, despite the cold, were not wearing headscarves.

The people of District 86 are Alawites, born into the same religious sect as President Assad. Alawites, sometimes also referred to as Alawis, have a set of beliefs that originate in Shia Islam, but many are secular.

For them being an Alawite is as much a badge of identity as of religion. Like many minorities, often they close ranks when they are faced with outsiders. Some conservative, traditionalist Alawites did not like Bashar al-Assad's decision to marry a Sunni who had grown up in London. Their heartland is in the highlands that overlook the Mediterranean in the northwest. When Syria became independent from France, in 1946, Sunni Muslims, who were big landowners in the countryside and merchants in the cities, dominated the country. Alawites were poor, living on the margins in the hills. Hafez al-Assad, Bashar's father, was part of the first Alawite generation to move properly into the mainstream of Syrian life. Like many of his contemporaries his way up was through the military, which the Sunni elite considered beneath them. That was not wise, as Hafez's generation, fuelled by ambition, with force behind them as well as the ideology of the Ba'ath Party, came to dominate the country.

Not all Alawites supported Assad's violent response to the uprising. One prominent member of the community, a highly educated, sophisticated woman, told me at a cocktail party in Damascus that there was real distress about the bloodshed. Like any community, the Alawites are not all the same. She said that families were divided, and that there was huge pressure to rally round the president because of the fear that if he went they would face violent reprisals. But as the uprising become an armed insurrection it was hard to be an Alawite and to speak out against President Assad.

One of Bashar's associates complained to me that Alawites were misrepresented abroad: 'If you think about Alawites it always has to be a security guy hitting someone in a cellar. But there are Alawi poets, sculptors, soap-opera makers.' But there is also no doubt that they dominate the security services, as a matter of deliberate policy. Hafez al-Assad chose to surround himself with fellow Alawites because he trusted them and they were loyal. He built security forces that were dominated by Alawites, and that is why many of the people who live in District 86 work for them. They have a distinct accent regarded by other Syrians (who say they have a distinct look as well) as one of command. A Sunni friend of mine complained that some people who were not Alawites put on their accent when they gave orders to get an extra air of authority.

I noticed a gate about 100 yards from where we had stopped in District 86, guarded by armed soldiers with the red berets of the military police. Behind them, on a rocky hill, a drive wound up to a concrete fortress that squatted on a crag. It was the building that used to be Mezze jail. In a country with an always forbidding and often brutal prison system, Mezze was particularly notorious. Political prisoners ended up in Mezze, and plenty of them were tortured.

Across the Middle East the secret police and their ruthless political masters have slotted comfortably into places with a long tradition of torture. In Jerusalem the Russian Czars built a compound for pilgrims to the Holy Land. The British made it into a police station and interrogation centre for Jews and Arabs they regarded as terrorists. Israel's Shin Bet security service would often torture Palestinian suspects in the Russian Compound until the Israeli High Court banned the practice in 1999. Palestinians allege torture continues.[1] The British Empire also bequeathed its emergency laws restricting civil liberties and human rights to its former territories in the Middle East, and sometimes its habit of sending people who took up arms against them to the gallows. The Crusaders, as bloodthirsty as any of the Middle East's masters, built a castle on that crag in Mezze. In the twentieth century French colonialists made it a prison. Bashar al-Assad closed Mezze in his first few years as president. It was a good symbolic way of showing that he aimed to be a different ruler than his father. It just meant that prisoners ended up in other jails. In Crusader days a village would have huddled at the gates of the fortress at Mezze, a place for camp followers and locals who were prepared to make themselves useful to the men of power. District 86 did not feel so different. It sat at the gates of the castle that was part of the regime's network of coercion and repression, which also employed many of the people who live in District 86. Rulers need their loyal fighters close at hand. Just across the valley from the former Mezze prison, on another crag, is the palace built for Hafez al-Assad as he created his dynasty and prepared his sons for power.

As we walked deeper into District 86 I wondered why so many people were carrying rolled-up Syrian flags and posters of Bashar al-Assad. They were expecting us, and the regime's local cheerleaders were going to put on a show. For a moment, Damascus felt like Tripoli in the days of the Brother Leader. Some of the chants were adapted versions of the ones Gaddafi's fans used. Instead of God, Muammar and Libya, but with the same rhythm, they chanted for God, Syria and Bashar. They kissed posters of their leader, screamed their love for him and their hatred of anyone who might want to harm him. But it felt more genuine, more deep-rooted than the claques in Green Square in Tripoli. The Alawites feared that their time at the top, their special position in Syria, was coming to an end. People were pushing forward, all trying to talk at once. It was a struggle to get them to take turns. A man in his thirties with ginger hair, powerful-looking and with an assurance that must have come from a good position in one of the Security branches, obligingly laid out the official line.

'Syria is always strong and will remain strong with the will of our president, may God protect him, and the people. Everything will be over soon. We'll claim victory in a few days [...] Protestors aren't getting killed. Everything you're seeing on TV is fabricated [...] Syria has always been like a steadfast castle and we've proved to the Americans and the British that we're strong.'

A middle-aged woman pushed forward to take her turn to talk to the foreigner, clutching a framed portrait of a man in uniform.

'That's my husband, Muhammad al-Sayyid. They killed him in Hama on 8 October 2011. He was doing his duty. The terrorists shot him in the head and the body and they chopped him. God will never forgive them.'

I asked her what she thought about people who condemned President Assad for ordering his security forces to open fire at protestors.

'They're liars. Bashar is the most human person on earth and the most cultured and educated president in all the Arab world. From day one he's been saying he doesn't want any blood. He was saying, "I will sacrifice my army to protect the citizens." But they're killing us and killing our army that is protecting us. We're worth nothing without the army. Without it we would have ended up like Libya or other places. We're one people with one God and we will never give up on Bashar, no matter what.'

She blamed foreigners and exiled Syrians for stirring up trouble. Like most of the others I spoke to in District 86, she singled out three men often condemned as bogeymen by state television. They were Hamad bin Jassim al-Thani, the prime minister and foreign minister of Qatar, who was leading the charge against the Assad regime in the Arab League. He was the first Arab leader to call for foreign military intervention. The next was Burhan Ghalioun, the secular Sorbonne professor who was then the head of the deeply factionalised Syrian National Council, the most prominent opposition group outside Syria. And then there was the Sunni Alawites hated most of all, Adnan al-Arour. He was a fire and brimstone television preacher who broadcast a notorious sermon threatening Alawites. In it he said that, once Sunnis took over Syria, Alawites who had been neutral in the conflict would not be harmed. Any of them with the sense to support the Sunnis 'would be one of us. But those who violate all that is sacred, by God we shall mince them in meat grinders and we shall feed their flesh to the dogs.' As Arour made his blood-soaked point he got out of his seat in a television studio in Saudi Arabia and waved his finger at the camera to show he was serious.

'May God never forgive them!' the woman raged. 'Hamad and Ghalioun and Arour will be responsible for the blood of our martyrs until the Day of Judgment. They're sending arms to kill us and our husbands and children. Why should they make us orphans and make me a widow?'

Plenty of Sunnis dismissed Arour as a hothead. Alawites and Christians and members of other minorities took him much more seriously. The regime's message that bearded Sunni extremists would take over if the Assads went was widely believed, and often reinforced on state television.

Another woman in the crowd in District 86, who said she had been forced out of her house in Homs ten days earlier, could barely get through a sentence without abandoning normal speech and chanting her hatred of the people who had risen up against the president.

'These terrorists did not let us live peacefully. Our children couldn't go to the streets even to buy a biscuit. We can't breathe in Homs, we can't open a window; all we can find is fighting and gunfire. We just need the army, and God and Bashar. The terrorists are dogs, they killed our people and pushed them out of their homes [...] Bashar should take off his civilian suit and put on his uniform and go to the streets to rescue the world from terrorism.'

The minder from the Ministry of Information added helpfully: 'She wants him to kill them.' It wasn't exactly what she said, but I had the feeling she would not have objected.

The reality of fighting the uprising was hurting them. One man said he was a driver whose busload of government employees was stopped by armed rebels in a suburb of Damascus.

'They beat me and took the bus and left me on the floor bleeding [...] It's because I was working for the government. Whoever supports Bashar they kidnap and torture. He's our leader and the leader of the whole world.'

Another man joined in. He was older than the others, with a Bashar badge pinned to his anorak and the air of a political organiser from the ruling Ba'ath Party.

'We all love Bashar. He's the protector of the Arab world, of Jerusalem, he is the imam of everyone. The Arab League is the betrayer and has nothing to do with Arabism [...] The infiltrators have nothing to do with Syria. They're just being paid [...] I'm not in the army but four of my sons are. I'll sacrifice them for Hafez and Bashar. And we'll nominate him as leader forever because he is the leader of the Arab world. He really lives up to the Ba'ath message: love, friendship and brotherhood.'

Two boys in their late teens with wet, sad eyes stood with a framed picture of their dead brother. The younger one was close behind the other and rested his chin on his shoulder as if they were comforting each other. The older one spoke first: 'My brother was killed in al-Qusayr by armed terrorists. He was killed and he's thirty-five. He has two children. Who's going to raise them? What shall I tell his children? They're asking where he is. His wife is ill in hospital; what should we do? What mistake has he made? I want to be in his place now. I want them to let me do his job.'

The other one chimed in: 'I just submitted my papers to volunteer at State Security. It's for the sake of the country.' Volunteering, one of the Syrians explained, was code for joining the Shabiha and a quick route to a Kalashnikov and a job. I wondered what he would do the first time his squad was called out to deal with a demonstration. I believed their stories because a few days before I was in Homs, in northwestern Syria, at that time the centre of the armed uprising by the rebels who called themselves the Free Army. In the military hospital I had seen the regime's dead soldiers as more casualties came in from al-Qusayr, the place near the border with Lebanon where they said their brother was killed. While I was there a laconic soldier was sitting in a van waiting for three uniformed corpses, blooded and twisted, to be unloaded.

'They were killed an hour ago ... They're hard, the clashes down there. We've brought in these three dead and there were two others before them this morning. And fifteen wounded so far today.' It was mid-morning. Inside the hospital doctors were working on the casualties, filling a tray in the operating theatre with shredded sections of a soldier's liver and intestines. Some of the doctors were Christians – who make up about 10 per cent of the population – and, like most of their community, sometimes out of conviction, sometimes because it seemed the least bad option, had sided with the regime against rebels they said were dangerous Sunni extremists. Outside in the hospital yard coffins were brought out of the mortuary, draped in the Syrian flag and sent with the blessing of a military band back to their villages to be buried. Inside the morgue, a man shouted with rage close to a box of body parts he said were the remains of his cousin.

By the beginning of 2012, one of the terrible ironies in Syria was that, while Bashar al-Assad and his regime were being condemned by large parts of the world for the violence they were using, at home his supporters were asking – demanding – that he use more. The pressure did not just come from Alawites. I spoke to a Western diplomat in Damascus who said he had met one of Syria's Christian bishops who was in the city to see President Assad. The diplomat asked what message he would be taking to the palace.

'He told me my people are totally scared. They look at what happened to Christians in Iraq and Egypt – and they want the rebellion crushed.'

In Syria it was never the Assad regime against all of the people. He had genuine support from some of Syria's minority communities, not just the Alawites. Like Lebanon next door, Syria is a mix of different sects. Arab Sunni Muslims are in the majority, around 66 per cent. Alawites are around 12 per cent, Christians about 10 per cent, Kurds 9 per cent and Druze around 3 per cent. Some Sunni members of the middle classes supported the regime too, as they feared the chaos of a civil war.

As the uprising continued, the sectarian cracks widened. Most supporters of the rebellion, and most of the fighters, were Arab Sunnis. Assad's core support came from Alawites and Christians, up to 90 per cent of both communities, including the diplomat in Damascus. He estimated that two-thirds of the Druze and a 'large minority' of Kurds were with the regime. The reasons were a mixture of fear about what would happen to them without the regime, and self-interest. Some Kurds saw a chance to take over security in their areas and to start creating a de facto mini state. Even those who were repelled by the regime's violence were more terrified of what they saw as the alternative, which the diplomat called the 'Salafi nightmare', the fear that Syria would be taken over by Sunni extremists, a vision that the regime did all it could to foster. Over the years the Assad regime used its secular ideology to hold together a country of different religious groups, comforting minorities because the ruling family was itself part of a minority and encouraging powerful businessmen from the Sunni majority to make money. An Alawite woman in District 86 recited the authorised version, almost as if it had been wisdom she had learnt at school.

'We don't have any sectarians; there's only one sect and that's all the Syrians. We don't love the president because he's an Alawite like us, we love him because he is faithful, he loves his country and he's not a liar like the other leaders. He's not like Hamad[2] and the others who are all animals. It is only Bashar and his father who protected us [. . .] my cousin is an only child and a sniper killed him with one shot. Isn't that a shame? Bashar should be the president of the whole world.'

A Syrian official who was horrified by the violence but still supported Assad on the grounds that the alternatives were worse put it like this:

'Seventy per cent of the people are against the government. That doesn't mean that 70 per cent are for the insurrection. Maybe 30 per cent of the anti-government side are with the opposition. The rest say we need peace and reform. I can take five more years of government corruption, five more years of harassment by the intelligence services. But not thirty years of mullahism. If beards take over it will be the end of it.'

Secularism was vital glue to hold together Syria's jumble of communities and sects. But as the violence increased, cracks started to show, as the regime lost support that was not part of its Alawite core. Sunni merchants in Damascus were not opposing the regime – not publicly anyway – until they went on strike to protest at the massacre at Houla in May 2012 that killed more than 100 people including many children. The regime insisted that it had nothing to do with the killings, but the merchants did not believe them. Neither did many others outside the country.

The response to the uprising, the decision to spill blood to protect the regime, looked to be a classic Assad-family decision. Understanding the extended Assad family, the pinnacle of Syria's Alawite community, was the only way to work out how power was wielded in Syria. Over forty years the Assads kept private business private, so Syrians made a science out of interpreting fragments of information, using guesswork and the Damascus rumour mill. Some foreign diplomats in Damascus used to say, only half joking, that it helped to watch the *Godfather* films or a box set of DVDs of *The Sopranos* television series. Simon Collis, British ambassador in Damascus, called the Assads a mafia family after the British government pulled him with his staff in March 2012 on safety grounds. Bashar al-Assad might have appreciated a bit more time to wait before he took over the family business. He was thirty-four when his father Hafez al-Assad died. Ever since 1970, when the first president decided being a member of a military junta was not enough and took control of the country on his own, power in Syria had been kept close to home. In the narrow lanes and covered alleys of the old city of Damascus, you could buy fridge magnets showing black-and-white photos of Syria's first family in the seventies when its patriarch was in his pomp. On the magnets Bashar and his siblings pose on their bikes, watched lovingly by their smiling parents. Just like any other happy family, except that Dad was an airforce general who had seized power in one of the coups that were regular events in Syria for twenty years after the trauma of the Arab failure to stop the creation of Israel in 1948. While the kids were having fun on their new bikes, Assad senior was redefining the phrase 'iron grip'.

Hafez al-Assad was the kind of Middle Eastern leader about whom people used words like 'calculating', 'ruthless' and 'dominating'. He was a formidable negotiator, who made himself the necessary man in the Middle East, the spider king sitting at the centre of the web of war and peace. His shrewdness, determination and lack of compunction gave Syria an influence and power way beyond its poor natural resources and feeble, closed economy. The first President Assad dealt with attempted revolts by crushing them, if necessary by sending in the tanks. He ended the regular reshuffles by coup of successive military juntas after he seized power, and by the time he died in 2000 no one could challenge his wish to pass the presidency on to his son. His system stood up to the first year of the uprising but by 2012 the pressure was showing, in big and small ways. When I walked into the Ministry of Information in Damascus the gigantic bust of the first President Assad that adorned the entrance hall was, unthinkably, covered in dust and small bits of rubble from building work. The ministry's prudent employees used to keep it shiny. Now they had other things to think about. By then the system Hafez built for his son to inherit was under strain, but still holding.

Bashar al-Assad is a very different man. A Syrian official, a fan of the President, despaired, discreetly and quietly.

'When Bashar was growing up he didn't live in a palace, they had a relatively humble middle-class home, but he was treated like a prince. He's a decent man, but he's surrounded by idiots. His father knew what it was like to be an ordinary person. He came up the hard way. He had been poor. His dad could deal with people on the streets because he had been there himself. Bashar's not like that.'

The couple of times I met Bashar al-Assad before the uprising started he was amiable, polite and charming, self-confident as well as well informed, and answered the questions he was asked. He seemed to be the man in charge, apparently secure inside his own skin, though some former associates have said that he is anxious with sudden mood swings.[3] He claims to have had a happy childhood, playing on his bike with his brothers and sister. Bashar told a sympathetic biographer that 'we had a very normal family life. We had two very caring parents, and our happiness derived from those two caring parents.'[4]

Bashar conducted interviews with foreign reporters in a walnut-panelled library in a guesthouse next to the presidential palace, on a hill overlooking Damascus. A famous Japanese architect designed it as a family home back in the 1980s, though the Assads never lived there. It feels like a small and luxurious Middle Eastern hotel, lots of marble and mother-of-pearl-inlaid furniture. It is said in Damascus that it was a gift from Rafik Hariri, the Lebanese billionaire tycoon, in the 1990s to please Hafez al-Assad. Hariri was the prime minister of Lebanon, trying to rebuild his country at a time when it was still a domain of Syria. Hafez al-Assad was its feudal overlord and Hariri was bringing him a tribute.

Syria under Hafez and Bashar became a country whose fate was settled around the Assad-family dining table. I kept a picture in my head, imaginary but I suspect not too far from the truth, of them all sitting down together to eat, with Bashar at the head. He was the president, the chairman and chief executive of the family business he inherited from his dead father, who still glowered down on the country from innumerable portraits, busts and statues. Bashar's word mattered most, more than that of his siblings and cousins. But he had to carry the family, the board of directors, with him. Defying the collective will would break the system his father built.

The EU recognised that Bashar was the boss when in May 2011 it added him to a sanctions blacklist along with most of Syria's top leadership (many of whom also happen to be members of his close family). The EU said he was the 'person authorizing and supervising the crackdown on demonstrators'. It is necessary to point out that he was the top man because many people, inside and outside Syria, saw him as a reformer when he came to power and believed that he was stopped from changing Syria by his father's old friends. A year into the uprising some Syrians still hoped, plaintively, that he would keep the promises he made to modernise the country. One blamed the defunct shell of the Ba'ath Party for blocking him. Others – serial opponents of the Assads and some intellectuals – never bought the idea that Bashar wanted real change, which would mean the regime and the family giving up slices of the power that his father had taken and held. He never stopped talking about political reform, but his words became more hollow as the killing went on. At first his youth and sometimes awkward appearance made some people think he was weak, lacking in confidence and stubborn to try to cover that up, a man who would stick to an idea even it was proved to be wrong. His Syria was dismissed as a dictatorship without a dictator. But by 2012 Syrians who were opposing Bashar, and others who supported him, believed he was as prepared to spill blood as any other Assad.

Next to the president at my virtual Assad-family dinner was his younger brother Maher. In the family business he was the chief operations officer, a soldier seen by most Syrians as the family's chief enforcer. A Syrian journalist in Damascus summed him up succinctly as the 'psycho-violent one in a brutal family'. The European Union agrees. When it added his name to its sanctions list in May 2011 the EU described him as 'the principal overseer of violence against demonstrators'.[5] Maher commands the army's two top units, the 4th Mechanised Division and the Republican Guard. The relationship between Bashar and Maher has uncanny echoes of the one between Hafez and his younger brother Rifaat in the early days of the first Assad presidency. Rifaat led a force called the Defence Companies, which put down trouble for his brother. Maher's 4th Division has its roots in Rifaat's old unit. In February 2012, when Bashar ordered the Homs offensive, the 4th Division was the regime's spearhead. Maher al-Assad, like Rifaat, was also interested in business opportunities, and made deals with a number of Sunni businessmen. Unlike Rifaat, he had not, at the time of writing, tried to mount a coup to overthrow his brother, leading to his exile in a string of luxury houses in Paris and London. Maher's business partners grew rich, but they were also exposed to his rage and to the caprices of a family that has got used to getting its own way. Damascenes talk about what happened when he had a disagreement with one close ally, his brother-in-law Muhammad Hamsho. He was a tycoon who owned, among many other things, the local rights to sell Nokia phones, as well as al-Dounia Television, a loyal mouthpiece for the regime. Maher, the story went, decided that the best way for his view of the business to prevail was to put Hamsho under house arrest and to ring his house with troops.

Maher's rival as enforcer in the group around the dining table was Asaf Shawkat, the brother-in-law of the Assad brothers. In 1995 Shawkat, an army officer, married Bushra, Assad's sister, who is said to be an ideologue, making sure the family does not forget how much it is against Israel and Islamists. She is also strong-willed, apparently insisting on the marriage despite her father's opposition. Shawkat always made himself useful, helping his father-in-law to make sure nothing stopped his son's succession. He was put on the EU sanctions list on the same day as Maher, for being 'involved in the crackdown on the civilian population'. But at the beginning his relationship with his wife's family was not always easy. He was the newcomer in a group of men that had grown up together. One unconfirmed story that is often heard in Damascus is that during a row in 1999 Maher shot Shawkat, an uncanny echo of the former ruling family in the other Ba'athist paradise, Iraq. Saddam's son Uday was notorious for pulling guns and sometimes using them at family parties.

In 2008 the German paper *Die Welt* reported that Shawkat had tried to overthrow Bashar. The theory he might have tried to seize power is contradicted by other signs, especially the fact that, apart from his wife, Bushra, his main ally in the family was the president himself, who made him head of intelligence. His continued presence at the top table, and a move from intelligence to another key job as deputy chief of staff of the Syrian army, suggested that he was trusted in a way that a disloyal plotter could not be. In the early summer of 2012 the Syrian Foreign Ministry was forced to deny rumours that Shawkat and his top advisers had been poisoned by one of his bodyguards who had gone over to the opposition. People in Damascus became more convinced there was something in the rumour when the two main mobile-phone companies sent out text messages from two senior generals, one who was assistant vice-president and the other who was minister of the interior, denying that they had been killed in the same poisoning attack. In the end Shawkat was assassinated in a bomb attack, along with two other senior generals, in July 2012.

The president's cousins were always a big part of the family business. Atif Najib, the former head of the Political Security Directorate in Dera'a, and Hafiz Makhlouf, a senior officer at State Security, were also on the EU sanctions sheet for being 'involved in violence against demonstrators'. Atif, the White House among others alleged, gave the orders to break up the first demonstrations in Dera'a with live fire. Hafiz Makhlouf survived the car crash that killed Basel al-Assad, the heir apparent, in 1994. So did the chauffeur, who was sitting in the back seat so that he could take the car back from the airport where they were heading to catch a flight.

The scene around the dinner table was a long way from the lives of the poor Alawites in District 86. Over more than forty years of power the Assad family has acquired certain financial expectations as well as the arrogance of power. Wealth is part of the equation. Another first cousin on Bashar's mother's side was Rami Makhlouf, the family's money man and the brother of Hafiz. Rami had big stakes in what was the best of the Syrian economy until the uprising began to destroy it – property, tourism, construction, insurance and banking, as well as a controlling stake in Syriatel, the biggest mobile-phone operator. His fortune was estimated in billions of dollars. A well-connected Sunni businessman told me he was having lunch with an Alawite friend in April 2011, as the uprising gained pace, when he was beckoned over for a private chat with yet another Assad cousin, one more Makhlouf brother who was a player in the Damascus power game. He delivered a message from the ruling family: that Alawites should stick together. And he complained, exasperated, about the people's ingratitude 'after all we've done for them over forty years'.

Rami might well have been sitting at the family dinner table near his mother's sister, the family matriarch, widow and mother of a president, the former first lady Anisa Makhlouf. Alawites – and other Syrians – believed that she stayed highly influential. A contact in Damascus described her as 'the mad mind behind the scenes'. Others say she has been unjustifiably accused and instead is old and ailing and still mourning her dead husband and son. Opponents of the Assads in Syria liked to repeat the story that she first told her sons to get tough after protestors in Dera'a early in the uprising uprooted a statue of her late husband. In the operation that followed, her family's opponents insist, more than twenty people died. Anisa was determined that even in death her husband would not be humiliated. When Bashar came to power she was also anxious to preserve her own position, and not to be upstaged by his beautiful Sunni wife, Asma. The new Mrs Assad grew up in London, the daughter of a doctor, and worked as a banker at J.P. Morgan before she met and married Bashar, who was still the heir. For the first few years after he inherited the job Asma was not known in the official media as the first lady, because that title was still reserved for Anisa. Asma had to accept the workaday title 'the wife of the president'. An opposition group leaked emails it said it had hacked between Asma and her husband the president. Some of them were requests for friends to go shopping for her. For the wife of an Arab potentate, her tastes were relatively modest. Like many Londoners, she had a strong faith in John Lewis; and one of the emails pointed out that it was sale time at Harrods.

The family was sustained by the power of the police state built by

Hafez al-Assad and passed on to his son. It rested on the directorates of State Security, Political Security, Air Force Intelligence and Military Intelligence, the last two being directed by Alawites.[6] The Syrian security services were pervasive, overlapping and intimidating. In 2006 I went to see a lawyer in Damascus, a critic of the regime called Anwar al-Buni, who had just been released from prison and was heading back there fast. He had a black eye, given to him by a couple of thugs who had jumped off a motorcycle outside his block of flats and beaten him up without saying a word. Their fists were doing the talking and he assumed the message was from the secret police. Walking up the narrow steps to his small flat felt like going to see a dissident intellectual in Eastern Europe in the seventies or eighties. In the flat, with a worried wife and young children who could not have known their father as well as he would have liked because of his prison time, we discussed the way the Syrian intelligence services operated, the way they worked night and day to maintain the barrier of fear that the regime had put up around itself. What changed with the uprising was that barrier became so battered it broke. Once a regime uses force against its people and fails to crush them its life-force starts to drain away. I felt bad about getting Anwar into more trouble, and warned him that speaking to the BBC openly might send him back there. He shrugged, and told me to get on with it. Of course he knew better than anyone the risk he was taking. He had done time, and his brothers, who he had defended, had spent more than thirty years between them as political prisoners. Not long after we met he was arrested again and imprisoned. He was released in 2011 and went back to working for political detainees.

The pattern of keeping power as close as possible to home – with sons, brothers, cousins, in-laws and, after that, members of the Alawite sect – was set by Hafez al-Assad. His system was designed to withstand and to destroy threats to the regime. The best counterweight, the first President Assad decided, was to make sure that men he could trust

were in the top jobs. Very often that meant Alawites, and best of all
Alawites who shared his blood.

An uprising by Syria's biggest religious group, the Sunni Muslims,
was always seen as the biggest internal danger. When it came, in 1982
in the town of Hama, the event defined the Assad family's approach
to internal security. The officers who had seized power in 1963 were
members of the Ba'ath Party. The Arabic word *ba'ath* means 'renais-
sance', and from the time it emerged in the 1920s and 1930s the
party's message was attractive to poor, ambitious youngsters like Hafez
al-Assad. The Ba'athist ideology taught that Arabs could once more
lead the world if they were united, free of colonial rule and socialist.
That meant a challenge to the traditional Sunni landed classes and
merchant elites. Some Sunnis who felt that they were not being dealt
into the nation's wealth joined the Ba'ath, but the party had an obvious appeal to members of minority groups. One of its founders,
Michel Aflaq, was a Christian. The Ba'ath's natural rivals came from
the Sunni Muslim Brotherhood. The young Hafez would get into
street fights with them as he emerged as a student politician.[7] For
Assad and a generation of his fellow Ba'athists the way ahead was to
join the armed forces. It was the only way up, and they went all the
way, outwitting the Sunni elites who considered military service dis-
reputable.

After the coup in 1963 the Brotherhood kept pushing back against
the Ba'athist state. The centre of Sunni discontent was Hama, an
ancient city famous for its waterwheels on the banks of the Orontes
River. Hama was a citadel of Sunni Muslim tradition and dogma,
utterly opposed to Assad's secular, Ba'athist ideology. The first
uprising in the city happened in 1964. By the eighties the Muslim
Brotherhood in Hama had a long record of opposition to the Assad
regime. In 1980 the Brotherhood tried to assassinate the president in
Damascus with hand grenades. He saved himself by kicking one of
them away. The next day troops from Rifaat al-Assad's defence
companies killed hundreds, perhaps more than a thousand, Muslim

Brotherhood prisoners in Palmyra jail. Rifaat always denied any involvement. Two years of tension and violent competition followed between the Brotherhood and the regime. By February 1982, both sides were ready for a showdown. After Muslim Brotherhood gunmen killed a unit of regime troops who were on a sweep through Hama's old town, Hafez al-Assad ordered Rifaat to crush the uprising. Assad was building his Syria into a regional player by intriguing against the United States and Israel and taking chunks out of Lebanon. That was not going to work if he could not secure his base. The time had come to deal with his most obdurate internal enemies once and for all.

It took three weeks. Amnesty International made one of the first reports piecing together what happened and said estimates of the dead went from 10,000 to 25,000. Even after they regained control of Hama the killing went on.[8] According to Patrick Seale in his classic biography of Hafez al-Assad, 'entire families were taken from their homes and shot'. Most of the old town, which for a time the insurgents turned into a killing ground for the regime's troops, was bulldozed flat.

It prompted some nasty memories. Thirty years on, Amnesty International went back to some of its original eyewitnesses.[9] It took Hafez al-Assad's forces only four days to claim victory, but the centre of Hama stayed sealed off for another two weeks. Amnesty points out that there were conflicting accounts of atrocities, including some by the Muslim Brotherhood. Conditions for the people caught up in the fighting were horrific. Maha Moussa, then nineteen, had regime snipers stationed on the roof of her family house. When her grandmother died of natural causes 'we asked the military men in our house what we should do with the body. One told us we should just put it outside our door on the street. But I remember looking outside our window and seeing dogs feeding on the old corpses already all over our street, and thinking, *We cannot put my grandmother out to be eaten by the dogs.*' After the fighting was over, her uncle was arrested on suspicion of being a member of the Muslim Brotherhood. His interrogators killed him, then returned his body to his family. His eyes and fingernails had gone. The same tactic was used by the regime of Assad the younger as he fought to maintain the barrier of fear that was vital for the security state.

When the uprising started in 2011 its torturers did not try to conceal what they had done. Mutilated bodies were returned to families as a message, and to deter others from any more dissent. It was an old tactic but it backfired, increasing anger not fear. Something similar happened in Cairo before the uprising against President Mubarak, after police filmed themselves torturing minibus driver Imad Kabir then gave the video to the other drivers – an event that touched off public fury. In Syria a chubby thirteen-year-old boy called Hamza al-Khatib was arrested by security forces on 29 April 2011 in a village called Jizah near Dera'a. His badly mutilated body was returned to his family a month later. As well as bullet wounds he had burns, and marks that human-rights activists said were likely to have been made by electric torture devices and whips. He had a broken neck and his penis had been cut off. But the regime, perhaps concluding a display of any weakness would only encourage its enemies, brazened it out. A special one-hour television programme claimed that insurgents had killed Hamza. A doctor on the show said opponents of the regime had mutilated his body so they could create a symbol as powerful as Muhammad Bouazizi, the vegetable seller who set light to himself in Tunisia and started a revolution. The dead boy's father was also paraded on the TV programme, saying he believed a promise made by President Assad to investigate what had happened.

After a video showing Hamza's broken body was put on to YouTube, activists claimed that his father, brother and uncle were detained. The irony is that the boy's appalling injuries did make him into a symbol of the uprising, in Syria and around the world, via the internet. Firm confirmation of exactly what happened to Hamza will be impossible until the time comes when journalists, or perhaps war-crimes investigators, are able to visit his family and town and find the men who arrested and held him. But there is strong evidence that the regime was up to its brutal ways, taking a page from the Hama play-book. The problem President Assad and his security chiefs had was that the world had changed. 'Hama Rules', as the *New York Times'* journalist Thomas Friedman called them in his book *From Beirut to Jerusalem,* do not have the power they once did. At the time of the Hama operation thirty years ago, returning the body of a boy who had died in agony and terror might have intimidated the people close to him – though of course it would have also incubated hatred in their souls for the regime. But in May 2011 the video gave a boost to the uprising, which was only six weeks old. Within days 60,000 people were following a Facebook page called We Are All Hamza al-Khatib. The title of the page was a homage to the Facebook campaign We Are All Khaled Said, commemorating the young man killed by the Egyptian security forces, which became a crucial part of the Egyptian Revolution. Hamza's name was chanted at demonstrations. The regime's torturers had not just murdered a child; they had also made a serious political error.

In Hama, thirty years earlier, the regime was also sending messages and warnings. According to Maha Moussa, the security forces cut off the fingers of sixty men they had killed and put them along the walls of a mosque. No one dared to remove them. Abd al-Hadi al-Rawani, one of the witnesses to the Hama killings in 1982, told Amnesty that what was happening thirty years later in Syria was for the same reason: because 'the people want freedom and the regime is suppressing it'. Brutal killing still intimidates. But as a way of terrorizing the popu-lation it works best in a sealed, closed society, amplifying the feelings of isolation and fear among the regime's enemies, aiming always to give the impression that the power of the army and the intelligence services is absolute and all-seeing, that any transgression will be pun-ished with spectacular brutality. Hama Rules needed darkness and privacy from the rest of the world in order to work best. In 1982 it took Friedman, a highly industrious reporter, two months to get to

Hama, and even then he had to sneak in. Reporting revolutionary Syria first-hand thirty years later was no easier. But the difference was that modern digital communications meant that an idea of what was being done was emerging on the internet from local people's phones and laptops, almost in real time. One of Amnesty's original intervie-wees said it took a week for people in outlying villages around Hama to find out what was happening in the city. Exactly three decades on people all round the world could get a graphic impression, at the very least, of Syria's slide towards civil war.

Bashar al-Assad, without any prompting from me, referred to Hama and the killings when I met him two years before the uprising began, at the time of Israel's war on the Palestinian armed Islamist group Hamas in Gaza at the beginning of 2009. Before an interview President Assad liked to sit with his guest for a private chat, without any aides in the room. First he questioned me closely about the atmosphere in Israel, which I had left the day before to travel to see him. Officially foreigners who have been in Israel are not supposed to enter Syria, but he was curious about what was happening there. Bashar regarded himself as pragmatic.

'I have to be flexible,' he said, 'to do what is best for the country. Take our alliance with Hamas. It helps Syria, and our fight with Israel. You know how we believe in a secular society, but we're getting involved with political Islam. Why? Because it suits us.

'You might not expect us to be close to Hamas,' he added with a smile. 'You know my family's relationship with the Muslim Brother-hood.' Hamas is an offshoot of the Brotherhood. He might have been talking about a dispute between neighbours, but I took it to be a ref-erence to what had happened in Hama in 1982. Perhaps that throwaway remark about so many deaths showed a certain detach-ment from the flesh, blood and bone reality of what his family has done in the name of Syria. The bigger game was Syria's strategic posi-tion and above all the security of the regime. One led to another. Not many years after the Hama massacre, in 1990, a much more secure Hafez al-Assad was being persuaded by the first President George Bush to join a coalition against Saddam Hussein. The message from one generation to another was do what's necessary, because in the end stronger Assads make Syria stronger. Perhaps the belief that the world would turn again and he would be back in favour reassured Bashar as the world turned against him in 2012.

The most charitable interpretation of Assad's actions was that growing up as the son of an authoritarian Arab leader, inheriting the highest office in the land the way that a prince succeeds a king, always going to places where people cheer and bow, might make it hard to comprehend the killing, the torture, the savagery that was done in his name. The other interpretation is that Assad inherited from his father the realisation that keeping power means showing no weakness and killing anyone who poses a threat.

My best guess, based on many conversations with Syrians for and against the regime, is that Bashar knew exactly what was happening in the country and decided it was necessary. Maybe President Bashar al-Assad, and the rest of the family, just wanted to be as tough as Dad.

8

THE FALL

This time walking up to the low blue gate that separates Tunisia and Libya was very different. 'Who's in charge over there?' I asked the Tunisian border policeman.

'*Les Revolutionaires.*' A burst of gunfire and some whooping drifted over the border. The hatchet-faced Gaddafi gunmen had been replaced by cheerful rebels, shaggy-haired, triumphant and blasting at the sky. They greeted Libyans returning home by firing their Kalashnikovs into the air, and the returnees high-fived them back. One man was so overjoyed to be home he hugged the man who had greeted him with a volley of bullets, then borrowed his gun to make his own attempt to shoot down the sun. The bullets were endless, always more boxes to break out, taken from the old regime's arms dumps or delivered by the Qatari Air Force.

'Welcome to free Libya,' said a young man with a beard.

So we went down the road to Tripoli. The landmarks were familiar by now. The sculpted, elegant curves of six half-built fishing boats rising out of the sand, beached and abandoned between the road and the sea. The petrol queues and the checkpoints, protected by sand chicanes to slow the traffic in case anyone planned to run their cars right through without stopping. The checkpoints were in the same old places, with the portraits of the Brother Leader scratched out and replaced by the revolutionary flag. The men checking the cars were younger and more cheerful than Gaddafi's people. In the winter his men had been there stamping their feet in front of fires made with scraps of wood, hulking and sour under long greatcoats in the desert cold, Kalashnikovs pointing, with the kind of face you get when you have been cruel to far too many people. They would wave through the regime's cars, which had special number plates. Trying to cross the checkpoints without the regime's seal of approval guaranteed a sick nervous churning in the gut and could mean arrest. The new guys reclined on the small, half-broken swivel chairs that seemed to be at every checkpoint in Libya. My mind wandered to offices reopening, and staff without seats as every chair was at a checkpoint. We drove through Zuwara, the first big town, a stronghold of the Amazigh people, better known as the Berbers, bustling again with some new damage freshening up the debris left from February and March. Sobrata was busy too, full of people shopping for Eid al-Fitr, the feast that marks the end of the holy month of Ramadan. The custom is that families buy new clothes for the festival. The shop-keepers were already opening their doors, putting the war behind them, rediscovering their sense of tradition and love of profit.

By the time I got to the capital a few days after the rebels, the regime had been scattered and was trying to regroup around Sirte, Gaddafi's birthplace. Tripoli's soundtrack was a mix of gunfire and prayers. From early on mosque loudspeakers were buzzing across the city's sprawling skyline, and as the sun rose higher the words of the Koran merged with the clatter of gunfire. Libyans liked to shoot in the air when they were happy, sad or angry, and all three emotions were spilling out around Tripoli. Almost two more months of fighting still had to be done in and around Sirte, but the war was ending, as wars always end, with extravagant hope, numbing fear, winners, losers and the bereaved. Gaddafi and Saif al-Islam, his son and presumed heir, had disappeared. The colonel's wife, pregnant daughter and two other sons with their families and retinues had been able to drive unmolested across a big stretch of Libya to cross into Algeria. In

Tripoli it was too early to talk about a return to normality because Libyans were trying to work out just what normality should look like. Colonel Gaddafi had been dominant since 1969. Libyans had to be well into their fifties to remember the king. But the Brother Leader was gone, and so were his portraits, posing in a series of increasingly elaborate uniforms, apparently made to his own design, or backlit in ochre robes against a pastel sunset, hands clasped in triumph and benediction. The cult of personality that had put his image just about everywhere had evaporated. In my first few days back in Tripoli I saw only two Gaddafi portraits. One was propped up in a dustbin as a fighter emptied his Kalashnikov into it for some grateful photographers. The other was positioned carefully on the threshold of the hotel where most of the journalists were staying, so all the guests had to tread on it to get inside.

In the days leading up to the fall of the regime the captives inside Abu Salim prison in Tripoli sensed Gaddafi's endgame was closer, even though they had very little news from the world outside. The prison was the most feared place in the country. Libyans felt a creeping sense of threat if they had to drive past its gates, and would not even look at it in case they made eye contact with the wrong person. By the end of July, according to Muhammad al-Ziani, the man I had interviewed just before he was arrested and sent to Abu Salim in March, the jail was seething with discontent. The regime had shown in the past how it would treat revolt in Abu Salim. In 1996 an estimated 1,200 prisoners were massacred there after a failed uprising. But by the end of July, in Abu Salim's stifling, airless atmosphere, Ziani and his fellow prisoners were desperate enough to try again. I walked with Ziani along Abu Salim's long corridors and in the exercise yards, walled with concrete and roofed over with steel mesh. Some prisoners were not even allowed out for a glimpse of the sky through the barred roof. Ziani showed me the collective cells where he was warehoused with other threats, real and imagined, to the regime. Each could hold around twenty men without serious overcrowding. But Gaddafi's security services were hauling in more suspects every night, and Ziani said that more than fifty men had been packed into his cell.

'There was one night it was so hot we couldn't sleep. We kept hitting the doors, the guards came here, and they kept yelling at us to stop and go to sleep. We told them we can't sleep.' A guard opened the door to one of the cells, and the men inside surged out. 'The guards ran away because they were so scared. After an hour they told us go inside your cells. We said, "If you're real men, force us..." We were so scared, we thought they would shoot us, or take us out and torture us. At that time there was no difference between death and life [...] I thought, *Before you kill me I just want to do what I want.* So we took control of this place on that day.' The territory they seized was just a corridor but the fact that they held it was also a sign that the regime had weakened. In 1994 mass dissent meant death. In 2011 the guards must have realised that the end for Gaddafi was coming and let the prisoners stay where they were, in control of their corridor.

In the early hours of Saturday 20 August a NATO airstrike flattened the administration block at Abu Salim. Ziani said the men in his corridor decided to break out. He pointed to the door that was still lying there on the ground.

'Yes, we said, "God is greatest, it's time. It's our time, we will go out." We broke the door [...] It didn't take a minute, I swear it.'

'You were supercharged that night?'

'Like a Ford Shelby GT500.'

From a barred window he showed me a view of the road outside, where on that Saturday in August they could see armed men in civilian cars cruising up and down outside the prison. The Gaddafi regime had settled the families of many men from the security forces in the Abu Salim district from which the prison took its name. There was still the best part of a day before rebel fighters reached the edge of Tripoli, so it was a fair bet that the men with guns in the cars were Gaddafi loyalists. The prisoners broke through another door to get to the entrance of the cellblock, and looked cautiously out on to the barrack square. The guards were no longer in the block but the watchtowers were still manned, and so was a heavy machine gun that was mounted on the top of a porch leading to another block, with a clear field of fire across the square. A colonel called Jamal, who had brought them food, soap and shampoo after they took over their corridor at the end of July, came back with soldiers who had already changed sides, and persuaded the remaining guards and armed loyalists to stand down. Elsewhere in the jail, which was a sprawling series of compounds, families and friends of prisoners were breaking in with sledgehammers and crowbars to free their men.

The prisoners based themselves in better-equipped cells with televisions that had been used by trusted prisoners. The news was a revelation. The rebels were getting closer to Tripoli. Messages reached Ziani and his friends that there was a plan for a general uprising in the city, and that it would start after the evening prayer.

'We knew the zero hour. We kept crying. We couldn't believe that we were winning, that Tripoli was free. At that moment I wanted to fight. I wanted to be in it, to help to make Tripoli free [...] I didn't want to stay in the cell and watch al-Jazeera on TV.'

Colonel Jamal warned that for now Abu Salim prison had gone from a place of potential death to the safest place for them. Gaddafi's men were still roaming around. The streets outside the gates were too dangerous, especially for anyone with a Benghazi accent, regarded by Gaddafi's men as the mark of a rebel, and a death sentence for anyone who fell into their hands. Colonel Jamal told them that if they wanted to chance it after his warning they should shave their beards, if they had them, and change out of their prison uniforms. By Sunday morning Muhammad al-Ziani was back home in Tajoura, most of which was already in the hands of home-grown rebels who rose up before the advancing fighters reached the city.

Some of them had guns that had been obtained by Salem al-Fituri, the auditor from PricewaterhouseCoopers who we had met in

Tajoura in late February when parts of Tripoli were still in open revolt. Fituri had become a gunrunner, as well as clandestinely feeding information to the BBC about the resistance throughout the months of bombing. His first Kalashnikov was bought from a man in Bani Walid, the stronghold of the Warfalla, Libya's biggest tribe, which along with two others, the Gaddafa, Gaddafi's tribe, and the Magarha, were always considered to be vital buttresses for the regime. Plenty of men from the tribes carried guns for the leader. But such big groupings – the Warfalla claimed around one million, a sixth of the population – could never be monolithic, and some of them had bad blood with the regime before the uprising. Powerful men close to Gaddafi from the Warfalla had attempted a coup in 1994, which ended with the execution of many of their leaders. Early in the uprising Akram al-Warfelli, a leading member of the tribe, demanded an end to Gaddafi's rule. On al-Jazeera he said, 'We tell the brother he's no longer a brother; we tell him to leave the country.' So in Bani Walid, Fituri found people who would sell him guns because they wanted the money and owed the regime no favours. It helped that one of his contacts in the town had a cousin in the regime's forces who would always follow the money.

'He's loyal to the dollar. So they get weapons out of the military warehouses, and they sell it to the revolutionaries – high prices – they get money but we get weapons.'

As usual in times of war, the Middle East Kalashnikov price index reflected how bad things were getting. Fituri paid around $2,500 for a single Kalashnikov in Bani Walid, which was full of weapons, before prices went higher as demand increased. Orders of more than ten could mean a reduction of about 15 per cent. Bullets cost around thirty cents each. As a favour to the Warfalla leaders the regime had put an assembly plant in the town, where stripped-down Kalashnikovs would arrive from Russia for assembly. That helped Fituri's supply chain. To buy the guns he collected more money from people who wanted to find a way to help the revolution. It came in small amounts, as the regime had ordered banks to allow maximum withdraws of only 500 dinars, less than $400. Fituri used his own savings too.

'When the revolution started the last thing you care about is money, all you care about is freedom so you will pay all you saved to get your freedom back [. . .] We brought the weapons to Tajoura one by one, stripped down into pieces. We opened up the lining of the car door and then stuck parts of the weapon inside it, with tape, and with plaster, the kind you use to set a broken leg [. . .]

'We did it like that because in the checkpoints the forces were knocking on the door to make sure nothing was hidden inside [. . .] so we needed to make sure that nothing moved when they tapped it [. . .] It was very scary. For the first time I was shaking and I was sweating and I was afraid of them stopping me to search the car, but most of the time they searched only the boot, and then they let you go [. . .] We became more confident.'

Fituri started by buying one Kalashnikov for himself, then one for his brother and then 'tens' for other people. Sometimes, because petrol was so hard to get, he could not make a pickup, so he would act as a middle man, transferring the money to the men selling the guns, arranging for them to stash them somewhere discreet, like an empty house, then telling the buyer where to collect them. They realised phones might be tapped, so they used a simple code.

'For example, I don't say, "I bought the goods so come and get them." We get ourselves in conversation like he wants to buy a bike – because, you know, there is lack of fuel, so if you can provide a good bicycle . . . I would say, for example, "It's for three and a half" or "350", and he would recognise it's 3,500. He says, "Can't you get a better price?" I go, "No, this is the final price, so if you want to buy one I'll bring you one, if not it's your decision."'

The people building up the anti-Gaddafi underground in Tripoli had a very realistic fear of being betrayed. Fituri said they tried to keep the numbers low, and to operate in small cells. 'I worked with ten, fifteen people maximum. And these people have a leader. And this leader was coordinating with another group in Tajoura. And all the groups in Tajoura had a leader who was coordinating with other places – for example, Souk al-Joumha. It was like that.'

'Did they take orders from Benghazi or did they decide themselves what to do?'

'No it was from themselves. They weren't taking orders from anybody. It started from the base. People were working randomly but after that they were getting themselves organised day by day.'

Outside the city on the weekend of 20–21 August, rebels were pushing hard from all sides; but the biggest thrust came from the west, meeting only pockets of resistance as they advanced on Tripoli. Until the very end, Colonel Gaddafi's sons never allowed themselves to believe that their father's regime would fall. The culture of self-deception that had grown up around the omnipotent, all-seeing leader over forty years affected them too. Their senior aides knew better. Saif al-Islam's closest adviser was a shrewd and intelligent man called Muhammad Ismail. He had been at the centre of the diplomatic overtures to the West to negotiate a way out of the crisis. Muhammad Ismail had discreet visits to London where he visited the Foreign Office with the message that the regime would like to talk. The reply was always the same: no deals until Colonel Gaddafi goes. That did not stop him trying. In Tripoli he would often be at the Rixos hotel, muttering into his mobile phone, speaking perfect English, grappling with the fact that his world had shifted on its axis. A few weeks earlier he had been liaising with friends in the West, allies in the war against jihadist Islam, who now had his country in their sights. When I spoke to him he seemed to be a man under huge strain, giving tense, impatient answers. But if the sons were prepared to follow their father to the end, their advisers were not. Muhammad Ismail, seemingly loyal to Saif al-Islam, surfaced briefly in Cairo with his family on what seemed to be a diplomatic mission in July and then disappeared from view. The way he went to ground so seamlessly, and then stayed there, suggested to me that he had help. Perhaps he was discussing his future as well as Colonel Gaddafi's during his trips to London. The foreign minister Musa Kusa had defected to Britain at the end of March. After a short period of questioning he was allowed to leave for a comfortable exile in Qatar. Britain said it had no grounds to hold him, but if there was a case for Colonel Gaddafi and his son Saif al-Islam to answer then it is hard to see why one of the colonel's closest associates during his time in power could be declared blameless so quickly. The tribunals on war crimes in former Yugoslavia and Rwanda indicted many people of lower standing in their countries than Musa Kusa had in Gaddafi's Libya. By allowing Musa Kusa to leave, Britain had set a precedent showing how well defectors could be protected. The Gulf, with its sticky summer heat and icy air conditioning, was a much better bet than a dusty desert road in Libya and truckloads of rebels looking for revenge.

When the ground war came to Tripoli Saadi al-Gaddafi was in the Corinthia hotel. It is about the tallest building in the city, a luxurious, twin-towered five-star hotel built between the sea and the old city in a faintly Arabesque style with a pointed arch over the entrance, more like a building in the Gulf than on the Mediterranean coast of North Africa. Being there was a big problem for Saadi, as the Corinthia, a favourite hangout for the regime's people, was on the side of town that fell first to the rebels. They had fought their way in from the western mountains, and they could smell victory. They came into the Corinthia's lofty foyer, and went room to room to find out who was there. Saadi's adviser and assistant, a feisty American called Jackie Frazier, told me that she had begged him to make a contingency plan in case he had to leave Tripoli in a hurry. It was not disloyalty, she told him; it was simply a matter of being prudent. Even in the last few days, the Gaddafis made no plans for the fall of Tripoli. Nothing was prepared for a day the Gaddafis had decided was unthinkable. Saadi managed to slip out when the rebels were already in the hotel, according to Jackie.

'It was lucky for Saadi that the regime guys knew the Corinthia better than the rebels did.'[1] He rang Jackie on his way out of the city. He didn't have anyone from his family with him, but he had his retinue, and they were protected as usual by Tuareg fighters, desert nomads who were loyal to the Gaddafis. She was at a wedding in the United States when her deeply worried boss rang, from the road to Bani Walid, wondering what he should do next.

Saadi and Saif al-Islam believed their father's regime was too strong to be toppled. To make matters worse for Saadi, according to Jackie, he had fallen out with his father over his violent response to the rebellion. Father and son, she claims, hadn't spoken for three months. Some rebels – and journalists – say that Saadi was deeply implicated in violent attempts to put down the first rebellion in Benghazi. Saadi travelled down through the desert to cross into Niger, escorted by the Tuaregs. Their ability to find their way through the Sahara without appearing to use maps or compasses mystified Jackie and made her a little uncomfortable. She had been out into the desert with Saadi and his friends, in convoys of 4×4s. Their Tuareg drivers, heads wrapped in black cloths so that only their eyes showed, would race across the dunes, cackling with laughter and taunting each other, for hours at a time without getting lost.

Colonel Gaddafi put an audio message on state television, trying to rally his supporters against the 'rats'.

'I am giving the order to open the weapons stockpiles,' he said. 'I call on all Libyans to join this fight. Those who are afraid, give your weapons to your mothers or sisters. Go out, I am with you until the end. I am in Tripoli. We will win.' But by Monday 22 August only fighters in Gaddafi's compound in Bab al-Azziziya and a few other loyalist pockets were offering any resistance. Saif al-Islam made a last defiant appearance in Tripoli, and then disappeared. By Tuesday there were still bursts of gunfire but it was over in Tripoli for the regime, and Gaddafi had disappeared. Rebel fighters, and journalists, ranged around Tripoli, going to places that had been forbidden,

opening up prison cells and document stores, discovering dead
bodies and the paper trail left by murder and deception.

The heart of Colonel Gaddafi's security state was Abu Salim
prison. One man I spoke to after the fall, still too frightened to give
his name or show his face publicly while Gaddafi was alive, told me
bleakly: 'I felt my last link with life was cut when they took us to Abu
Salim. The guards told us our existence meant nothing. I thought I
could be killed at any time.' The fear of being sent to Abu Salim was
used by the Libyan regime to control people, to deter them from
making trouble. I made repeated trips to the prison, because in
many ways it was a microcosm of Gaddafi's power, and his fall, and
walked through hundreds of yards of corridors of abandoned cells,
steel doors gaping open where the locks were broken when the
prison was liberated. The ceilings of the cells were about twenty feet
high, and the windows at the top of the walls were small. In my notebook I wrote:

> Clothes still hanging where they had been left to dry. Improvised
> mirrors made of the shiny lids of food boxes, shelves made from
> milk cartons, and ropes made from blankets going up to high
> barred window – for exercise? Or just to see the sky? Some graf-
> fiti. Barcelona championship 2010–2011. The future will be us.
> I ♥ Libya. 17 February 2011 [the day the uprising started] the
> way to utopia. We will never surrender. We will win or die. If you
> want to be a king, first you should be a man.

In some of the administration blocks Libyan lawyers from a human-
rights group were collecting boxes of documents and taking them
off to a safe place. Ironically it was an uncompleted technology park
that had been owned by a close associate of one of Gaddafi's sons.
The day before, someone – presumably a Gaddafi loyalist – had managed to set fire to a storeroom of documents at the prison. They were
still smouldering, thousands of pages of potential evidence reduced

to ashes. So the lawyers were taking away what was left, files, documents, audio and video tapes and photographs, forty-two years of frightened faces stored in old fruit boxes as well as pictures of some of the inmates' children – which they must never have seen, as they were confiscated on the way in. One of the photos was ripped almost in half. It showed a boy of about four years old, posing in front of vases of pink plastic roses and yellow soft toys, dressed in his best clothes for an absent father who probably existed for him only in his mother's stories. He had a traditional waistcoat, shirt and cap and wide eyes. A note attempting reassurance was scribbled on the back of the snap.

My dear brother Bahjat

I ask God that we will be together as one family very soon. In all we are fine and in good health. Hi from everybody. We don't miss anything except we badly want to see you.

Depriving prisoners of their children's faces was just another small cruelty perpetrated by the regime on top of all the brutal, murderous ones. Or perhaps the photos and letters were not delivered because the people they were sent to were already dead. I spoke to Salah Margani, a well-known Libyan human-rights lawyer and activist, as we watched his colleagues covered in dust and dirt pulling out more boxes of documents. He said they were looking for evidence to build a case against the men responsible for the 1996 massacre in the prison.

'Thousands of families have lost loved ones in this place, and many other places across Libya. It is important that their families know all the facts about what happened to them.' That was certainly true, but it occurred to me that there could be documents which would embarrass Western governments among the evidence they were collecting and safeguarding.

The reasons why were part of the fallout from the response of the United States and Britain, its main ally in military matters, to the 9/11 attacks and the declaration by President George W. Bush of the 'war on terror'. The attacks, and the invasions of Afghanistan and Iraq that followed in the next eighteen months, shifted the tectonic plates of the Arab world. Colonel Gaddafi and his advisers, prompted not just by the belligerent mood in Washington and London but also by years of sanctions and diplomacy, agreed to a plan that looked as if it would navigate them to a safe, richer place in a dangerous world. In a series of deals in 2003, Libya pleaded guilty to organizing the attack that downed a Pan Am jumbo on to Lockerbie in Scotland in 1988, and agreed to pay $2.7 billion dollars in compensation to the families of victims. In return sanctions were lifted and then, just before the end of the year, in a move that stunned arms-control experts around the world, Libya agreed to give up its attempt to build weapons of mass destruction and to allow inspectors in to dismantle everything it had.

Colonel Gaddafi, President Reagan's 'mad dog of the Middle East', was in from the cold. He became an invaluable ally in the war on terror, a partner in a process known as 'extraordinary rendition'. It was the way in which the United States and its allies bundled suspects into cars and on and off planes to move them around the world without the bother of going through tiresome procedures like court hearings, arrest warrants and extradition appeals. They would then be delivered either to places immune from the safeguards built into the US legal system, like the American bases in Guantanamo Bay in Cuba, or at Bagram in Afghanistan, or to friendly countries (Libya was one) that were not squeamish about interrogation procedures. Information extracted in the stuffy, stinking cells and corridors of Abu Salim prison in Tripoli was fed back to Colonel Gaddafi's new friends in London and Washington. One bonus about unsavoury friends was that they were less than transparent about the details of what they did. Campaigners were never going to extract information from autocratic governments that denied human rights and legal protection to their own citizens.

But after the fall of Gaddafi the cell doors and filing cabinets at the heart of his security state were thrown wide open, and within a few days of my first visit to the prison details of the connections between London, Washington and Tripoli started to emerge. The most important cache of documents was found at the former offices of Musa Kusa, Gaddafi's former intelligence chief and foreign minister. Peter Bouckaert of Human Rights Watch, an indefatigable sleuth whose investigations produced a stream of stories, uncovered the hoard. He photographed piles of documents that showed in great detail how much cooperation there had been between Libyan intelligence and MI6 and the CIA. The boasts of the regime had been correct. They had worked together closely, and Musa Kusa had been at the heart of it. He had become the most useful man in Libya for the British and the Americans after Libya's relations with the West thawed in 2003, because he was one of Colonel Gaddafi's closest advisers. But cooperation – even friendship – with Musa carried a cost. For Western governments he was damaged goods, a political risk because of allegations that he had been involved in some of the outrages most associated with the Gaddafi regime in the 1980s, from the killing of the police officer Yvonne Fletcher in London in 1984 to the Lockerbie bombing.

Intelligence chiefs like to work discreetly, away from prying questions about a secret business where it does not pay to have too many scruples. Even before Tony Blair paid a visit to Colonel Gaddafi in Libya at the beginning of 2004, Musa Kusa was in close touch with MI6, Britain's secret intelligence service. His main contact was Mark Allen, the head of counter-terrorism at MI6. Until Allen left MI6 with a knighthood in 2005 after he did not get the top job – known inside the service as 'C' – he was Britain and the West's main connection with Gaddafi's Libya. After MI6 he became an adviser to BP, which had signed a huge oil deal with Libya during the time that he was shuttling back and forth between London and Tripoli. I managed to see Colonel Gaddafi's last foreign minister, Abdulati al-Obeidi, while he was being detained by rebels. When I asked about the connections between Libya's rehabilitation in 2003–04, the negotiations over the future of the convicted Lockerbie bomber Abd al-Baset Ali al-Megrahi and the BP deal, Obeidi told me to contact Mark Allen.

'He was very important as a counterpart to Musa Kusa. And as a close personal [adviser] to Blair and adviser to BP. He was always speaking about BP you know.'

'So he was involved in all sides of the diagram?'

'Yes, yes.'

'What's he like?'

'What do you expect an intelligence [man] or a spy to be?' Obeidi was elderly, unwell and exhausted because he said he was being forced to share a bed with another former minister. But he managed a half smile when he talked about the man from MI6.

Mark Allen had spent his working life absorbed in the politics and culture of the Arab world, studying the language and its calligraphy – and even falconry, the traditional pastime of desert princes. His contacts were legendary, and they were not just with Arabs. I bumped into him later in 2011 in the Kyria, Israel's defence ministry, in Tel Aviv. Sir Mark was smiling and charming and gave very little away. It so happened I was going to see the same man he had just left, one of Israel's most senior security officials. He spent the first ten minutes of our meeting lauding Sir Mark Allen, a man he called his friend, praising his absolute affinity with the world of intelligence and his achievements and talent. My Israeli contact also expressed incredulity that Sir Mark's private papers could have got out, and wondered how any intelligence officer could ever hope to work effectively if he thought what he did would not stay secret. Some of his MI6 colleagues in the Middle East were less complimentary. One of them told me he was as 'mad as a sack of frogs'.

The relationship between MI6 and Musa Kusa was not just a long-distance one, carried on through messages that were meant to stay confidential. He would visit London too. Muhammad, my friend in Gaddafi's office, once reminisced about a meeting with senior British officials, including the head of MI6, in London at the Travellers Club, one of the old-fashioned gentlemen's clubs on Pall Mall.

'One of us, Musa Kusa I think, didn't have a tie. So the club provided one.' He smiled at the eccentricities of British life.

Musa Kusa became a close colleague and even a friend of senior figures in London. One of Mark Allen's messages – signed 'Your friend, Mark' – expresses regret that Musa Kusa could not join him for Christmas lunch. It does not matter whether Allen's friendship with Musa Kusa was genuine or a professional necessity. Once the information of what had been said got out the relationship was a political embarrassment. The moral ambivalence around Musa Kusa had been building since he defected to London at the end of March 2011, when a *Daily Mail* headline summed it up:

Why did we give this murderer sanctuary? He's up to his neck in Lockerbie, WPC Fletcher's death and arming the IRA. Yet ministers hail Libyan's defection as a coup.[2]

But the cache of documents was about much more than some political awkwardness, which could on its own have been brazened out. After all, they might have said, spies need to mix with all kinds of people and they are not always clean and nice. The documents were not just about social contacts. They also detailed the process of extraordinary rendition, which many lawyers say was illegal. The most detailed case concerned a man called Abu 'Abd Allah Sadiq. He had been taken off a flight to London in Bangkok, and transported to Libya by the Americans.

It so happened that I had met Abu 'Abd Allah the day before I saw the documents, only I knew him by his real name, Abdel Hakim Belhaj. He was the new military commander of Tripoli, no longer the powerless man who the documents said had been sent back to Colonel Gaddafi's gulag by the United States and Britain. Belhaj and his men were in control of Mitiga airport, about four miles east of the former Green Square, to which the rebels had restored its old name, Martyrs' Square. Among the guards on the gates were some of the expat Libyans who had come home to fight. They were always keen to talk. One friendly fighter from Manchester called Sami Areibi showed off his gear, mostly bought from the city's Smithfield Market, though the Kalashnikov, Sami said, came from Libya. A Boots first-aid kit, the kind a well-organised parent might take on holiday, poked out from one of his pouches.

'I got the AK-47 here. Look I'll show you, it's easy to learn how to use it.' He cocked it and fired half a dozen shots into the air. Another fighter with a long black beard called over in a broad Manchester accent from the roadblock on the main gate, 'You're not supposed to do that.' He had a huge grin. Orders were often issued to stop firing in the air. But mostly they were ignored, and the men doing the firing were not at all bothered that bullets come down almost as fast as they go up. Slowly, they were persuaded to fire out to sea instead of into the air at imaginary planes. It made fishing even more dangerous but the chances of a spent bullet killing someone on the ground went down. Sami had video on his phone of the fighting around Gaddafi's compound. It showed a man being dragged back past the camera.

'That was one of our boys. Dead. But we were twatting them.'

Until Colonel Gaddafi came to power in 1969 and expelled American and British troops, Mitiga had been Wheelus US Air Force base. Low-rise brick-built pieces of Vietnam-era military architecture still stand. I wondered if American officers almost fifty years ago buzzed around the same buildings keeping the world safe from communism in the same busy way that bearded men in desert-camouflage uniforms were seizing their capital city. In the 1990s and first years of the new century Abdul Hakim Belhaj had been head of the Libyan Islamic Fighting Group and as such was condemned as a fellow traveller of al-Qaeda by the British and the Americans. Now that he was military commander of Tripoli, he was a key man and officially an ally of countries that once hunted him as a terrorist. Belhaj and his staff were well aware of the rich irony and it did not amuse them one iota.

In the foyer of his headquarters at the airport was a timeless tableau of the weak, the ambitious, the needy and the conniving flocking to the court of a chief. Outside on a long veranda at the top of a broad flight of steps was a crowd, some uniformed and armed, others civilians looking for favours, trying to get past two armed guards just inside the main door. They stood like bouncers behind the velvet rope outside a club, only instead of black overcoats they had desert uniforms and Kalashnikovs with double magazines taped together pointing at chest level, fingers on the triggers and one of them with his boot planted against the door to stop anyone forcing their way in. They were a little too alert for my taste. They stiffened a little more when four blind men, with white sticks and dark glasses, arrived and felt their way up the steps to get some of Belhaj's time.

The face of my new friend Anes al-Sharif appeared in the doorway. He nodded to the edgy-looking men on the door, who raised their guns just enough for us to get in and keep the other supplicants out. Anes was another veteran of Libyan Islamic Fighting Group and was the right-hand man of Belhaj. He was the most amiable former Islamic fighter I had ever met – perhaps because he put himself on the British wavelength during years of exile from Libya, when he had supported himself by working as a chartered accountant in Pinner, a short drive from his adopted home in Harrow in northwest London. The speed of their advance into Tripoli had taken Anes by surprise.

'We'd prepared very well. I knew we'd win when we were still in the western mountains. But I thought I had time to get back to my family in Harrow for a quick break for Eid. I'd even bought an air ticket for the 28 August from Tunisia!'

His boss and friend Abdul Hakim Belhaj was a quietly spoken, intense man in his forties, with occasional flashes of a smile. He denied that the Libyan Islamic Fighting Group was ever allied with al-Qaeda. All they wanted, Belhaj said, was to overthrow Gaddafi. I told Belhaj, via Anes, about the British and American documents when they emerged from Musa Kusa's former offices, to get his reaction. He invited me back to his office and by the time I got there Belhaj was at his desk, half-moon spectacles on the end of his nose, going through the MI6 and CIA files, which he had ordered to be sent over to his office.

A CIA document dated 6 March 2004 described some of the planning for the rendition of Belhaj. It asked for a Libyan agent to be present on the plan 'to provide legal custody' of his wife. It thanked the Libyans for agreeing to grant the Americans 'direct access' to him after he was back in Tripoli. The document also contained a paragraph demanding that Belhaj be treated humanely and that his human rights be respected.

> We must receive these assurances prior to any assistance our service can provide to your service regarding his debriefings. In addition, it is our standard practice that our officers cannot condone any significant physical or psychological aspects, such as direct physical contacts, unusual mental duress, unusual physical restraints, or deliberate environmental deprivations beyond those reasonably required to ensure the security and safety of our officers and to prevent the escape of the detainees.[3]

Gaddafi's intelligence services were notorious for not just torturing but killing prisoners at Abu Salim jail. Intelligence professionals from the CIA and MI6 would have known that, which makes the assurances the CIA demanded sound like a hollow, box-ticking exercise. But the Bush administration's vocabulary was increasingly debased. It had, after all, invented the phrase 'enhanced interrogation techniques' to describe what many people would call torture.

On 7 March 2004, the day after the document was sent to Musa Kusa's office from the CIA, Belhaj was travelling to London from Kuala Lumpur with his wife. He had been to the British High

Commission in Kuala Lumpur to ask if he could apply for political asylum in the UK, and, he said, had been told he would be allowed to fly to Britain, where the Libyan Islamic Fighting Group was not illegal. It was not proscribed under Britain's Terrorism Act until 14 October 2005. But Colonel Gaddafi was becoming a friend of the West, and Tony Blair was about to seal the new alliance with a visit to Tripoli. Britain passed the information about Belhaj's travel plans to the Americans. In a warm message to Musa Kusa, Mark Allen wrote: '... this was the least we could do for you and for Libya to demonstrate the remarkable relationship we have built over recent years. I am so glad.'

During a scheduled stop in Bangkok, Belhaj and his wife were taken off the aircraft. Belhaj told me that he was taken to a room at the airport and beaten by Thai agents and by Western men he presumed were Americans (he doesn't speak English so he would not be able to recognise their accents). Eventually the couple were put on another aircraft, which the documents say was American, and flown to Tripoli. Belhaj's wife, Fatima Bouchar, who was four months pregnant when they were detained, told the *Guardian* that her body, including her head, was wrapped in tape to bind her to a stretcher during the flight back to Libya.[4] She was released not long before the birth of her son. Belhaj was held at Abu Salim jail for six years until he was freed under one of Saif al-Islam's pet projects, which was aimed at 'de-radicalizing' Islamists. While he was there, he told me, he was tortured, sometimes interrogated immediately afterwards by foreigners, and was not allowed to bath or shower for three years, though he managed to wash with cups of water. Musa Kusa, he said, visited his cell, told him he would die there and ordered the guards to reduce the size of what was already a small window high up in one of the walls. At one point, Belhaj said, he did not see sunlight for a year. Belhaj was still full of cold fury about the way he had been rendered back to the Gaddafi regime. Six years in jail had given him plenty of time to think about it.

'What happened to me and my family is illegal, and they should apologise for what happened to me when I was captured and tortured, especially since they're people who claim to work with human rights.' The Americans? 'Yes, the American people and those who helped them capture me.' The people who helped the Americans were the British. MI6's Mark Allen was keen to claim credit, and let Musa Kusa know that Britain had been a full partner in the operation. Belhaj is referred to throughout by his *nom-de-guerre* Abu 'Abd Allah Sadiq.

> Abu 'Abd Allah's information on the situation in this country is of urgent importance to us. Amusingly, we got a request from the Americans to channel requests for information from Abu 'Abd Allah through the Americans. I have no intention of doing any such thing. The intelligence about Abu 'Abd Allah was British. I know I did not pay for the air cargo. But I feel I have the right to deal with you direct on this and am very grateful to you for the help you are giving us.[5]

Most of the message, headed 'for Musa in Tripoli from Mark in London' and dated 18 March 2004, was about the impending visit by Tony Blair to Colonel Gaddafi in Tripoli. Allen passed on a request from Number 10 Downing Street for the meeting to be held in Gaddafi's tent. His comment was:

> I don't know why the English are fascinated by tents. The plain fact is that the journalists would love it. My own view is that it would give a good impression of the Leader's preference for simplicity which I know is of importance to him.

A few months after I told him about the documents, Belhaj and one of his former colleagues in the Libyan Islamic Fighting Group, Sami al-Saadi, started legal action against Mark Allen and Jack Straw, who was Britain's foreign secretary when the two Libyans were rendered back to Tripoli. Belhaj alleged complicity in 'torture, inhuman and degrading treatment, batteries and assaults', claiming that the attacks were carried out by Thai and American agents as well as during his time in Abu Salim.[6]

If power in Tripoli had any address in the first chaotic months after the fall of the regime it was at the headquarters of Abdul Hakim Belhaj. Inside the lobby were men in their thirties and forties with an air of assurance, and command, and victory. All of them had beards, and many of them were Belhaj's old comrades from the Libyan Islamic Fighting Group. A few younger men were there too, some of them recovering from wounds. One of them stumped around with external fixation bolted in and around a shattered leg, the metal clamps and rods sprouting like Meccano from his trousers. They all looked tough and disciplined. The funding, mainly from the Qataris, was very apparent. Their boots and uniforms were excellent quality, and matched. About half the men in the crowded room were carry-ing Kalashnikovs – I had seen people coming in and clearing and checking their weapons on the way in – and the rest had pistols in holsters on their belts. The weapons were well looked after, and many of them looked new.

Tripoli was in its revolutionary honeymoon, the streets heavy with militias driving around furiously, dripping with weapons. Like so many fighters around the world, they had styled themselves on the films that once had been speeded-up fantasies of real life and in their minds had come true. That meant as many guns and knives as they could carry, bandanas wrapped round their heads, double bandoliers of ammunition draped over their shoulders, and shades, an urban-pirate look somewhere between John Rambo and Mad Max. They draped themselves over pickup trucks that they had customised into fighting machines. We called them 'technicals' after the ones in Mogadishu. On the backs of their trucks they had welded anti-aircraft guns, or heavy machine guns, or sometimes even a missile pod looted from a helicopter, fully armed and with cables leading down to car batteries to try to power the launcher. Rebel fighters and sightseers were picking through and looting Bab al-Azziziya, Gaddafi's compound, which had been Tripoli's looming, threatening forbidden city. The residence that he had kept as a ruin and a museum of American evil after it was wrecked in a US air raid in 1986 had been turned overnight into a monument to the monster. Sightseers were queuing up with their children to write insulting graffiti on the walls. One woman without a pen used her nail varnish. Libya, like it or not, was going to have a new beginning. The leading figures of the regime were either on the run, in exile, or dead.

The NATO powers had recognised the rebel National Transitional Council as the sole, legitimate governing authority in Libya. But the top men from the NTC were still in Benghazi, apparently too over-whelmed by the job facing them in Tripoli to leave the city that had become their safe haven. Even though Gaddafi was still at large, and big parts of the country were still under the guns of his loyalists, it was clear that Libya was going to have the most complete Arab revolution of the year. The colonel had created a quirky and unique form of gov-ernment that was dependent on his presence and the enforcement of his police state, both of which were gone. Its new leaders would have to start again from scratch and take the people with them. Mustafa Abdul Jalil, the leader of the National Transitional Council, and Gaddafi's justice minister until the start of the uprising, spent most of his time either in Benghazi or abroad. The NTC explained that it did not want to give the impression that it was stealing the lime-light from the militias who made the blood sacrifices to unseat Gaddafi. But it was also missing a huge political opportunity by not grasping Libya's enormous, daunting challenges more decisively. Instead Jalil sent Ali al-Tarhuni to Tripoli as an emissary with the rank of deputy prime minister. He was a university economist who had spent years in the United States, a friendly, rumpled man who had the air, not of a politician, but of a college professor. He had set himself up at the Corinthia hotel, just outside the Old City, the place where Saadi al-Gaddafi just evaded the rebels as they entered Tripoli. It had a very different atmosphere to the gun-toting Radisson where the BBC and most of the international media were staying. Its security was not run by rebel fighters, who would sometimes, with an angry lecture, remove bottles of whisky from the baggage of incoming news teams but by mainly British contractors, which allowed the Corinthia's lobby to have an atmosphere of quiet political endeavour. It was about the only place in Tripoli where you could find men in suits having discreet conversations with other suit-wearers while their close-protection teams loitered nearby. They represented powerful forces, states and corporations, but real power in Libya was still somewhere else, on the other side of the plate-glass doors, metal detectors and beefy retired British servicemen, out where it was noisy, violent and turbulent.

In his suite high up in the hotel I asked Tarhuni about the huge number of guns on the streets of Tripoli.

'I'm not too concerned about the guns right now. We need the guns to hunt this thug, this killer. But my concern is that when you talk about democracy, civil society, peaceful discourse you don't really want to do that with anti-aircraft guns.'

It was a polite way of saying that they needed to get the guns under control, but they had some jobs for the young men who were carrying them to do. In the next year, once Gaddafi was captured and killed, the biggest challenge in the new Libya was talking the guns out of politics. Progress was slow. Some militias were absorbed into various official formations but they continued to be the key players in the new Libya. Nine months after the fall of Gaddafi militias still answered to no one except themselves, still having shootouts with the rivals. Some based their power in towns that had resisted Gaddafi and now regarded themselves as city states. Others were more closely based on tribes and ethnic groups that came from much broader areas, or had elements of both. Some were just gangs who had grabbed some of the weapons washing around the country.

From the windows of his suite Tarhuni could see Tripoli sprawling into the distance on the flat coastal plain, full of activity despite the absence of a central government and for the first time in forty years without the regime, its secret police and the threatening, snooping curiosity of the Revolutionary Committees. People were running their own lives. Muhammad al-Ziani, who had broken out of Abu Salim and gone home to Tajoura, spent some of his time organizing bands and political events in Martyrs' Square, and the rest of it turning himself into a freelance vigilante. He was blithe and dismissive about the people who had been genuine supporters of Gaddafi.

'Well, most of them got killed. Those who didn't get killed are inside prison, and those not inside a prison are hiding in farms, or outside Libya. They've got nothing; they've got nowhere to go. Even those who went to Tunisia or Algeria, even if they've got 15,000 dollars, they will finish it and they will come back and we will catch them [. . .] It's not revenge, just justice.' But Muhammad, for all his talk of justice, had his own prisoner who he was keeping in his own personal jail. 'Yes I'm treating him so well, so good. He's eating the best food in the world. He's sleeping in a good place.' He thought the man might lead him to the people who arrested him, and in the process intimidated and humiliated his parents. The conversation I had with Muhammad about his prisoner might have been bizarre in any other city, but in Tripoli just after the fall of the Brother Leader it seemed quite normal.

'Muhammad, you've deprived him of his liberty. Shouldn't you take him to the police? Why did you take the law into your own hands?'

'Do you believe that there are real police now? Do you believe it?'

'There are people with police uniforms.'

'I'm smarter than them. I can play with his emotions, with his feelings, to make him say what I want.'

'So you're interrogating him?'

'Well I will do my best. I love cinema, I love Hollywood – I've learnt a lot. I'm not just watching movies for fun. There is a saying: act like a professional you will be a professional. So I will act like a professional and I will investigate him and will take what I want from him without beating him.'

'So he will give you information?'

'He will do.'

'What do you want from this guy?'

'I want only one guy: the man who insulted my mother and pushed my dad.'

'You want his name?'

'I want him.'

'And what will you do?'

'I don't know my reaction.'

'But you're going to find out who he is first of all?'

'I just want to see him. To see his face, scared, is enough for me.'

'You don't want to kill him?'

'No I didn't kill anyone. Even to kill a chicken is not something easy for me. But I'll feel proud when I remember his face when he caught me and when he smashed my dad and he smashed my head, and then I'll see his face when I catch him.'

'So you want him to realise now that things have changed?'

'Yes, I believe in change. I will make him believe in change, I will make him believe in Libya, I will make him believe in revolution.'

'And you're still looking for other Gaddafi people?'

'Yes. If the control room tells us there is someone hiding, bring him here, we go and bring him to the Katiba [paramilitary headquarters] and they investigate him.'

*

The most common scapegoats were black Africans, who were regarded at the very least as suspects and quite possibly mercenaries for Gaddafi. Every day, dozens were arrested on sight. Black men were automatically suspicious. If they were caught out in the open by some of the rebels who were cruising the streets, reclining around the guns they had welded to their pickup trucks, there was a strong chance they would be picked up. Much paler-skinned Libyans from the coast also suspected their black countrymen from further south. I saw some being dragged in off the street at a school in Souk al-Joumha that had become the headquarters of the local anti-Gaddafi militia. Three terrified men, one from Ivory Coast and two from Ghana, were accused of being mercenaries on no evidence other than their black skin. When one of the Libyan rebels asked the younger of the two Ghanaians what he was doing in Tripoli, he dissolved into tears and shook with terror. They insisted they were domestic servants. One of them said he was just going to see a friend when he was captured. If they were soldiers, they weren't very tough-looking.

Gaddafi's regime certainly employed black soldiers, and the rebels assumed they were mercenaries, though I was never shown any direct evidence to prove the charge. Racism was part of it. I saw rebels treating blacks with contempt plenty of times. Perhaps it was also a reaction against Colonel Gaddafi's statement in *The Green Book* that blacks would rule the world. He turned his back on his fellow Arab leaders after they showed no desire to be told what to do, and used Libya's oil billions to buy new friends in Africa south of the Sahara. Muhammad, my friend from Gaddafi's office, said that 'the leader' had been betrayed by President Jacob Zuma of South Africa, who had not supported him even though, Muhammad alleged, Zuma had accepted large amounts of money to pay for his defence when he was accused of rape. And Muhammad claimed that another African president had left Gaddafi's offices with his pockets and briefcase stuffed with wads of dollars. 'Ungrateful!' he fulminated.

'The Leader did everything for them and they did nothing in return. And when he needed support they abandoned him.'

Whatever the reasons for their suspicion of blacks, in Tajoura an improvised jail was created by local people who, like Muhammad al-Ziani, believed they had every right to protect themselves by taking the law into their own hands. Across the city militias were setting up their own, generally very primitive, detention facilities. In the course of the next year they were the closest thing Libya had to a criminal-justice system, as the police and the courts were essentially without power.

Just outside the prison yard in Tajoura I stood next to a couple of pine trees that gave some shade.[7] The only good view was up through the branches into the blue sky, and close to the trees the wind smelt fresh and sappy from the cones and the bark. The Mediterranean was almost close enough to hear and it was easy to imagine the sand on the beach and the waves. My mind and senses were trying to escape, because in the lock-up a brutal lesson was going on about defeat and victory and the meaning of power. The metal gates of the compound had been painted in red, black and green strips like the revolutionary flag. The paint was fresh, the fumes still a little heady. Half a dozen women stood outside, trying to get news of their men. They were not city people. Their hands were rough from work, and one of them had tribal tattoos on her face.

The gates opened into the first compound, surrounded by high walls of concrete and stone. Armed men stood around another metal gate, smaller this time and half open. The man who appeared to be in charge sat on a broken office chair outside the gate, with a Kalashnikov balanced across his knees. Beyond was yet another walled compound where men, lots of them, perhaps 100 packed together, were sitting on some steps in the September sun. I went in, with my BBC colleagues. More guards, some in assorted uniforms, others in civilian clothes, all with Kalashnikovs, were staring down at the prisoners, giving them orders and raising and pointing their guns when they disobeyed. One of them lit a cigarette and as he puffed on it threw half a dozen more down on to the ground. Some of the men dived down and fought for them. The guard took another puff, and watched. His face showed superiority and contempt. He was a winner, a conqueror of the sunken regime, and the men fighting for cigarettes were jetsam.

All the men outside in the sun were black Africans, mostly Ghanaians and Nigerians. The yard where the men fought for smokes was just in front of the camp's main holding centre. It was about the size of a small aircraft hangar, wide enough for a couple of light planes to stand wingtip to wingtip, and about fifty yards long. The stench of unwashed bodies and blocked lavatories was overpowering. The guards wore surgical masks, and they handed them out to visitors too. The guards, toting their Kalashnikovs, swaggered in, and I followed. Discipline, it seemed, was strict. When one group of prisoners didn't get out of the way fast enough, one of the guards ostentatiously cocked his weapon. The group scattered. The guards, local men from Tajoura, looked very confident, strutting as if they were a higher form of life. They weren't bothered about the risk of the prisoners seizing one of their guns and trying to shoot their way out. They hadn't heard of the rule in American prisons about not allowing guards to carry guns inside the wire, in case they are taken and used against them or the other prisoners. But this was not an organised prison, with watchtowers with gun positions and secure areas for weapons and reinforcements. It was improvised and miserable. I put the mask on, but immediately felt bad about walking in on several hundred human beings behind a couple of armed men, masked against the stink of the sweat and the shit. I took it off and put it in my pocket. The place stank but I felt a little less like a conqueror. For once I was glad of the fumes from the cigarettes being smoked by everyone who had them. They killed some of the stench.

Salem al-Fituri, the man who had run guns and fed the BBC information about the resistance to Gaddafi, was our guide. He was in the medical team that was the one decent part of the operation. Their sickbay, basic but clean and humane, operated out of a room off the yard with the pine trees. A line of black African women had been standing outside it, waiting to have medical examinations. Some of them were pregnant. They were the wives and girlfriends of some of the men who were held in the stinking shed, arrested with them. The prison was in a walled compound that had once been used to house drug addicts. It must have had a punitive treatment regime. At heart the place must always have been a prison camp, made for this moment. A Libyan human-rights campaigner was there too, horrified by what he was seeing in the main camp. This, he said, was not what the world after Gaddafi should be like.

'It's about safeguarding important and essential basic human rights! If the new Libya fails to deliver this, all the sacrifices will be in vain.'

In a separate, caged-off room was a young man who was accused of murdering two captives and burying their bodies. He looked distracted, and I wasn't sure he could understand the accusations against him. It was early days. Countries take years, even generations to get over civil wars and dictatorships; and Libya had both. But neither the suspected killer nor the other men and women in the camp were facing any formal charges. No legal process had started and there was no immediate prospect of one. It was not an auspicious beginning for the new Libya.

Not all the men inside the hangar were blacks from Africa south of the Sahara. Libyan Arabs who had fought for Gaddafi were held too, staking out their own sections of the bare-concrete floor of the building, where they had spread out thin mattresses and piles of grubby clothes to mark their territory. The Nigerians, Ghanaians, Ivoirians and the rest kept clear of the Libyans, and vice versa. A lot of the men were dressed in blue-and-white striped pyjamas and night shirts, official Libyan hospital issue, which made them look as powerless as they were.

Fituri defended what they were doing. It was good local

organisation. The prison guards were carrying their own guns. They had agreed to have them licenced, and the deal was that if you were not prepared to do a job with your gun for the new Libya then you would have to give it to someone who would. Yes, it was tough at the camp, but if the men inside the camp were allowed out they would be killed by the citizens of Tajoura, who had forty-two years' worth of revenge in them. The people, Fituri said, had been furious when the prison was set up about ten days earlier, because they saw prisoners getting free medical care.

A group of Nigerians wanted to talk. They were men ranging in age from their late teens to late thirties. They had been captured on 1 September, when they left their hiding places to try to get to Tunis to get a flight home. I asked them if they were mercenaries. An older man answered.

'No, never. We are workers. They have taken all our money, and our van. Our wives are here too. It would be lovely to see the faces of the women. Can you help us to see them?' We couldn't. The Africans, the suspected mercenaries, had no access to lawyers, had not been charged and had no idea how long they would be incarcerated. One of the chief guards said they would be held until 'investigations' had been completed. But no investigation had been started. The Libyan Arabs did not try to deny that they had been in the regime's military, as they had been captured at the barracks of Khamis al-Gaddafi's 32nd Brigade. But they claimed they were just in it for the money. I was prepared to believe some of the teenagers. I did not believe many of the older captives, watchful-looking men in the late twenties and thirties. I had passed the Khamis Brigade's main headquarters many times on the main road into Tripoli from the west. It was supposed to be part of a 'ring of steel' around the capital, with long sand-coloured walls, a high gate and battlements. After the headquarters fell, fighters took away truckloads of weapons.[8] The brigade, in its pomp, was frightening. In March I saw it deployed around Zawiya, about thirty miles west of Tripoli, when the regime was busying itself putting down an uprising by the people of the town. It was before the no-fly zone was declared, and before NATO started to use air power to destroy the Gaddafi side's heavy weapons. The Khamis Brigade was cutting the main coastal highway between Tripoli and Tunisia, and at every junction there were tanks or self-propelled guns. I could imagine some of its beaten veterans in the prison doing their own swaggering with Kalashnikovs when they had the power, and in the last mad months of the regime chanting Gaddafi slogans and joining in the frenzied fire-in-the-air afternoons in Green Square. No wonder the men from the Khamis Brigade were denying that they had been fighters, and claiming that they were in it only for the money. The Khamis Brigade had a fearsome reputation, and its barracks in Tajoura fell after it was softened up by NATO bombs.

'Who are the rats now?' one man said to a reporter. 'It is them who are fleeing like rats.'[9]

At the time it looked as if they had no stomach for the fight. And no doubt there were plenty of men who managed to lose themselves, and their uniforms, in the confusion, and then try to head for home. But a hard core was still in an organised formation, and set out for the regime's strongholds in Sirte and Bani Walid. As they fell back, men from the Khamis Brigade showed that, while they had decided that the time had not yet come to make their stand, they were still feeling strong enough to kill their prisoners. On 23 August, according to witnesses, members of the Khamis Brigade shot detainees at a warehouse that was being used as a prison. Four days later investigators from Human Rights Watch found the remains of around forty-five bodies south of Tripoli, next to the Yarmouk military base. A survivor called Abdulrahim Ibrahim Bashir said that, as the sun was setting on the twenty-third, men from the Khamis Brigade opened up on him and dozens of other detainees. They shot through the sheets of tin on the roof, while another Gaddafi soldier threw hand grenades in from the entrance. Bashir said that he escaped by jumping over a wall while the guards were reloading.[10] The Tajoura prison camp was an unpleasant and humiliating place. The guards were enjoying every ounce of the power they had over their detainees, some of whom complained that they had been beaten. But at least they were not being killed.

It took almost two more months, until 20 October, for the rebels to find Colonel Gaddafi and kill him. He was trying to break out of Sirte, his hometown, when his convoy was hit by NATO planes. One of the men travelling with him was Mansour Dhao Ibrahim, a trusted member of the inner circle of the old regime. Ten days after Gaddafi's death he gave a remarkable interview to the BBC's Katya Adler while he sat on a slightly blood-stained mattress at a detention centre in Misrata.[11] Mansour Dhao was alleged to have ordered killing, rape and torture in the name of his leader – and he was one of only a few witnesses to Gaddafi's last days.

'Gaddafi was nervous. He couldn't make any calls or communicate with the outside world. We had little food or water. Sanitation was bad [...] He paced up and down in a small room, writing in a notebook. We knew it was over. Gaddafi said, "I am wanted by the International Criminal Court. No country will accept me. I prefer to die by Libyan hands."'

Speaking during a break in his interrogation, Mansour Dhao said that Colonel Gaddafi tried to get to his birthplace, the Jarref Valley.

'It was a suicide mission [...] We felt he wanted to die in the place he was born. He didn't say it explicitly, but he was going with the purpose to die.'

He thought his people should love him until the end. He felt he had done so many good things for them and for Libya. He also felt betrayed by men who had seemed to be his friends, like Tony Blair and Silvio Berlusconi.'

Gaddafi set up in a convoy of around seventy-five vehicles that left District 2, the centre of loyalist resistance in the northwest of Sirte, after first light. Fewer vehicles moving at night might have stood a better chance.[12] The reckless behaviour bears out Mansour Dhao's theory that Gaddafi believed he was rolling the dice for the final time, expecting to be captured and killed. At around 8.30 French aircraft attacked the convoy, which split into smaller groups. Gaddafi's fragment moved south, until it was attacked from the air. Once again Gaddafi survived the attack.

After the airstrike Gaddafi and a few of his men tried to hide in a water pipe. They were soon spotted. One of the rebel fighters, Salem Bakeer, said:

'At first we fired at them with anti-aircraft guns, but it was no use [...] Then we went in on foot. One of Gaddafi's men came out waving his rifle in the air [...] as soon as he saw my face he started shooting at me. I think Gaddafi must have told them to stop. "My master is here, my master is here," he said. "Muammar Gaddafi is here and he is wounded."'[13]

Katya Adler also interviewed Huneish Nasser, who was Gaddafi's driver. He was still wearing the same blood-stained shirt that he had on when Gaddafi was killed.

'Gaddafi got out of the pipe. I stayed inside. I couldn't get out. There was such a crowd of fighters [...] Gaddafi had nowhere to go. He was one man amongst many and the fighters were shouting, "Gaddafi, Gaddafi, Gaddafi."'

The driver said that when he saw the crowd of rebels Gaddafi seemed resigned rather than surprised. It was around midday. Some of the men filmed the scene on their phones. The pictures are broken and jerky, but they show the dictator being tormented by the men he had called rats and threatened to exterminate. Nasser also said that the men who approached them did not kill Gaddafi, but Katya Adler noted that as he spoke to her in the Misrata detention centre that he was 'nervous and clearly mindful of his captors, two of whom stood with us in the room, their arms folded. His black eyes darted around the room.' Their authorised version at the time was that they tried to get him medical help. Someone must have realised that the pictures of the mob around him might not go down entirely smoothly with Libya's Western allies. Gabriel Gatehouse, who was the BBC's correspondent in Misrata, spoke to one of the commanders who said that his unit found Gaddafi hiding in the water culvert. He said he stopped some of his men killing Gaddafi there and then, but their vehicle came under heavy fire as they were heading for Misrata and Gaddafi was hit. The commander claimed that he was turned away from one field hospital that was overwhelmed with casualties and that Gaddafi died as they drove towards another.

It was certainly true that he was not killed immediately, because there is more phone video of him being beaten after he was captured, when he was already bleeding badly. It shows crowds of men surrounding him, all armed with Kalashnikovs. Then a smaller group drags him about ten yards away from the camera. One of them bends down near his backside, and pushes something through his trousers. The intention seems to be to sodomise him, with a sharp metal rod or maybe a knife or a bayonet. Gaddafi's assailant doesn't pull the trousers down. The seat of the colonel's pants, a military shade of beige, is immediately soaked with more blood. Another piece of video shows Gaddafi dead, arranged on the bonnet of a vehicle like a blooded hunting trophy and surrounded by dozens of exultant rebel fighters.

The precise circumstances of Colonel Gaddafi's death are confused. He was captured at around midday. A man who said he saw what happened told the BBC that Colonel Gaddafi was shot in the stomach around half an hour after he was captured. By 4.30 in the afternoon Mahmoud Jibril, the prime minister of the National Transitional Council, confirmed his death. The body was put on display in a cold store in Misrata, to allow as many people as wanted to check that the man who had dominated their lives really was dead. Libyan TV showed close-ups of at least one bullet hole in Gaddafi's head, which surely would have killed him straight away. It wouldn't have been a question of trying to get medical help. The video evidence points to a summary execution.

Gaddafi's son Mutassim, also captured in Sirte, appears also to have been shot out of hand. There is video of him after he was held. He is wearing a torn vest and he has been lightly wounded. He's drinking something, and talking. His wounds do not seem to be bothering him much. Yet not long after that he was dead. Mutassim had a personal militia and stories circulated that once he had tried to seize power by breaking into his father's Bab al-Azziziya compound. He had to go abroad until he was forgiven. But he was united with his father in death. His body was put in the cold store in Misrata next to Colonel Gaddafi's; both were wrapped in blankets, only their faces showing. Mutassim was a striking-looking man, handsome in the way that his father was in his young days and before his personal eccentricities – and perhaps something pharmacological or surgical – changed his face. The son had shoulder-length dark hair and a beard. After his death pro-Gaddafi broadcasts that had restarted from a new home in Damascus compared him to Che Guevara, deliberately burnishing his image as a martyr, even showing pictures of Che and Mutassim next to each other. The comparison worked with the few people who supported the Gaddafis and were still prepared to admit to it. Back in Tripoli a young woman called Noor who had helped out occasionally with translation at the Rixos smiled with delight and her eyes shone when she talked about him.

'I think he's great [...] When I see Mutassim you could say someone gives me another spirit. I feel power [...] I told my father that if Mutassim was still alive I would go to him and ask him to marry me!'

It is ironic that his tormentors were as brutal with Gaddafi as his men had been with several generations of Libyan suspects. Every Libyan I spoke to about what happened saw it as entirely appropriate rough justice. Europeans and the UN especially are more squeamish. Many Libyans just wanted to see him dead, and were just not bothered how it was done.

The killing of Colonel Gaddafi and his son imbued the new Libya with original sin it may regret. The leaders of the National Transitional Council during the months of the fight against the colonel often spoke about building a country based on rights, not revenge. But the iconic image of their moment of national liberation was of Colonel Gaddafi, a man who spilt oceans of other people's blood, not accounting for his crimes in a court, but being set upon by fighters who killed him. I met only one Libyan who told me Colonel Gaddafi should have been spared to make him face justice. But everyone else I spoke to was just pleased he was dead, and they didn't care how it happened.

If the new rulers of Libya wanted it to be a country of rights, then they should have investigated the death of the Colonel. The wholesale imprisonment of black Africans as alleged mercenaries, on little or no evidence, without being given access to a lawyer, needed to be investigated too. The black prisoners were a regular sight in Tripoli towards the end of 2011, hands bound, blindfolded with cloths of Gaddafi green, in the back of rebel trucks next to the welded-on artillery.

Colonel Gaddafi was a cruel dictator who ordered appalling acts of murder. He built a system that ran on fear and brutality. He deserved to face punishment. The justice he received came from the barrel of a gun, exactly the same as his own henchmen had meted out for years. States that have been through deep and violent change tend to do best later on if there is a process of national reconciliation. Old enemies need to learn how to work together. Maybe dispatching Colonel Gaddafi and his son will make that easier. Or it might make the promises of fairness the National Transitional Council made during the fight against the regime harder to believe. Right or wrong, killing him quickly solved a problem for the NTC. It was hard enough to agree what to do with the body and where to bury him. In the end, at the request of Gaddafi's tribe, they took the bodies of Muammar and Mutassim to a remote, unmarked spot in the desert. Had he lived, there would have been months of rows about his crimes, his trial and his punishment. And there would have been the nagging fear that Colonel Gaddafi's existence, and his public and no doubt defiant appearance in court, would have been a focus for the old regime's loyalists who are now quietly keeping their heads down.

Some Libyans who had been educated abroad understood the squeamishness of their Western allies, especially Europeans, argued that the rapid death of Colonel Gaddafi removed a big problem for this country's new rulers. They had visions of a long trial, with Muammar al-Gaddafi defending himself for years in the same way that the former Serbian president Slobodan Milosevic spun his trial out for so long it ended only when he died of natural causes. 'He'll terrorise people from the courtroom,' one Libyan said to me in Martyrs' Square. 'No one in this country would feel safe if he was alive. They'd always think that he could come back.'

The death of the Colonel changed the atmosphere in Tripoli beyond recognition. On an evening stroll through Martyrs' Square it felt as if it was a different city. During the bombing campaign what was then called Green Square was the centre of the Gaddafi cult, and it was not a comfortable place to be for anyone who was not an acolyte. The crowd would work themselves up to a pitch of anger against NATO. Thousands of bullets would be fired into the sky, and tens of thousands on a Friday. Ask someone a question and you'd be surrounded by a jostling, yelling mass of people competing to condemn the West and express their love for Muammar al-Gaddafi. As soon as the Gaddafi regime fell at the end of August, it changed. The faces were different. I had started recognizing the noisiest regulars in the Gaddafi rallies. The new ones often said they had not been to the square for years. As in all police states, the best thing to do was to keep your head down, to be grey, unnoticed.

Some things didn't change. Libyans are never going to be quiet when they get into a crowd. People celebrating the death of the Gaddafis, just like his supporters, drove overloaded cars around the city at speed, hanging out of the windows and chanting. And Libyans still had an alarming love of expressing their emotions by firing into the air. But I had never seen Tripoli so relaxed. A heavy weight had been lifted. While he lived, many Libyans could not quite lose the fear that he might come back. But they had seen his body, and videos of his death. According to Saadi al-Gaddafi's assistant Jackie Frazier, the colonel's surviving sons always believed they had a way back while the old man was alive and on the run. They realised the game was up only when they too saw his last moments on television, and video of his body lying alongside their brother Mutassim on the floor of the cold store in Misrata.

Libya's neighbours in Egypt feared that they had chopped the head off the regime, only for it to start growing a new one. Libyans did not need to have that fear. Gaddafi's Libya was smashed.

9

SLIDING INTO CIVIL WAR

Outside, Damascus was locked into winter, freezing cold, drizzled with rain that wanted to be snow and in the grip of an uprising that was turning into a civil war. I sat down in my hotel room to write my diary.

25 January 2012

A year ago Egyptians marched to Tahrir Square on Police Day and started their revolution and the fall of Hosni Mubarak. The revolution is not complete. You can see that with Field Marshall Tantawi, Mubarak's defence minister for years, appearing on television to lecture the people in full uniform, with rows of medal ribbons and a beret. He looked like a pensioned-off veteran dressed in his old finery for an old soldiers' parade. In fact he is the most powerful man in the country, head of the ruling Military Council. He was saying that the emergency law would be partially lifted – hardly a huge step to take a year after a revolution that was supposed to sweep away the old order, and a sign that much of the power is in the hands of the same people, all of them in uniform.

I was watching it here in my room, 612, at the Four Seasons hotel in Damascus. It is a big hotel, and almost empty. I had breakfast with one of the European ambassadors yesterday, who told me that they used to have problems getting rooms here for delegations because it was usually close to being full. Not anymore. The marble foyer is hardly populated. The pianist keeps playing. As far as I can tell, most of the staff have been laid off.

It is hard from here to get a grip on what's happening on the streets. I get emails, sometimes two or three every hour, from Syrian opposition groups sending out updates with links to videos that have been posted on the internet. I sit in my expensive room and read about terrible events, if the emails are true, and that is not certain either. Another Western diplomat here told me that some of the news coverage in Europe has been terrible, ignoring the fact that, love it or hate it, Assad still has a following and a powerbase. Videos had been shown that were not what they claimed to be.

Here's a selection of this morning's headlines from the opposition emails. The SRGC [Syrian Revolution General Commission] has a message from someone in the Bab Qibli area of Hama to the UN Security Council, the Arab League, the Syrian National Council and what he calls the free world.

He says: 'the Syrian dictator gang [. . .] bombed houses indiscriminately with mortars and artillery; in addition to shooting thousands of heavy bullets randomly at the neighbourhood homes they also cut the water, electricity and telephone in this very cold night. More than 4,000 [. . .] thugs, criminals and soldiers attacking the entire neighbourhood amid the cries of women, elders and children to save them from genocide.'

The messenger from Hama ends by saying to his audience, whoever they are, 'do not kill us twice with your carelessness and silence'.

And here is a small selection on a random day in the uprising, Tuesday 24 January 2012. A mortar on a building in Karm al-Zaitoon in Homs, killing at least seven. The security forces also apparently opened fire on a funeral in Jabal Az-Zawieyeh in Idlib, in the north not far from Homs. It was the funeral of Rudwan Hamadi, an activist who had been arrested and killed. According to the report, one of the soldiers involved in the operation was so horrified that he tried to defect to the opposition there and then. The email says that 'he was followed by the army and was executed on the spot in front of all people, then the security forces started a revenge operation on the town', shelling buildings and burning 'most of the cars in the street'.

And so it goes on. Three wounded by snipers in al-Hamidiyah in Hama, eighteen wounded by tank fire elsewhere in the city. In Nuwa City a sheikh from a mosque was apparently arrested along with his eighty-five-year-old mother 'when the neighbours in the streets begged for their release the security forces replied with opening gunfire on the residents'.

And from Damascus the 'Revolutionary Leadership Council' says that the al-Midan quarter was 'besieged' by security forces and the Shabiha militia after they heard that one of their victims, a seventeen-year-old boy called Talal Terkawi, was going to be buried after a prayer at a local mosque. The security forces, it says, arrived in Abu Habel Street in four cars and two big buses, set up checkpoints and attacked people in the street, beating and arresting passers-by. It says that they were trying to stop people going to the funeral. The Shabiha are accused of cruising the streets in their cars, and arresting people in nearby al-Zahera Street, even when they said they were locals who were just going about their business. That report I know is largely true because a colleague was there, and had to shelter in a house for six hours while the security forces were carrying out their sweep through the area.

By the end of yesterday I had tweets and emails from campaigners saying more than sixty protestors had been killed in the previous twenty-four hours. One estimate was sixty-eight dead.

What I don't have are figures for how many regime soldiers are dead. Judging by what I saw at Homs Military Hospital the other day there must be some. But they've stopped publishing their own casualty numbers. Perhaps there are too many. Perhaps it is becoming an embarrassing sign of weakness for the regime.

The point is that we don't know. A lot of it is guesswork. The information on the emails cannot be checked. But if only 25 per cent of it is true that is still a lot of bloodshed. Later on this morning we're planning a trip out to Douma because it is the only way to try to find out what is really happening.

You cannot find out what is happening in a country gripped by a violent insurrection by sitting in a hotel room. The problem in Syria was getting to the places you needed to see. Colleagues who had crossed illegally into Syria without visas, from Lebanon or Turkey, had to move with extreme caution, sometimes getting to where they wanted to be for only a handful of days on a trip of two to three weeks. I was on the government side with a valid visa, officially having to go everywhere with a minder from the Ministry of Information. But I was discovering that, with some contacts and some luck, it was possible to see much more than I had expected. It felt much looser than Tripoli under Gaddafi. On that winter day we were trying to get to Douma, a satellite town on the edge of Damascus, with a population of around 120,000, which had become one of the main centres of rebellion in and around the capital. I was sitting in my room writing my diary because we were waiting for our contacts to get in touch.

Two hours later I was with my colleagues trying to find a way in. Douma was one of the first places the uprising spread to after it started in Dera'a in southern Syria. It was the centre of regular, big demonstrations that often ended in bloodshed, which led to more funerals, more demonstrations and then another round of funerals. It was a classic cycle of violence that by then had been stoking hatred in Syria for almost a year. That week Douma was the focus of the regime's security operations around Damascus, as the Free Syria Army, still a ragtag band of fighters, was said to be moving openly in the streets. If that was true it meant that armed insurgents were operating within twenty minutes' drive of the centre of Damascus and presidential palace. The regime was strong, and not about to fall, but losing control of any part of his capital was never going to be good news for President Assad. We had to go to take a look, but it was not going to be easy because the regime's security forces, as far as we knew, had checkpoints on all the obvious ways into Douma. Without permission and an official minder – and we had neither – we would never get through the roadblock and might even end up arrested, which would have wasted a day's filming.

Some opposition activists inside Douma had promised that they would meet us to guide us in through back roads. A few days earlier the regime's forces had opened fire on a funeral, killing six. As usual, video of what had happened was circulating on the web within a few hours. In it a crowd of men filled a rundown street lined with grim-looking concrete buildings and old cars, sometimes breaking into chants of '*Allahu Akbar*' – God is greatest – but mostly producing a hubbub of angry shouts. Their fury was aimed at a blur of men in the distance grouped around armoured vehicles. Then the firing started, the echoes of it crackling back from the high buildings as the men scattered.

We sat in our van with sheets of rain drumming on the roof and cascading down the windscreen outside a petrol station on the main highway near one of the turnoffs to Douma. Two men in a car with darkened windows seemed to be paying us too much attention as we waited, in a bubble of tension, for the contact to arrive. Every few minutes he would ring, complaining that new roadblocks around Douma had the place locked down. My body felt rigid, inflexible, immobile inside my flak jacket. DC, the cameraman, was carrying very light-weight camera gear, but after seeing the video of the shooting and

killing in Douma it seemed foolish not to wear some body armour. We
didn't want the mukhabarat officers who were always posted in the
hotel lobby to see us carrying it, so we walked past them wearing the
flak jackets under coats, with scarves around our necks so that they
could not see the protruding ballistic collars that were supposed to
protect the carotid artery.

A white minibus slowed down in front of our van, some of the deep
puddles splashing black water on to the wheel arches. It stopped
around twenty-five yards ahead, next to a bald man with a black
leather jacket, tan trousers and a Kalashnikov held in his right hand
so the barrel bumped casually against the outside of his thigh.
Straight away the doors opened and around twenty soldiers in combat
gear, flak jackets and helmets climbed out, fast and with purpose. The
bald man directed them down a narrow road that led into Douma.

'*Imshi*. Let's go.' Our driver was calm and moved our van slowly forward towards the highway. The soldiers were not after us, but it was
not a good place to stay. If the driver had taken off like a guilty man,
Baldy would have noticed. The mukhabarat in Syria are programmed
to smell fear and guilt. They work on their reputation. People who
come out of their custody without being tortured often describe how
they were kept close enough to less lucky prisoners to hear their
screams. He was alert, and his eyes followed our vehicle moving away,
and he seemed to be staring harder as we joined the flow of traffic on
the highway. It felt as if he had made eye contact even though the
rain and the spray coming up from the traffic meant it was impossible. Something was disturbing his secret policeman's antenna. Why
did we move off the moment he appeared? His look was mean,
inquisitive and alert. George Orwell was right. By fifty, every man has
the face he deserves. All around his black moustache the bald man's
glare showed what happens if you spend too long working for Syrian
State Security.

We wanted to get into Douma too, but nowhere near the baldy and
his soldiers. By then Douma's residents had spent almost a year in a

grinding routine of protests, killings and funerals. Most of the world's only link with what was happening there was through videos on YouTube. Every video released on to the web needed to be treated with scepticism. Some were what they claimed to be. Others were not. Rebels can be just as keen to manipulate, spin and lie as regimes. The only reliable way to find out what was happening in Douma and all the other places like it was to send in a reporting team with good eyes and ears. No news organization, human-rights group or international observer had been able to do much more than scratch at Syria's surface since the regime was working so hard to keep us all out. That was why we were nibbling at Douma's edges trying to link up with the people who had promised to get us in there. Our car bumped slowly along a side street. On the left a big entrance arch came into view, topped with portraits of the two Assad presidents. Below it were more soldiers, more green uniforms, more Kalashnikovs. It was Adra prison, another infamous part of Syria's gulag. The prison was built inside a massive compound, with a population estimated at around 10,000. Adra holds criminals as well as political prisoners. Just before the uprising started Muhannad al-Hassani, a human-rights lawyer, was badly beaten by a prisoner, a violent criminal, who was put into his cell. Afterwards Hassani was moved to a solitary-confinement cage underground.[1] Adra's walls stretched on into the damp murk. It was no place to hang around and certainly no place to meet any activists from inside Douma.

In almost constant phone calls, on a phone we hoped was secure, the contacts said they were trying to find a place to rendezvous but each location became suspicious and they had to move on. Armoured personnel carriers mounted with heavy machine guns were moving round the area. The activists, via the phone, directed our driver down a road that turned into a checkpoint manned by half a dozen soldiers, long rain slickers over their uniforms, with their Kalashnikovs, which have a legendary ability to fire when they are wet and muddy, hanging down in the open. Luckily, and without looking like we were panicking, the driver took a fork off to the left, back down the other side of the prison. The activists on the other end of the phone passed on rumours that a big operation was being planned by the regime, perhaps even that night. They said they were getting information from sympathizers inside the regime who were staying on as moles instead of defecting. The driver thought we were being tailed, and stopped the car at a fruit stall to pretend to buy some bananas, while looking to see if the suspicious car had slowed down too.

It was a false alarm and we went back to the Four Seasons hotel in the centre of Damascus. It was like the old joke: *How long have you been paranoid? Ever since they started following me.* Paranoia, like panic, can be an infectious disease. Something about Syria incubates it, perhaps with good reason. A businessman who was building a chain of three-star hotels in Syria told me that mukhabarat had come to him just after construction started, wanting to wire every room for sound and vision. Under the Assads Syria became a country where your night-mares could come true. It was always sensible to assume that someone was listening. Or even watching. One of the major contractors for the hotel we were using was the billionaire cousin of the president, Rami Makhlouf, the Assad family's own tycoon. It is hard to imagine him turning down a polite request from the secret police. So we used our usual code. Trips to places the regime might not want us to visit were always described as shopping.

We talked about what we might buy into the microphones that we assumed were in the hotel, and strolled out on a bitter evening for another attempt to reach Douma, pretending to be off duty, the only tourists in Damascus, strolling past the Shisha place where men sat in overcoats and woollen hats to smoke and drink tea, checking for tails, being propelled by the BBC's valiant Damascus correspondent Lina Sinjab into an optician to pick out sunglasses on the darkest night of January to see if we had anyone following us who would hang around outside waiting, until a car pulled up and we hopped in. Behind the wheel was a woman in her thirties, a Christian called Joumana.[2] She knew the back ways into Douma because she had been smuggling in food, fuel and medicines. She did the same delivery service to the parts of Homs held by the rebels, sometimes twice in a day. Joumana was brave to the point of being contemptuous of danger. The mukhabarat were on to her and she was often pulled in for questioning. Sometimes they told her to report to their offices. Sometimes she was just picked up. So far they had not touched her, physically. But every Syrian knew what they could do, and the interrogators must have enjoyed the weight of the threat that they carried into the room with them. But it did not stop her. Suddenly, on the way to Douma, on the highway that goes from Damascus to Homs, Joumana accelerated hard and started weaving between the traffic. Something in her rear-view mirror had not looked right. After about a minute she stopped careering through the wet, crowded road and slowed down. The suspicious car wasn't following.

Joumana drove on to the place where the bald man had been ordering the soldiers down a side street. It was a back road into Douma. She had an arrangement with a family who lived in a house just off the main road, behind a high wall and tall steel double doors. They would leave her a signal if there was trouble on the road ahead. A cord tied to the padlock on the front gate meant danger. If it was not dangerous, no cord. The padlock shone in the car headlamps. Nothing was tied to it. It was dark, and my stomach was churning. What if Baldy was waiting down the lane, angry, cold and tired after a day in the rain with his soldiers? If Joumana had her spies in the district so would whichever branch of government security was operating in the area. Would they shoot at anyone moving towards them? Other contacts on the phone inside Douma were saying to move ahead. A lot of news reporting in dangerous places comes down to a question of how far you are prepared to drive down a dark and frightening road. We were trying too hard to stop, and had come too far. Joumana was nervous that her sign was on danger. But she moved forward, slowly. First one bend, and then more of them. I rolled down the window to see if there were voices, or gunfire. The rich smell of a cowshed drifted in. Some torches flashed ahead. Masked men with guns appeared out of the damp cold mist. For one nauseating moment I thought they were from the Shabiha, the plainclothes militia the regime was using to do its dirty work.

But then a man with a mask made from the green, white and black flag loomed out of the fog. These were the colours Syria used when it became independent from France in 1946. The independence flag was the banner of the uprising, and they burnt all the black, white and red horizontal tricolours of the Assads that they could find. We had reached the Free Army. More men with guns and masks appeared, some with the Kalashnikovs they brought with them when they defected from the regular army. Others had an assortment of hunting rifles, pistols and a few ferocious-looking pump-action shotguns. The sounds of heavy gunfire, fairly distant, came from the edge of Douma. A man who said he was the commander had a Kalashnikov, a walkie-talkie that was crackling and fizzing, and a black balaclava with slits for his mouth and eyes. All the men were cheerful. They seemed glad to see people from the outside world. He was optimistic.

'We're in control of Douma and we have been for a while. Douma is ours, thank God, Syria is ours and we're going to win [...] The security and the army try to come in. We defeat them, but they keep trying. I can't tell you how many men I have here, but we are the Free Army and we're going to win – soon!'

'And what should happen to Assad?'

'We need to hang him.'

If it had been possible to drive straight to Douma, without roadblocks, farm lanes and fear, it would have taken about twenty minutes from the centre of Damascus. Until that first winter of the uprising, there was still a stark difference between parts of Syria that were favoured by the regime and the places that wanted the Assads in hell. But by the New Year of 2012, Damascus was starting to feel the pain of the uprising and the collapse of the economy. Shops in the centre of the city were cutting prices by 70 or 80 per cent. Plenty of people were looking at the piles of unsold goods but not many were buying. The bubble protecting the illusion that central Damascus could escape the violence had burst on 23 December 2011, when bomb attacks, according to the official count, killed more than forty people. After that the security around public buildings and the homes of top people was doubled and trebled. Roads were cordoned off behind coils of barbed wire and piles of sandbags. Soldiers wearing the red berets of the military police milled around the checkpoints. Sometimes menacing-looking men with Kalashnikovs – pals of Baldy from the mukhabarat – loitered in the background. Despite all of that, the lights were on and the traffic was moving. People would be hurrying home by seven or eight in the evening, but it still felt bright and busy compared to the menace on the streets of Douma.

We drove in down a cold and dark road, the car headlights picking out sunken, dead windows and doorways in the blocks of flats that lined the route like tombstones. The plan was to meet a guide at a small mosque. Its glass and steel doors were splattered with bullet holes. Months of death notices, names and faces of people killed in the protests, printed on small posters, were pasted layer upon layer on top of each other on the stone doorframe. The dead whose faces stared from the notices, and the hooded figures who started materializing around us in the cold night, were Syrians who wanted – or had wanted – to smash what the Assads had built. Some of them had been displaced to the dismal, desperate suburbs of the capital by the worst drought in Syria's recorded history, between 2006 and 2011. According to the UN, it wiped out the entire livelihoods of 800,000 people. In the northeast, 85 per cent of the livestock died, which affected 1.3 million people. The regime failed to deal with the problem, even making it worse by subsidising big farmers who intensively farmed crops like wheat and cotton that needed a lot of water. The people affected burned with anger, had no stake in the status quo, and became desperate enough to challenge it.[3] Before I went to Douma I wondered what was making Syrians go out to demonstrations even with the certain knowledge that by the end of the day they might be dead. They stopped doing it in Tripoli after Gaddafi's crackdown. In Tripoli Gaddafi's enemies among the people waited for NATO's bombers to do their work, and for the fighters who already controlled Benghazi to the east and the mountains to the west to reach them. In Douma and the other grim suburbs of Damascus they had decided that no one was coming. They would have to do it themselves. Risks change when life seems to have nothing left except more pain.

Most of the streetlights in Douma were out. Light pooled on the mosque steps from inside. They must have had a generator. The walls were daubed with paint blotting out graffiti against the president, rewritten on top with insults like 'Bashar is a dog' – fierce words for Muslims, who believe that dogs are impure.

A man with his face hidden by a scarf appeared out of the shadows.

'Hello, I'm Adam.' It didn't take a degree in Middle Eastern Studies to work out that Adam was not his real name. He said, almost like flashing an ID card, that he had been born into an opposition family.

'Of course our views always had to be secret when we were with others.' Being conspiratorial and careful were habits from childhood. He saw me looking at the death notices. 'We've had more than 100 martyrs here since it started.' Adam spoke in good English. 'The area where we have the big demos is two minutes from here. Let's go.' He talked about the last time the army had been in Douma, less than a week before.

'Last Friday the army was on the outskirts. On Saturday it was inside Douma. They attacked the funeral. Six martyrs were down. The next day we had three martyrs and three martyrs were killed in the prison.'

'So what has changed?' I asked. 'Why were we able to get in?'

'Some army defectors are protecting us. That's what happened [...] It's more comfortable; it's safer now for us to move in and out.

The army's still on the outskirts, and they've got snipers, but we're feeling a bit safer.'

He had no idea how long their fight was going to take. The regime, he said, was strong, but not strong enough to beat them, and Bashar would, eventually, be hanged. It would be better if foreigners intervened to set up a no-fly zone, like NATO had done in Libya, but if they didn't it would just slow things down, not change the outcome. But he too was expecting a push into Douma by the army. Harasta, the neighbouring suburb, was under fire. Douma had to be next.

The call to the evening prayer started crackling out of the mosques. Dark figures emerged from the dead-looking buildings, nervous shadows hurrying to a place where numbers made them feel more secure. The regular evening demonstration was going to happen after the prayer. A man came up to say that their revolution was not Islamic, even though the demonstrations would start from the mosque. They had heard President Assad condemning them as religious extremists. They might not have been extremists, but in the blighted cold suburbs of Damascus most of the people feeling so much resentment towards the regime were Sunnis and the people who listened to the president were Alawites from his own sect, Christians and other minorities. The country was splitting on sectarian lines. Nobody said they wanted it, but at the same time sectarianism was being embraced. People felt safer with their own kind. Some boys were warming themselves on a fire they had built in the middle of the street. The smoke was acrid and poisonous, from plastic packaging they were burning. The fumes did not stop them huddling around it. Douma was being starved of fuel, another pressure point for the regime, and any warmth was worth having.

What looked like a permanent mourning plaza, with a big plastic shelter and a wooden stage, had been set up in a square next to the mosque. Someone had made a glossy banner of the latest martyrs, the men who had been killed at the funeral. Immediately we were surrounded by more young men, shouting in the excitement of seeing foreigners who had somehow made it in from the outside world. They milled about, yelling their defiance, outdoing each other in their hatred of the regime. Older men were filling up long lines of chairs on the side of the square. They were the fathers and other male friends and relations of the young faces on the martyrs' banner. Some of the men had small children with them. One baby of about nine months had been dressed as a revolutionary. His face was painted with the colours of the independence flag and with the slogan 'Go leave us, step down, Bashar'.

The only women I saw that whole night were Lina and Joumana, the two who had come in with us. They kept to the side of the square, staying discreet. It was not simply that it was dangerous to be out and the men were making sure their wives, sisters and daughters stayed at home for their own safety. Douma, like so many centres of rebellion, was a traditional Sunni Muslim society. Public mourning was a job for men. I asked one of the bereaved fathers about his son.

'He was shot by the army last Friday.'

'Will your son's sacrifice bring freedom to Syria?'

'Yes, of course.'

'How long will it take before you have freedom?'

'The whole of my life. It's going to be a long fight.'

'How old was your son?'

'Twenty-five years old.'

'What kind of boy was he?'

'He was strong, he was brave, and he wanted freedom.'

A man in his mid-twenties standing next to the bereaved father started speaking in English.

'Last Saturday we came out to move the body of a young man about fifteen years old, Muhammad Sayeed Arabi, to the grave. And the fucking army just crushed everything and started firing on us [...] I'm a soldier. I escaped from the army. I make my service in Homs. I was a tank driver in a T-72. I escaped because I couldn't see my people and my Syrian family get killed by our hands.'

'Did you have to kill people?'

'No, I didn't because when they ordered me, I just escaped.'

He claimed that members of the regime's security forces had shot some of the soldiers.

'Most of the heroes of our army, they died and went to paradise for that reason, including six of my friends. They were killed in the first three months of revolution.'

'And they were killed because they refused to shoot demonstrators?'

'Not just that. The government tried to kill some soldiers to make the other soldiers shoot the people, to let the rest of the soldiers think that the people were killing us.'

The men in the square were nervous about an attack. They had seen the army moving its tanks, armoured personnel carriers and heavy weapons around the edges of Douma, and they guessed what might be coming next. A few of them started muttering that we could be spies, and demanded to see our BBC ID passes. The others apologized, but I was always conscious how fast the mood of an excitable crowd can change. None of them wanted to give their names and I took the hint and stopped asking. I didn't want to inflame any suspicious minds. One of the young men appointed himself spokesman.

'The situation is very, very bad. The regime's army is killing us every day. The Free Army is fighting but there's news about the tanks coming to Douma. But we're not scared. We're not scared by anything.'

I asked him what should happen to Bashar al-Assad.

'He has to be killed. We want to kill Bashar. He killed our people, he killed our families; he has to be killed.'

'Are you going to win this war?'

'Of course!' He pressed a metal badge into my hand. It was some sort of mascot, a cheery cartoon character with a football on his head. He wanted me to take something from Douma back into the world of safety, warmth and electricity.

Then some men ran through the crowd towards us. It was time to go they said. Harasta, as they had predicted, was under fire. They had heard the army might be moving forward into Douma. If we did not get out now it might be too late. With my colleagues I followed the men back through the crush of Douma men.

With more shouts of '*Allahu Akbar*', they went on with their nightly protest. A couple of young boys were doing a stylized sword dance, crashing the blade into the other's shield. For getting on for an hour they had been clapping and chanting against the regime. 'Douma forever,' one of them started, then the rest of them clutched their necks and roared, 'Put the head of Assad on our shoes!' It was the Syrian equivalent of an American pep rally, with the same purpose of gathering their side for the fight that was coming. But they were talking about life and contemplating death, not boosting the football team. The ritual of call and response warmed up the night for them, a protective pocket of noise in a pool of light created by a generator, in a town that was dark and still and waiting for the regime's next move.

We moved fast through the dark streets to get to the car, piled in, and followed another vehicle out to the edge of town. The driver slowed down and signalled every fifty yards or so to small groups of armed men on street corners. Once we crossed the last rebel roadblock getting out was not easy either. Two army checkpoints had sprung up on the road back to the highway and we had to talk our way through them. Lina and Joumana turned the radio on, to Western pop music, and pretended to be two scared and lost girls who had taken a wrong turning and now were desperate for a strong soldier to put them on a safe road home. They did it so well that one of the men offered to get into the car to show them the right way back. Smiling, even giggling, they politely turned him down. In the back seat DC and I tried not to breathe. It was a dark night and the soldiers at the checkpoints showed not a sign of noticing that the two damsels in distress had a couple of foreign men in tow.

Two things struck me about Douma, as it did about other rebellious suburbs I visited around Damascus. First of all the uprising had strong support. Second, the men on the street corners with Kalashnikovs looked determined and ready to fight and die. But their light weapons would not take them very far against a properly equipped professional army with heavy artillery and armoured vehicles. Most of the rebels with guns claimed to be part of the 'Free Syria Army'. It announced itself with a video in July 2011 that showed deserters from the regime's forces saying they were going to protect the mostly unarmed demonstrators and fight against the Assad regime. A man who called himself Colonel Riad al-Asaad said he was the commander. But early in 2012 I saw no evidence of any kind of effective central command and control. The fighters I spoke to were mainly local men who had picked up guns, or farmers with hunting rifles. Some were army deserters who had come home from their units and not returned. They had their training, fragments of their old uniforms, and if they were lucky their Kalashnikovs. The men seemed glad to be part of a bigger idea, but they decided what they did in their own areas. Sunni Muslims made up the backbone of the armed insurgency. Most of the fighters I met claimed to be part of the army, but at first it was more a question of adopting its name and branding than being part of a coherent military formation. By the early summer of 2012 that was changing. The Free Army was getting bigger, and stronger, and more organised. Major General Robert Mood, the Norwegian head of a UN observer mission that had by then deployed, was impressed at a meeting with Free Army officers when they put a UN flag at his seat and a Syrian flag at theirs. He thought that showed they had a military mind at work, which when added to more than a year of fighting experience was finally bringing them victories in the field against the government's army.

The observer force, called the United Nations Supervision Mission in Syria, or UNSMIS, was supposed to supervise the implementation of a peace plan put together by the former secretary general Kofi Annan. The plan did not work, but for a while the observers fed out precious accurate information, as Syria was still closed most of the time to journalists. They managed to document massacres, including the evidence of killers going from house to house in the village of Taldou, near Houla, shooting civilians. The UN observers counted the bodies of at least 108 people, including forty-nine children and thirty-four women. A widespread assumption abroad was that the regime's militia, the Shabiha, had killed them, which was hotly denied. Some witnesses claimed to see the Shabiha arrive, and the UN observers were shot at when they tried first to get to the village. A report commissioned by the UN Human Rights Council concluded that Syrian government troops and militia carried out the massacre.

By July 2012 the conflict went into a new phase with an attack on the heart of the regime. The Free Army launched its first offensive in downtown Damascus. Its fighters tore into parts of the city centre. On the eighteenth, four of President Assad's closest advisers were killed by a bomb at the headquarters of the National Security Bureau, the place where the regime co-ordinated its military campaign. The explosion killed President Assad's brother-in-law Asaf Shawkat, along with three other generals, the defence minister, Daoud Rajiha, the head of the president's crisis management office, Hassan Turkomani, and Hisham Ikhtiar, the director of the National Security Bureau. The Free Army claimed it had planted the bomb. Conspiracy theorists immediately speculated that the regime had killed its own men to stop them mounting a coup d'état. But President Assad was not seen on state television for forty-eight hours after the attack. His regime showed its first signs of panic, in way that looked too genuine to be part of a plan. The president's side still had more firepower than the rebels. But the balance of forces was changing, and that was critical. The rebels were on the up, and the regime was not. A fortnight before the bomb Manaf Tlass, a general from Syria's most powerful Sunni family, had defected to Paris with the help of French intelligence. In the weeks after the attack more diplomats and soldiers deserted the Assads.

*

In London I walked around the Serpentine, the lake in Hyde Park, with a Syrian businessman who had formed a syndicate to buy weapons for the Free Army. He described how they had started by paying for communications equipment that opponents of the regime could use to upload pictures to the internet. He pointed out that the quality of video coming out showed how much help Syrians were getting. Phones were smuggled in with foreign SIM cards that ran up huge roaming bills as they sent out video, which were paid for by Syrians abroad. As we walked past couples and families who were strolling by the Serpentine, he would stop talking. Running weapons into Syria was expensive, and they had to be careful about who knew. Tripoli in northern Lebanon was the hub of the business, the centre from which weapons were taken over the border. As early as the summer of 2011 I met a Sunni businessman from the city who complained that it was getting impossible to find warehouse space. The reason for this, he said, was that they were full of weapons. Much of the hardware was heading for Syria, but some of it was being kept back for the local market.

Syria, after a year of rebellion, was sliding into a civil war. More and more Syrians heard shots fired in anger. Every major urban area was affected, along with scores of villages and small towns. For civilians, it was terrifying. For the dictatorship, it was the failure of its harshest sanction. It used violence against what started as peaceful protests. But instead of crushing the rebellion the killing made it stronger and more aggressive as the armed opposition organised itself. Until the spring men still left the mosques on a Friday to demonstrate, but increasingly armed men were not far away. I saw them in Zabadani, a small town in the mountains between Damascus and the border with Lebanon, emerging with their Kalashnikovs from the shadows around a knot of about 500 protestors. They were treated like heroes, given babies to kiss, and surrounded by admiring, chanting townspeople.

The security agencies would conduct sweeps that arrested thousands of people over the months of the uprising. People who were sent for interrogation sometimes emerged scared but physically unharmed. Others had terrible stories about what happened to them. One man who made it out to Lebanon after he was released spoke on condition that his identity was not revealed. He was accused of taking part in anti-Assad demonstrations, which was true. He stopped denying it after his interrogators said he had been filmed. Many demonstrators covered their faces when cameras were around, but he had not. The prisoner said that he was taken to a room where a big tyre was suspended from the ceiling.[4]

'Before they did anything they said, "Look well into our faces because one day when you see us in the street you will want to remember this." I was tied up and put inside the tyre. My feet were inside as well as my head. At some point they just flipped me over so that my back was on the ground and my feet were up in the air. Then they started beating me with sticks. Whenever one would get tired the other would be there to take over.

'I was dragged into the interrogator's room. I was dragged because I couldn't walk. The soldiers said, "Sir, this guy is ready for questioning." The interrogator asked me, "So did you demonstrate?" and I said, "Yes, we did," and he said, "Why did you demonstrate?" I said, "Because we want our freedom." Then he said, "What kind of freedom do you want?" I said, "The freedom to say whatever we want without you bringing us here." "So you don't want Bashar al-Assad?" he said. "No, we don't want Bashar al-Assad." And then that's when he said, "I'll show you why you should want Bashar al-Assad."'

The former detainee claimed he was beaten repeatedly. After a particularly savage assault by a group of men, some in police or army uniforms and some in civilian clothes, he was pushed down a flight of steps.

'My leg was unusable and I couldn't stand up anymore. I told the officer but he just got another stick and started beating me, dragging me along the floor. He looked at me and he said, "You want freedom? This is freedom. See how much freedom has given you. We treat you like animals now!"'

The man said he was kept in a small, overcrowded cell with twelve others.

'It was in the middle of summer and the floor was wet with perspiration. We kept calling out for help because we were suffocating but no one came. An old man, who was about seventy, actually suffocated and died while he was with us. At that point they opened the door and took his body away. Two hours later we discovered someone died in another cell because we heard the same screams that we were shouting being shouted all over again.

'The next day my name was called and along with others I was taken to the air-force security base. You were only allowed to go to the toilet once a day and only to the count of five. So the guard would say, "One, two, three, four, five." It meant that you were in, did your business and had to be out by the time he counted five.

'By then I had only my trousers, since my shirt was ruined. One of the officers told them to stop the beatings so I could heal and they would be able to send me to the judge. He used to ask me to show him my back and he would say, "You still have a couple more days and then we will let you go." He was actually nice to us.'

The man was charged with weakening national morale, creating fake videos and undermining the state. Then he was released. When he heard a few days later that the mukhabarat were looking for him again, he escaped to Lebanon.

'There was only one accusation. They would tell me, "You were sending clips to al-Jazeera News." And I would say, "I didn't do anything." And they would say, "No, you did, and we want to know who financed you; who was sending you money from Saudi Arabia, the UAE or from Qatar?"'

That question, in one of the regime's interrogation rooms to a man who had been tortured for weeks, went to the nub of why the uprising in Syria, and its slide into civil war, contained more danger for the region than any other. The uprising in Syria was not happening in isolation. It was inextricably linked to the big issues of war and peace in the Middle East by a network of political and religious fault lines. Al-Jazeera, which is owned by the royal family of the Gulf State of Qatar, plugged into those connections because of its power to form opinion. The Qataris supported the rebels, and the Assad regime believed the Arabic broadcasts of al-Jazeera were a tool of their foreign policy.

The regional connections were a major reason (though not the only one) why the international response to the uprising in Syria was so different to the one in Libya. Intervention by NATO and Qatar in Libya in 2011 was feasible because Libya is big and relatively isolated, without the same ethnic, political and religious grid that runs through Syria and its neighbours. Syria is at the centre of the small and politically complex central core of the Middle East that over the years has probably generated more blood-soaked headlines than any-where else on the planet. Intervention there was much more daunting, even for powerful Western countries. The closeness of cap-itals in that part of the world, and the connections between them, make local crises international, and international crises local. Libya is buffered by its deserts. Syria stares directly at its neighbours. I could not quite believe my eyes, as a new arrival in Jerusalem in 1995, when I saw in the garden of the YMCA one of those multi-fin-gered signposts showing the distances to other big cities. From Jerusalem to Damascus is 135 miles. Amman, the Jordanian capital, is 44 miles from Jerusalem, and Beirut is 146 miles. Somehow I had thought that an area that produced so much world news would be bigger. If inconveniences like heavily armed frontiers that most people cannot cross were not in the way it would be possible to start the day with breakfast in Damascus, drive to Beirut for lunch and then have dinner in Jerusalem. The triangle between Damascus, Beirut and Jerusalem is the place where tectonic plates of history, culture and religions collide, and the world's big powers find it impossible to ignore this small patch of the globe. Its interconnec-tions, its fault lines, are a major reason why, as the American commentator David Ignatius put it, the Middle East 'sometimes resembles a string of detonators wired to explode together'.[5]

Before the Arab uprisings began to remake the political map of the region, there were two main competitive sets of formal and informal alliances: friends of Iran, and friends of the United States. Syria was Iran's most important ally, on an axis – its members called it the axis of resistance – that ran to the west, from Tehran, to Damascus, on to Hezbollah in Beirut. The friends of Iran were also Shias, on the same side of the schism that has bisected Islam for 1,400 years. They added the Palestinian Sunnis of Hamas to their alliance, because of shared hostility to Israel and the United States.

The friends of America had a much more sprawling network, and some of its members were officially each other's enemies. Its Arab members were Sunni Muslims. The alliance included some of the most notorious despots in the region, but, as American diplomats would point out to anyone naïve enough to question their choice of company, this was an alliance of convenience, not necessarily of friendship. By the end of 2010 America's network included its old enemy Colonel Gaddafi in Libya, President Zine al-Abidine Ben Ali in Tunisia, Hosni Mubarak in Egypt, as well as Israel, the Palestinians of Fatah, and the monarchies of Jordan, Saudi Arabia and the other Gulf States. The Saudis and the Israelis found themselves on the same side, which was only slightly embarrassing for either, because in Iran they had a common enemy. Both countries were deeply suspicious of Iran's nuclear programme, which they believed was aimed at creating a nuclear weapon – and they shared the hope that the Americans would destroy it. Israel made its own threats against what it said were Iran's genocidal plans for Jews, but always believed the best plan would be for the Americans to do a much more comprehensive job. Prime Minister Binyamin Netanyahu appealed for support in America by making comparisons with the lead-up to the holocaust, saying that it was 1938 and Iran's president, Mahmoud Ahmadinejad, was Hitler. King Abdullah of Saudi Arabia also pressed the Americans to attack Iran. An American diplomatic cable, dated 20 April 2008 and released by WikiLeaks, quoted the Saudi ambassador to the United States, Adel al-Jubeir, recalling 'the King's frequent exhortations to the US to attack Iran and so put an end to its nuclear weapons program [...] He told you to cut off the head of the snake.'

Once the uprisings started, the friends-of-America alliance had a change of personnel. To Washington's discomfort, the reliably pro-American presidents of Egypt and Tunisia were overthrown. No tears were shed over Colonel Gaddafi, but the chaos that reigned in Libya in 2012 increased the sense of regional instability. The Saudi King and royal family were shaken by what was happening, not just because elderly rulers would always have felt threatened by a revolt led by young people who were desperate to topple the status quo. They were also appalled by the way that the Americans and their other Western allies dumped their old friend Hosni Mubarak in Egypt. Saudi oil made it hard to imagine the Americans doing the same thing to them, but the precedent was not reassuring and made them feel even more nervous and exposed on Iran.

The Sunni rulers of Saudi Arabia, and their smaller Sunni neighbours on the Arabian side of the Gulf, feared that their Shia minorities could become a fifth column for Iran. The Saudis focused on a problem very close to home, at the other end of the 16-mile causeway that runs from Saudi Arabia's Eastern Province to the tiny island state of Bahrain.[6] In February 2011 an uprising started against the Bahraini royal family, the al-Khalifas, and from the start the Saudis saw Iran's hand at work. Not only had the Iranians once claimed Bahrain as its fourteenth province, but it also had a restive Shia majority and a Sunni royal family.

The Shias were not the only people demonstrating in Bahrain. Sunnis who no longer trusted the royal family to deliver the reforms that the king promised were on the streets too. But Bahraini Shias dominated the protests, as they were sick and tired of a political system that was tilted against them, with gerrymandered constituencies designed to devalue their votes. The royal family and a small, over-whelmingly but not wholly Sunni elite controlled most of the country's wealth. The system made it hard for Shias to buy houses and land. Demonstrations that sometimes turned violent were regular happen-ings in Bahrain. But, by early February 2011, there was a conscious attempt to emulate Tunisia and Egypt, with a Facebook page called 'February 14th Revolution in Bahrain' calling for mass protests. On the fourteenth the protests began – fifty-five of them, according to one esti-mate, in a tiny country. They occupied a road junction called the Pearl Roundabout to try to make it Manama's Tahrir Square. The Bahraini security forces eventually used deadly force to drive the protestors off the roundabout. The authorities demolished the Pearl's angular con-crete sculpture, trying to defeat the uprising by flattening its symbols. Months later the place was still surrounded by barbed wire and heav-ily guarded. Just like other authoritarian rulers in the Arab world, and other protestors, the Bahrainis realised that symbols mattered. Simply trying to re-enter the area could mean jail. A fourteen-year-old boy was among those sent to prison. The tough action preserved the govern-ment and the power of the al-Khalifa family, but left behind almost continuous low-level violence, especially in Shia villages, and increas-ing sectarian tension.

Bahrain's King Hamad bin Isa al-Khalifa commissioned an enquiry into what happened from a panel headed by Cherif Bassiouni, an Egyptian American war-crimes lawyer and former nominee for the Nobel Peace Prize.[7] Arab kings do not usually allow open scrutiny of the actions of their security forces, but Bassiouni defied the cynics to turn in an independent report, and King Hamad broke with the stereotypes to listen at its launch to a litany of abuse by his own secu-rity services, including unlawful killing and torture. This is just one paragraph from 500 detailed pages.

The most common techniques used on detainees included the following: blindfolding; handcuffing; enforced standing for prolonged periods; beating; punching; hitting the detainee with rubber hoses (including on the soles of the detainee's feet), cables, whips, metal, wooden planks or other objects; electrocution; sleep-deprivation; exposure to extreme temperatures; verbal abuse; threats of rape to the detainee or family members; and insulting the detainee's religious sect (Shia).

The Bassiouni commission found no evidence for the Bahraini authorities repeated allegation that Iran was behind the protests, inciting the Shias to revolt. At the Bahraini ambassador's official residence in London, an elegant townhouse in Mayfair a short walk from the American Embassy, a politician visiting from Manama, the Bahraini capital, held forth at the dinner table, suggesting that the commission's members should just have read the Iranian press.

'Bassiouni found no Iranian involvement, but listen to what President Ahmadinejad says in Iran! Shias have more rights in Bahrain than elsewhere in the Gulf. Of course we blame Iran. We've been blaming them since the Islamic Revolution in 1979.'

Wine was served at the dinner. Bahrain has cultivated a strongly secular image, and not just in the West. Alcohol and other worldly pleasures are widely available in Manama. Every weekend, Saudi drivers are nose to tail on the causeway, getting out of one of the most restrictive countries in the world for a couple of days to let their hair down. A senior Bahraini diplomat joined the conversation.

'We're a new democracy. The king has done a lot of things. Bahrain is a tolerant society, and now we're fighting to protect our way of life. I don't want daughters being forced to cover their hair and sons to have a long beard. Do you want what's happening in Egypt, or Iran in 1979?'

The threat from Iran was the reason Bahrain gave for agreeing to the deployment of an intervention force from the Gulf Co-operation Council, which rumbled across the causeway from the east coast of Saudi Arabia on 14 March 2011. The Saudis led the force, which also included contingents from the United Arab Emirates and Qatar. None of them believed that Bassiouni had reported the truth about Iran. The Saudis suspected that their thirty-year cold war with Iran might be turning hot. Qatar is a very small country that sits on a huge reservoir of gas, which makes its people even richer than Saudis. Estimates of the wealth of Qataris vary, but most say that between 9 and 15 per cent of them are worth more than a million dollars. Qatar has spent the last decade and a half making its money count in politics and diplomacy. By the summer it was playing a decisive role arming and training the rebels in Libya. By the winter it thought it could do the same for Syria's mainly Sunni rebels. The Saudis promised support too.

Their interest in defeating the Assad regime had nothing to do with the violence that it was using against the uprising. Instead the Sunnis of the Gulf, encouraged by the United States, were looking for ways to hurt the Shias of Iran, whose nuclear plans seemed to be progressing. An obvious way was to support any opposition to the Assad regime. Syria was Iran's only proper foreign ally, which hit one regional connection. Another connection was sectarian. The worries that Sunni Arab kings and princes in the Gulf had about the loyalty of their Shia minorities led to the old, crude logic about the importance of doing down the friends of your enemies. Whatever was bad for Iran, and bad for Shias (including the Alawites of Syria), had to be good for the Sunnis of the Gulf.

The view from the presidential palace in Damascus as the first anniversary of the uprising approached was not at all as bleak as Bashar al-Assad's enemies had hoped. His tactics looked to be sustainable. Force was being used, but at a level that for months kept contained international outrage. Twenty to thirty opponents of the regime were being killed most days, but the deaths were becoming part of the international political landscape, slipping down the news agenda. Ironically, many of his followers, like the Alawites I met in

District 86 in Damascus, were pushing their leader to do more, telling anyone who would listen that he was not violent enough, that he should roll up his sleeves and wipe out his enemies – their enemies – once and for all.

Then the diplomatic landscape changed. The Saudis, Qataris and their allies chose to act through the Arab League. Ironically, the League was not able to meet at its headquarters in Cairo, a solid 1950s building that stands next to the Nile, because it is right on Tahrir Square. Either side of the New Year of 2012, when the League convened to discuss Syria, protestors were back in the square, sometimes just demonstrating, other times fighting the police, as Egypt continued its tortured progress towards elections. The Tahrir symbolism, and the danger that the arrival of the foreign ministers at the League would turn into an enormous mass demonstration, was just too much. The Arab League slipped into much more secure five-star hotels to talk.

They approved sanctions against the Assad regime and a peace plan that required Bashar al-Assad to step down. For the second time in a year the League was acting against an Arab leader, though Assad and Syria's connections meant they could not do so as decisively as they had against Libya. Assad was not as friendless as Gaddafi. Syria's neighbours in Iraq and Lebanon abstained from the vote and Jordan asked to be exempted from enforcing any sanctions. The Arab League plan was incorporated into a UN Security Council resolution by Britain and the United States. But on 4 February the Russians and the Chinese vetoed it, to the impotent fury of London and Washington. Britain's foreign secretary, William Hague, said the vetoes would only 'encourage President Assad's brutal regime to increase the killing'. When the Russian foreign minister, Sergey Lavrov, asked what the endgame was going to be, the US secretary of state, Hillary Clinton, replied, 'The endgame in the absence of us acting together as the international community, I fear, is civil war.' Saudi Arabia and Qatar declared that they would provide the rebels with weapons. After a few months, the greater military efficiency of the Free Syria Army suggested they were getting in.

The vetoes by Russia and China were much more about Moscow than Beijing. According to senior Western diplomats on the Security Council, Beijing authorized the Chinese delegation to agree the text of the resolution on 4 February. But, because of a strategic under-standing they had on the Security Council to stand with the Russians against the Western bloc of France, the United States and the United Kingdom, they joined the Russians in vetoing the resolution. The Russians were flayed by Western leaders for not allowing action on Syria, but there was some logic in their position. They argued that removing Assad without working out what happened next would leave a vacuum that would lead to even more slaughter, and the descent of Syria into a broken, Somalia-style collection of feuding sects, with huge implications for the future of one of the world's most strategically important and unstable regions. The Western members of the Security Council did not have a coherent answer. Even as the internal military opposition to the Assad regime was get-ting its act together, the external political opposition to Assad in the Syrian National Council was still, despite the lavish attention of Western diplomats, disunited and ineffective. No viable alternative government had emerged. Despite pressure from some quarters for military action against Syria – the former Republican presidential candidate John McCain led the charge in the United States – there was no appetite for what would be a hugely complicated and dan-gerous military adventure. Besides, without a UN resolution it would be politically and legally impossible; and the Russians made it very clear that there would be no repeat of Resolution 1973, which allowed 'all necessary measures' to protect civilians in Libya. Moscow said the mandate had been stretched beyond breaking point into a charter for a NATO bombing campaign and regime change, which was turning Libya into an increasingly Islamist and chaotic collection of warring factions. The Russians believed that they had been deceived by the West over Libya. A Western diplomat on the Security Council said the message they were getting from the Russians was that 'there's still mistrust about you pulling the wool over our eyes last time and overshooting the mandate and we won't allow that again'. Something else mattered to the Russians. Its only overseas military base was in the Syrian port of Tartous on the Mediterranean coast, and it had lucrative arms and engineering deals with the Syrian government. It had lost billions of dollars of contracts with the fall of Gaddafi. But it was not just about money. Russia's president, Vladimir Putin, was determined to restore his country's position in the world. The alliance with Syria went back to the high noon of Soviet power in the Middle East. Giving it up would be a serious setback. Putin would not take dictation from Western countries in the way that his predecessor Boris Yeltsin had been forced to do after the fall of the USSR.

The diplomatic paralysis that followed the veto gave the Assad regime the opportunity it needed to move up into a higher gear. The Syrian army went on the offensive, first of all in Homs, and in Douma and other rebellious suburbs of Damascus, and then elsewhere in the country. Whole districts of rebellious towns were levelled with heavy artillery. My friend the *Sunday Times* journalist Marie Colvin was one of the courageous reporters who crossed illegally into Syria from Lebanon to get to Homs. She sent me an email from there, starting with a joke about racing past Syrian army positions at night on the back of a motorbike (it was fun until she realised how close they were), and then raging about the way that civilians in Homs were being killed by artillery fire from the regime. Her message said it was the kind of story we both had gone into journalism to report. I couldn't help but agree. The next day she was killed by shellfire, along with a French photographer, Remi Ochlik. Another French journalist, Gilles Jacquier, who I had got to know and like in Tripoli, had been killed in Homs a few days before I was there weeks earlier. His wife, Caroline Poiron, a photographer, was with him when he died. I didn't know Remi, but Marie and the others always believed that foreign journalists, who volunteered – even competed – to put themselves into danger should never become the story. What mattered were the people who had no choice about risking their lives. But the deaths of the journalists sharpened Western outrage about what was happening in Syria, and helped the story reach more people.

Epilogue

DOWN A FAULT LINE
TO THE FUTURE

Tehran, June 2009

The Basij militiamen stood waiting every few yards right along the avenues of central Tehran, fondling fearsome-looking clubs made of wood and rubber with thick hands. Not far behind them were vanloads of armed police. Every so often a posse of militiamen on motorbikes cruised by, accelerating off in a pack or slowing down to eyeball any group of young people who might have protest on their minds. Black cars with the words 'Special Police' painted on them moved steadily through the traffic, each one containing four or five men in camouflage uniforms. The authorities in Iran were in the last stages of crushing a public protest movement against a presidential election that the opposition said had been fixed. Tehran was much quieter than it had been, not because the anger had gone but because people were scared. One elderly woman told me it was the silence of the grave. She must have been past caring about what might happen to her for talking to a reporter. The huge protest marches that followed the announcement of the results had ended because of the power and ruthlessness of the Islamic Republic's armed men. Small demonstrations still flared up occasionally, but the most tangible protests happened, almost anonymously, for half an hour every evening. Opponents of the re-elected President Mahmoud Ahmadinejad and the Supreme Leader Ali Khamenei went on their roofs to chant '*Allahu Akbar*' – God is greatest – the words another generation had used against the Shah before the Islamic Revolution in 1979. Even chanting into the night was an act of considerable courage, and the sound would echo across the dark roofs of north Tehran where I was staying. Most of the foreign journalists who had been allowed in for the election had left as their visas had run out. Mine was still valid, but reporting from the streets was banned. A voice on the phone from the Ministry of Islamic Guidance had told me not to do it, or I would be punished. The penalty, he said, might not just be a simple trip to the airport followed by expulsion. He left the details to my imagination. I reckoned reporting did not cover just going for a walk without a camera or a microphone, so every afternoon I would stroll the streets of central Tehran with an Iranian friend. Before we went for our walks she would change out of her elegant strappy sandals into trainers – not, as I had first assumed, in case we had to run away from the police. She explained it would be much worse for us if we were arrested and they saw her beautifully manicured red toenails.

A few days earlier a young woman called Neda Agha-Soltan had been shot dead on the edge of a demonstration. Someone filmed her last moments on a mobile phone. A man shouts, 'Neda, don't be afraid. Neda, stay with me.' But very quickly her eyes stop moving and she dies with them wide open. The images were published on YouTube and Facebook and her death rocketed around the world. She became the face of the failure to overthrow the regime. Twelve months later, on the anniversary of her death, Iran jammed satellite broadcasts to stop its citizens seeing a film about Neda, including the first interviews with her family. Eighteen months later, the Arab uprisings began.

The failure in Iran was a dry run for the Arab uprisings. Some of the same patterns of protest that had been used in Iran re-emerged. Social media were important tools to spread the word about demonstrations and to subvert the official version of the news. Video taken by amateurs on their phones in places professional journalists could not reach found a way through the virtual wall of filters and jammers used by the state, proving that countries could not be sealed off and regimes could no longer kill in private. In the end Iran's protests could not withstand the power of the authorities and were forced so far underground that they became almost invisible. One reason why they failed was that they did not get a critical mass of the people behind them. Not enough people cared about the allegations of electoral fraud to risk a beating or perhaps their lives. The first big marches had a broader cross section taking part, and a temporary safety in numbers, but by the time Neda Agha-Soltan was killed most of the protestors in Tehran were the educated middle classes from the north side of the city. They did not have the numbers to swamp the Basij militiamen and take on the clubs and guns of the authorities. Revolutions need the poor, the excluded with no stake in the old world and nothing to lose by rising up. The power of the poor turned the Arab uprisings into an historic moment of reawakening. Poor men and women in the dusty provincial town of Sidi Bouzid started the revolution in Tunisia long before the middle classes in the capital had heard of Muhammad Bouazizi. If the protests in Cairo had been confined to what one well-off doctor in Tahrir Square called the 'Rolex brigade' they would never have overthrown President Mubarak. In Syria the bravery of demonstrators who continued to go out on to the streets, even though they knew there was a strong chance the regime's men would open fire, drove the first phase of the protests until a rebel army started to come together.

Before 2011, Arab dissidents – like the Iranians – had their failures. Like the Iranians, they tried to use the cyber tactics of modern revolutionaries. Until a critical mass came together in 2011 the regimes survived, but the fact that someone had even dared to try left them scarred and weakened. The fury about the 2009 elections in Iran broadened the fractures in the country's ruling elite. In Egypt, the attempt in 2008 to use the power of the internet to boost strikes and protests in the industrial town of Mahalla with the aim of crippling the regime was seen, even at the time, as a rehearsal for a bigger fight.[1]

Discontent spread through Arab countries because of more than a simple copycat effect. Every state had its own reasons to feel dissatisfied with its leaders. In turn, they did not respond in identical ways to dissent and defiance. But there were also tendencies and forces that ignored national borders. Frontiers made useless firebreaks. I was never very happy about using the phrase 'Arab World' to describe the diverse peoples who live in the twenty-two member countries of the Arab League. It seemed like a sloppy piece of Western shorthand. The uprisings in some countries and discontent in every other have once again shown the differences between them. When the Western media started writing about the events – which they persisted in calling a spring long after summer had turned into a bloody winter – some journalists tried very hard to join the dots between them. It was a struggle, as the countries concerned were much more diverse than outsiders assumed. Tripoli in Libya to Bahrain is more than 2,000 miles and almost five hours in a plane, assuming you can get a direct flight. Tunis and Algiers feel more than halfway to Europe. Sometimes it feels like most of the way to the eighteenth century in the spectacularly picturesque old city in Sana'a in Yemen, where many men wear traditional robes cinched in with an elaborate belt embroidered with tribal designs that instantly identify the wearer's origins and even his loyalties.

But what has happened since the end of 2010 shows that there is an Arab world worth talking about. Most of its people are under the age of thirty and are Muslims. Politically, they are much more disunited than, say, those of the European Union. But paradoxically everything else they have in common means that they understand each other better than Europeans do. Sharing a language helps. This meant that television viewers could follow direct, live coverage of the uprisings, especially from al-Jazeera, al-Arabiya and BBC Arabic, the channels that broadcast to the whole region. Viewers could see what was happening in Tunis, or Tahrir Square, and wonder whether they could do something similar. It was infectious and powerful. Language is a tie that binds – though, as Americans and British, Portuguese and Brazilians know, the fact that you share a language and some cultural roots does not mean that you always think the same way. But it did mean that it was easy to compare what these people had in common and what made them different. Living in a police state under an autocratic leader was something that every Arab knew about. So was dealing with the corrosive effect of corruption, from providing sweeteners to extract everyday official papers, like driving licences, from the bureaucracy, to watching as huge chunks of businesses that should have helped increase standards of living for all enriched ruling families and their cronies.

It wasn't just a matter of sharing experiences. The region's network of political and sectarian fault lines connected them. They make up an underlying web that will go on shaping the next acts of the Middle East's political, religious and social drama. Some of the fault lines are there because of the conflict between Israel and the Arabs. Others run between the Middle East and its former colonial masters in Europe, or exist as a result of the American-led invasion of Iraq in 2003. Often, they lie alongside each other, parallel lines, before splitting off to pull in another little piece of politics, history or religion.

No one saw the Arab uprisings coming the way that they did – not even the people who organized the first protests in Tunisia and Egypt and certainly not the tyrants who were overthrown. Some clues about the new world that they are producing have emerged, but it would be foolish to try to predict too much. So far, political Islam is a big winner; but, as politics reinvents itself and the Islamists are forced to try to deliver the nuts and bolts of better lives and jobs, not just dreams, they will find that re-election cannot be taken for granted. That assumes that there will be more elections, of course, which looks likely, as people who took on dictatorships in the streets are not likely to give up freedoms they extracted with such difficulty.

But there is a guide to where trouble lies ahead. It is the fault line between Sunni and Shia Muslims, the oldest in the region, and the one that might end up mattering most. It runs between Iran and Saudi Arabia, exits the top of the Gulf where Iraq meets Kuwait and continues north via Damascus and Beirut.

The Arab uprisings are shaking it in fresh ways. The troubles of a new era are grafting themselves on to an old schism. The Syrian civil war is the most serious tremor. But seismic change across the region affects the Shia–Sunni inheritance as well.

The split between Shias and Sunnis goes back to a succession crisis after the death of the Prophet Muhammad in 632. A majority of his followers, who became Sunnis, decided that the leadership would pass to his closest associates, known as the Rightly Guided Caliphs. But it was a turbulent time. Fellow Muslims assassinated one of the caliphs, Uthman, and the Umayyad dynasty from Damascus took over the Muslim Empire. A group of dissidents eventually became the Shias. They thought that their community's problems came from the way that Muhammad's successors were chosen. They believed the role of leader should have followed the family line, and gone to Muhammad's cousin Ali. The two sides went to war, and in 680 Ali's son Hussein and seventy-two of his followers were killed at the battle of Karbala, in present-day Iraq.[2]

Every year, Hussein's death – his martyrdom – is commemorated at the feast of Ashoura, a time of extravagant mourning and public grief that feels as fresh as if he had died last week. In some places men flay themselves until they bleed. In every Shia community people walk through their towns beating their chests rhythmically and calling Hussein's name. I stood once among perhaps 10,000 men and a few small, separated-off sections of women in one of the big squares that the Shias of Hezbollah use for demonstrations and public events in their stronghold in the southern suburbs of Beirut. They started in absolute silence, as a preacher retold the story of Hussein's martyrdom. As the voice coming out of the speakers cracked with emotion, more and more of the people around me began to weep, silently at first and then with great, deep sobs.

Comparisons are never exact, but a similar one is between Catholics and Protestants. Shias and Sunnis come from the same roots, some of them intermarry, and many live happily alongside each other. But their historical differences are embedded in their cultural DNA. They go well beyond religion and on to questions of power and identity. That can mean civilized discussion and political dialogue. It can also mean a deep dislike and suspicion of each other. Sometimes it leads to violence. During a burst of sectarian killing in Lebanon in 2008 that amounted to a mini civil war, I went to a mainly Sunni area in Beirut that was boiling with anger. Mourners at a funeral for a young Sunni had been chanting that Shias were the enemies of God. They turned on a Shia trader when he refused to close his shop out of respect. He took his Kalashnikov and opened fire at the cortege, killing two people. In their fury, Sunnis destroyed other Shia-owned property in the area. A reporter from the *New York Times* saw one of the Sunnis berating the rioters as they ate looted kiwis, strawberries and carrots at an abandoned juice stall.

'What are you doing?' he shouted to them. 'You can't eat these fruits: they are forbidden. They were bought with Shiite money.'[3] Their rage was not just directed at Shias. When I turned up with my BBC team our lives were threatened by a man with the beard and shin-length robes of the austere Sunni believers known as Salafists. We managed to escape when he turned away to threaten another TV crew.

Since the invasion of Iraq in 2003 the position of Shias across the Arab world has strengthened, and that has alarmed Sunni rulers. According to Vali Nasr, the author of an influential study of the Shias, it means 'a more even Shia–Sunni balance of power in the Middle East than has been seen in nearly fourteen centuries'.[4] The invasion removed a Sunni strongman, Saddam Hussein, who had gone to war in the 1980s against Shia Iran. It was the end of minority rule by Sunnis, a habit that the British had introduced when they controlled Iraq after the First World War. They preferred dealing with a small and traditional Sunni elite than with the majority, some of whom were discovering nationalism. The Sunnis kept their power in Iraq until the Americans brought in elections after the invasion in 2003. Many of the Shia politicians who were voted in, after lifetimes of anger and frustration at being excluded, had spent years in Iran on the run from Saddam Hussein's police state. One of the lasting ironies of the invasion of Iraq is that the Americans unwittingly flipped the local balance of power against themselves and their Sunni friends in the Gulf in favour of Shia Iran, their most obdurate enemy. They presented Iran with a potential ally and not an enemy in Baghdad. The Iraqis did not do as they were told by Tehran. They showed every sign of being Iraqis first and Shias second. But they knew Iran well, and had deep connections with the clerics in Tehran.

Shia politicians and their followers are delighted with their new power and influence. But the idea of resurgent Shia Islam worries the Sunni dynasties that have been the West's main allies in the region since early in the twentieth century, because it changes the region's sectarian balance and threatens their traditional dominance. King Abdullah of Jordan talked about the dangers of a 'Shia crescent'. Later, he extended his metaphor eastwards, telling the be-suited delegates at the annual celebration of Western capitalism in Davos in Switzerland that 'the fault line between Shias and Sunnis goes from Beirut all the way to Bombay and it's a catastrophic subject to play with'.[5]

At one end of the fault line, in Beirut in May 2012, the jacaranda trees were in blossom, their perfumed purple flowers swaying in the breeze off the Mediterranean. In some other time and place it might have been idyllic. But, even though it was twenty years since Beirut had been the Middle East's most war-torn city, they could feel the political and sectarian reverberations coming in via the fault lines from Syria. As usual, Beirutis were doing their best to distract themselves. For many secular Lebanese, early summer means the beach, the pool and the worship of the god of the suntan. I was staying at a hotel on the Corniche, the long, crescent-shaped promenade that runs along the Mediterranean. The hotel used to be pleasantly scruffy, with an old-fashioned oblong pool that was excellent for doing lengths. But new management with money and a good sense of what would be popular among the city's partying classes turned it into a place to pose, with a swim-in bar where customers could wallow to check out whichever sex they found most interesting, or to do a watery dance to the music pumping out of the speakers. Surgeons and silicon, not nature, shaped some of the flesh on display. It was trendy, bling central, and one of the places to go in a city where for some people image matters more than almost anything else. Right through the afternoon they downed cocktails and danced, while the music throbbed its way back to the Corniche past the canvas screens that kept out the prying eyes of the prurient and the austere.

For those who did not want to lose themselves in Beirut's hedonism, or couldn't afford to, identity mattered a lot more than the show. Power in Lebanon is split uneasily between eighteen religious sects, which is why sectarian tremors can turn into earthquakes. In that jacaranda week in Beirut the seams between Shias and Sunnis were straining in a way that made the Lebanese, with their history of civil war, feel deeply uncomfortable. Hanging out at the pool might have helped the fortunate few put it out of their minds, but not far away people had died that same week in sectarian incidents that were bringing back bad memories.

In Lebanon each sect gets a slice of power and government jobs depending on its size, as measured by the 1932 census. In 1943, when the deal was done, as Lebanon became independent from France, the demographic information was probably already out of date. Adjustments have been made since then, giving Muslims more power at the expense of Christians, but holding another census to get an accurate idea of population is so politically explosive that it has never happened. The big three sects get the bulk of the jobs. The president is always a Maronite Christian, the prime minister is always a Sunni Muslim and the speaker of the parliament is always a Shia. Lebanon works best when they can tolerate each other, and not forget that peace in the country depends on keeping it balanced. That is why the patrons of my hotel's beach club could carry on drinking, sun tanning and dancing wearing almost nothing, while a short drive away in the southern suburbs religious Shia women shop in voluminous black robes and their bearded husbands go about their business watched by the gimlet eyes of Ayatollah Khomeini, the venerated leader of the Islamic revolution in Iran. When they cannot agree, more often on the questions of power than on ones of lifestyle, the Lebanese have a habit of reaching for their guns.

One theory for the pursuit of pleasure and beauty in Lebanon's bourgeoisie, even at the cost of going under the surgeon's knife, is that history has taught them that it is best to live in the moment, because tomorrow everything could change. That weekend was full of reminders of uncertainty past, present and to come. It was the annual Liberation Day holiday, celebrating the withdrawal of Israel in 2000 from the zone it occupied in the south. Lebanon's most powerful man, Hassan Nasrallah, the leader of Hezbollah, the Shia movement whose fighters had made the occupation untenable for Israel, was the star attraction at a commemorative rally in Bint Jbail, one of the towns where Hezbollah took on the Israelis. Not far from where he spoke Hezbollah built a park, funded by Iran, overlooking the border with Israel and the irrigated fields on the other side of the wire, complete with Iranian flags, Khomeini portraits, picnic tables and barbeque pits. Israelis could look over and see hard evidence that Iran could project its power and influence right to their border, thanks to connections made along the sectarian fault line.

Christians and Sunnis and members of other Lebanese sects were invited to Nasrallah's speech, and given good seats at the front, but as usual what he said turned into a reminder of Shia power and

Hezbollah's alliances with Damascus and Tehran. Since the 2006 war with Israel security around Nasrallah, always tight, had become even tougher. He made his speech, more than two hours long, from an undisclosed location via a big screen. Hezbollah's communications were good enough to give him a feed of the crowd's response to what he was saying. When, uncharacteristically, he offered mild praise for Saad Hariri, the leader of Lebanon's Sunnis, the crowd booed. Nasrallah rebuked them, telling them that Hariri was helping in a hostage crisis that was happening at the time. Even through the big screen Nasrallah's glare was not to be ignored. Hurriedly, they applauded. Nasrallah was giving a shout-out to Hariri, the politically ineffectual man who had inherited the leadership of the Sunni community when his father was assassinated in 2005, because the sectarian tensions that are part of life in Lebanon were wound close to breaking point. All the community leaders wanted to reduce the tension, as upsets in the delicate balance between Lebanon's different communities tend to lead to war.

The trouble in Syria was causing the increased danger. Lebanon's second city, Tripoli, was affected badly. The city's own fault line was Syria Street, the scruffy, battered road that divided Bab Tabbaneh, a district of Sunnis, who were in the majority in Tripoli, from a small community of Lebanese Alawites. Since the civil war the two sides had been at loggerheads. The Alawites were fiercely loyal to the Assads, and the constant tension between the two sides, in a grindingly poor section of the city, led to years of regular exchanges of bullets and deaths. When I was passing through Tripoli a few months after the uprising started in Syria, I made the mistake of turning up in the Alawite district, Jabal Mohsen, without an appointment. Big posters of Bashar al-Assad were everywhere, and so were lookouts with walkie-talkies. Within minutes several carloads of muscular local men turned up. They were not carrying weapons openly, but I had no doubt they had them close by. The men's leader was deeply suspicious, and hostile, and told us that unless we gave him the tape they would smash the camera. Once they had the pictures they ran us out of their section of town. By early 2012 the shootouts across Syria Street were getting much fiercer, more people were dying and, most worryingly for the Lebanese, the contagion was spreading.

It hit Beirut for the first time after two anti-Assad clerics were shot dead by the army at a checkpoint in northern Lebanon. In the fury that followed a small faction of Sunnis allied to Damascus was forcibly expelled from a largely Sunni neighbourhood in the capital. Most Lebanese Sunnis supported the Syrian rebellion. Two people were killed in the fighting. A middle-aged woman called Hala Salhi had the misfortune to live in an apartment above the burnt-out offices of the pro-Assad Arab Movement Party. Her balcony windows were cracked and holed by bullets, and the glass-fronted display cases where she had put photographs and small sentimental mementoes were shattered and splintered by the gunfire. Hala sat in the wreckage of her best room, terrified that the street battles of the 1980s between Muslims and Christians could return as a straight Muslim fight between Sunnis and Shia. Lebanon had been cursed before as the battleground for bigger powers' proxy wars. They could be fighting, she said, 'for the sake of Syria, for the sake of Iran, for the sake of Saudi Arabia. We didn't get a lesson from the civil war. Nothing at all. Twenty years on and we're still the same.'

Lebanon was getting involved in Syria's war despite the fairly hopeless proclamation by Prime Minister Najib Miqati that it would stay out of the fight. Parts of Lebanon were acting as a rear echelon for anti-Assad fighters from the Free Syria Army. Arms were being moved across the border and wounded fighters and civilians, as well as refugees, were coming back in the other way. For Lebanon, staying aloof from the war in Syria was an aspiration, not an option. The reality was that the same religious and political fault lines ran through Lebanon as Syria.

From early on in the Syrian uprising, the country started to split on sectarian lines. As a civil war took hold, the mainly Sunni rebels as well as Assad's Alawites were driven by the fear that defeat would mean death, which left no alternative to fighting on. Sunni rebel fighters were mainly poor boys from the provinces or from the concrete jungle of suburbs around Damascus.

The regime lost the Sunni poor early on, but for the first year or so it kept its long-standing alliance with key members of the Sunni elite, which went back to the time of President Assad senior. The alliance strengthened and steadied the regime, and helped it deny that it was exaggerating very real sectarian divisions to keep its core support frightened and loyal. The alliance ended with the defection of the Tlass clan, the most influential Sunni family in Syria, in June 2012. It signalled that war had split Syria along even sharper sectarian lines. The Tlass family patriarch, Mustapha, spent years as minister of defence under Hafez al-Assad and helped make sure that Bashar's succession to the presidency was smooth. Mustapha went for what was described as medical treatment in Paris, a favourite place for Syrian émigrés. He was joined there by his son Manaf, who was a general in the Republican Guard, a unit whose main mission was safeguarding the regime. Manaf's brother, Firas, was a businessman who had grown wealthy on soft contracts from the state. By the time the family left Syria, much of his business had been quietly moved to Dubai. More damaging for the regime, though less dramatic, was the steady defection of Sunni soldiers and officers from the army, and the failure of young conscripts to turn up for their military service.

The Assad regime's most dangerous Arab enemies were the Sunni royal families of Saudi Arabia and Qatar, who were arming the rebels. Plenty of traditional great power reasons existed to fuel the rivalry, but the sectarian lens through which both sides viewed their differences increased the bitterness and suspicion, and reinforced the belief that Syria was part of a bigger, regional struggle between Iran and its Sunni adversaries.

Hamas also moved out of Damascus. It was impossible for a

Palestinian Sunni Muslim group to stay in Syria under the supposed protection of an Alawite leader who was getting deeper into a sectarian civil war against Sunnis. Hamas had been well looked after in Damascus for many years. Its headquarters was a heavily guarded house in one of the city's best neighbourhoods. When I visited the political leader of Hamas, Khaled Meshaal, in the years before the uprisings began, he seemed very comfortable in Damascus. He would give me something to mark the visit, usually a magnificent box of Damascene sweets and pastries. Sometimes I would take them to Jerusalem, where the BBC's Israeli staff would look at them, and take a nibble, with a mixture of suspicion and fascination.

All along the Sunni–Shia fault line sectarian tension was growing by 2012. In Iraq, Prime Minister Nuri al-Maliki, a Shia and an Islamist, headed a coalition that included Sunnis and Kurds. But then he accused the Sunni vice-president Tariq al-Hashimi of running death squads that were allegedly linked with the killings of 150 Shia officials. Hashimi fled across the border into Turkey, where the government, which was led by Sunni Islamists, refused to extradite him to face trial. Maliki also side-lined his own Sunni deputy, Saleh al-Mutlaq. Every Iraqi knew how easily the tension could lead to a return to the terrible communal violence they had suffered after the authoritarian glue that held Iraq together was broken down by the American-led invasion.

Trouble along the Sunni–Shia divide is already producing the Arab world's next great storm. The season of change is going to be long and hard. Saudi Arabia could become its next big focus. The political weather could turn against the House of Saud because of a crisis over Bahrain, or Iran's nuclear plans, or increased sectarian tensions, or a combination of all three. It might come when King Abdullah dies. The succession could be a natural breaking point. The king did not want Saudi Arabia to star in the next act of the Arab uprisings, but his own actions suggested that he accepted that no country was immune from what was happening elsewhere in the region. In late February

2011 Abdullah, then believed to be eighty-seven years old, flew home from medical treatment abroad as protests raged across the Arab world, and announced on his arrival that he would throw a huge amount of money at his people's grievances. Some 110 billion dollars were made available for job creation and housing. More money was also earmarked for the religious establishment that acted as a major dampener on discontent and the security forces who dealt with it.

King Abdullah had every reason to be worried. Saudi Arabia had some significant points in common with countries that had revolutions. Unemployment was usually described as a time bomb. More than 60 per cent of Saudis were under the age of thirty, and almost a third of them did not have a job. Their rulers were old. The money put into the system by the king blunted a lot of the anger, but Abdullah also needed his security services on full alert. Amnesty International said hundreds of Saudis had been arrested for daring to dissent since the start of the Arab uprisings, especially in the mainly Shia Eastern Province.[6]

Iran lost a lot of credibility among Arabs outside the ruling elites when it crushed its own attempted political spring after the 2009 election. But Sunni leaders remembered and still feared the way that their own people were exhilarated in 2006 when Hezbollah, with Iranian and Syrian sponsorship, took on Israel and fought it to a standstill. Later that year a man who sold pencil sketches of Arab leaders in Ramallah on the Palestinian West Bank told me that his bestsellers were Hassan Nasrallah, the leader of Hezbollah, and Mahmoud Ahmadinejad, the president of Iran, both Shias whose portraits were being bought by Sunnis. Across the region, Sunnis were looking with excitement and admiration at men who dared to do what their rulers could not or would not do. In Syria Bashar al-Assad taunted Arab leaders who did not support Hezbollah, calling them 'half-men' – an insult that was not forgotten or forgiven.

The attempted uprising in Bahrain still has to play itself out. When the rulers of the rich Arab states of the Gulf, driven on by their preoccupation with Iran, intervened in Bahrain they believed that putting a lid on its restive Shiites would be a way of crabbing Iran's political reach. But the attempt to crush the rebellion, rather than deal with its political and economic causes, made matters worse by ratcheting up sectarian tensions. Bahrain became a much more tangible focus for the long-running standoff between Iran and the Gulf Arabs.

Jane Kinninmont, one of the most authoritative analysts of the Gulf, spotted that Bahrain had changed.

'From being a country buffeted by sectarian tensions from elsewhere, Bahrain has begun to export them. Sunni–Shia tensions and mistrust have increased in Saudi Arabia, Kuwait and the UAE since February 2011.'[7] Iranian newspapers close to the Supreme Leader, Ali Khamenei, called for Bahrain to be annexed. Saudi Arabia, and its allies inside Bahrain, talked about unification. Bahrain, and its uprising have become dangerous triggers in the standoff between Iran and Saudi Arabia.

The Middle East's sectarian politics were snagging powerful Western countries too. The rumblings along the Shia–Sunni fault line reached Washington. The main US naval base in the Gulf is in Bahrain, inside a big enclave that is the headquarters of the Fifth Fleet. One of its potential targets is Iran. The fleet is a complex fighting machine, doing everything from flying strikes into Afghanistan to feeding the 6,000 sailors and airmen on each aircraft carrier. When I flew out of Bahrain to visit the USS *Eisenhower*, its spokespeople seemed as proud of the 80,000 eggs the crew consumed every month as they were of its nuclear reactors and its strike aircraft. Britain too had business interests, including arms deals, as well as historical ties with Bahrain. It all meant that Western powers showed patience and understanding towards what they insisted was the good faith of the royal family and its efforts to reform, despite the evidence of torture and the unlawful killing of civilians. And, just like their Sunni allies in the Gulf, they had their own deep suspicions of Iran and did not want to do anything more to strengthen its position as a regional power. The contrast with their response to the violent attempts to put down uprisings in Tunisia, Egypt, Libya and Syria was obvious, and the inconsistency was politically embarrassing. Western leaders thought it was necessary, though, to avoid alienating the Saudis any more than they had already by dropping President Mubarak in Egypt. The Saudis were stuck with the Americans, as their most important ally, but they trusted them less.

Sectarianism, of course, was not just a problem for Sunnis and Shias. It affected minorities across the Middle East and North Africa. Managing it, defeating it, and not being tempted to exploit it, will be a major challenge for the new Arab politics. Intolerance is a reflex in too many countries. As I write a video clip is trending on the BBC website. It was filmed in Jordan but could have happened elsewhere in the region. The clip shows a television presenter trying to moderate a debate between two irate politicians. Finally one of them takes off a shoe, throws it at his opponent and then pulls a gun. The guests push and shove, the presenter gets between them, the studio desks collapse, and the picture fades out.

The pistol went back into the politician's holster without being fired. But it was another small example of the reason why new habits have to be learnt. Democracy means more than winning elections. The next big job after voting is to create a country where the law rules, where people have freedom of speech and dissidents and minorities can feel safe. Sunni Islamists who won victories in Egypt and Tunisia, and who have become part of the mainstream in other countries, need to show that they can create tolerant societies. The constellation of forces in Syria might have been different if the Sunni-led rebels had persuaded Christians, Druze and Kurds that they would have as secure a place in a new Syria as they had under the Assad regime. A wise opposition leader – and there wasn't one, as the Syrian opposition remained hopelessly disunited – might have tried to undermine Assad's position by offering Alawites a better choice than an all-out fight to the death.

Respect for human rights was another demand of the Arab world's revolutionaries. They were sick of years of arbitrary arrests, of police and intelligence organizations that were above the law. Human rights can be patchy in countries with decades or even centuries of democratic politics. Creating a culture of rights from scratch is not going to be easy in states where none existed. Just after Gaddafi's downfall in Libya I spoke to a human-rights lawyer in Tripoli who had been brave enough to stand up for his beliefs in the colonel's time. Once the regime fell the lawyer's expectations were sky high. He was disgusted and disappointed when we visited a prison and saw captives being held in miserable conditions. No one there had legal representation, no one had been charged with any crime, and no policeman was investigating what they did or didn't do. The lawyer gave a roasting to the gunmen who controlled the prison, telling them that it was not what the revolution was all about.

'It is a very important and very essential and basic human right and if the new Libya fails to deliver this, all the sacrifices will be in vain.' Other lawyers in Tripoli, trawling through the remains of the old police state to seize and preserve its archives to amass evidence for future trials, accepted that it was early days but believed that more should have been done, from the very start, to uphold the rule of law.

Big losers were jihadists, the likes of al-Qaeda, its affiliates and fellow travellers, who were dealt a serious blow by the Arab uprisings. The power of the people proved to be much more effective than their murderous methods. As Fawaz Gerges explains in his excellent book *The Far Enemy*, men like Ayman al-Zawahiri, Osama Bin Laden's number two in al-Qaeda, switched to attacks on America and the West when they could not dislodge the 'near enemy', pro-Western rulers in iron-clad presidential palaces.[8] Hosni Mubarak was one early target for jihadists. But Mubarak, who had resisted extremely violent attacks designed to unseat him, in the end crumbled in the face of hundreds of thousands of unarmed demonstrators shouting slogans for him to go and refusing to return home until he did. Protest movements that grew out of years of humiliation and anger, and which were given a voice and a chance to grow by social networking, achieved political traction that the jihadists could only dream about. By the end of the year, men who had killed thousands of their fellow Muslims across the Middle East and the wider Islamic world were further than ever from the mainstream. It did not stop them continuing to plot and to kill. But they were isolated and reviled. Even the assassination of Bin Laden himself in May 2011 did not earn them any sympathy. The Americans handled the aftermath effectively, burying the body at sea, a long way from any cameras they did not control. Releasing photographs of Bin Laden in death, either freshly killed or being buried, would have made it much easier to prove beyond doubt that they had nailed their man, but the absence of any images, or a grave, made it much harder to build a martyr's cult around him. What was released was un-heroic enough. Far from running his jihad from a rocky hideout on a mountainside in Pakistan's tribal territories, as many had assumed, he was an aging, ailing man watching videos of his past triumphs in a squalid room with his wives and some of his children. Perhaps, before he was killed, he was glued to television coverage of the uprisings that were achieving results he could not.

But as Syria's civil war deepened, it offered jihadists opportunities. From the beginning of the uprising in Syria the Assad regime claimed that it was a conspiracy partly fuelled by the ambitions of Sunni jihadists. It did not produce any convincing evidence. But as the chaos and violence spread, reports began to surface that foreign fighters with a jihadist ideology were operating inside the country. At the time of writing the scale of jihadist involvement in the fighting against the Assad regime was not clear. It was another headache for the western countries who wanted to support the rebels.

The uprisings in the Middle East and North Africa also changed the game for the Americans and their Western allies. They were taken by surprise. Compare the hubris of 2003, when the United States, Britain and their friends decided to invade Iraq. Never mind for a moment whether they believed in the evidence they used to justify the invasion – though it has been clear for a long time that their assumptions about Iraq's supposed weapons of mass destruction were wrong. What mattered was that they believed then that an invasion was possible, and that it would be an easy victory and not a catastrophic mistake. Eight years later, with different faces at the top, they were more cautious, and more realistic. The searing experience of Iraq, and their commitments in Afghanistan, taught the Americans and the British some hard lessons. They calculated that what was possible in Libya, with good luck as well as a gambler's judgement, had no chance of success in Syria. President Obama was wise to indicate that there were limits to what the US could do. When NATO intervened in Libya, he insisted that the Alliance, and Britain and France, would have to take the lead. It was an unfamiliar experience. One senior British diplomat told me ruefully that announcing that they were letting go of the steering wheel did not stop Washington trying to be a back-seat driver. A sense of what was possible was only prudent. But it went deeper than that. By 2011 the Americans did not have the appetite, or the capacity, the consent of their people or the support of their allies, to act in the way that they did in 2003. Russia was trying to rebuild its position in the region. China's power as a trader and an importer of raw materials was making it more influential. The American people were fed up with wars seemingly without end. The invasion of Iraq was not quite the turning point for the US in the Middle East that Suez had been in 1956 for the British. The Americans still had the world's biggest economy and a military machine as dominant as any in history. But the United States is more of a spectator, less of an arbiter, more conscious of what it cannot do than it was in 2003. The next monumental challenge it faces in the region is whether or not to attack Iran if negotiations over its nuclear plans are finally pronounced dead. A mistake then could turn into America's Suez.

Israel, Washington's main ally in the Middle East, talking openly about its own attack on Iran by the summer of 2012, was forced to hang on and hope as the ground beneath its feet shifted. Almost every development since the beginning of 2011 has deepened Israel's concern about the way the region is going. When Muhammad Morsi of the Muslim Brotherhood became president of Egypt, one of Israel's top newspaper columnists, Ben Caspit, spoke for many of his fellow citizens. He declared that the Israeli security and political establishment's 'worst possible nightmare' was coming true. He recalled how Israel's president, Shimon Peres, nicknamed Hosni Mubarak 'the cliff'. Now, Caspit proclaimed, 'the cliff has been washed out to sea, and is being replaced by the Islamic flood, and all of that is happening in the largest Arab country, Israel's primary partner to strategic peace, the regional anchor, the country that used to balance out the neighbourhood. All of that is over.'[9] Egypt under Mubarak had watched Israel's back. The former president, sentenced to life in prison for complicity in the deaths of protestors by the time Morsi was elected, had been a full partner with Israel in the blockade of Gaza. Now Israel was faced with an Egyptian president who came from the Muslim Brotherhood, the political movement that was the mothership for Hamas, its enemy in Gaza. The Israelis, like the Americans, were spectators at an event that made them deeply uncomfortable. The government of Binyamin Netanyahu did not respond, as some Israelis and others suggested it should, by pushing harder for a peace deal with Mahmoud Abbas, the pro-Western Palestinian president. Instead they concentrated on building the walls around their state, physical as well as mental, even higher. Israel could only watch as Sinai, across its southern border, became more and more lawless after the Egyptian revolution destroyed the power of the police state. The civil war across the border in Syria, and the knowledge that the Palestinians had never accepted their fate, guaranteed more trouble ahead.

One evening in the early summer of 2012 I was in the gym in Cairo on the running machine, watching the news on the Saudi-owned satellite channel al-Arabiya. It struck me as I puffed along that the message coming from the big screen had none of the optimism that would have been there the previous spring. The process of change, the emergence of a new Middle East, was turning out to be long and hard. Libya's civil war ended with the death of Colonel Gaddafi, but the country was still violent and the killing in Syria was getting worse. On the screen families wept over the bodies of dead children that had been wrapped and prepared for burial. Graphics were framed by barbed wire.

The bulletin I was watching led with a suicide bombing in Yemen that killed ninety-six soldiers. The pictures showed hundreds of uniformed men moments after it happened, surging away from the site of the explosion where scores of still bodies were piled up together. I know that particular place in Sana'a. It is a wide, straight parade ground that is used as part of a highway most of the time. Until it was overshadowed by the turbulence and uprisings in the rest of the region, I thought that Yemen would be close to the top of 2011's agenda. It had an insurgency in the north, a separatist movement in the south, was running out of water and oil, its only export, and it had become the home of al-Qaeda in the Arabian Peninsula, an aggressive and ambitious jihadist group, which had been forced across the border from Saudi Arabia. After Tunisia and Egypt, Yemenis started their own uprising against Ali Abdullah Saleh, who had been president since 1978. Parts of the army defected to protect the protestors, but many people died before Saleh agreed to a deal where he would leave, in return for immunity for prosecution. For a while, a Saleh-style solution was seen as a prototype for an exit from Syria of Bashar al-Assad. The flaw in the Yemeni deal, which also made it possible, was that it left Saleh's sons and nephews entrenched in power, controlling elite units in the military. Al-Qaeda in the Arabian Peninsula, the same group who were close to blowing up airliners with bombs hidden in underwear and printer cartridges, said they carried out the attack at the parade. The attack was a heavy blow for Abed Rabbo Mansour Hadi, the former field marshal who had replaced Saleh as president. He was struggling to establish control of the capital city, let alone the mountains and deserts where al-Qaeda had its strongholds.

From my vantage point on the running treadmill in Cairo, via a-Arabiya's television cameras, an awful lot had happened since the extraordinary few weeks in February 2011 when Arab dictators seemed to be the new dominoes, tumbling as they had in Europe in 1989. But it was clear too from the news bulletin – and from any other that night, week or month – that irreversible change was happening. In Yemen jihadist gunmen and bombers were still killing their fellow Muslims. But I was in Cairo for the presidential election, which was a proper vote, the kind where no one knew the result in advance. It was not perfect democracy. No new constitution had been agreed, which meant that the voters did not know what powers the president would have. The ruling Military Council looked to be very reluctant to give up its power as the controller of the so-called 'deep state' and was shaping up for a confrontation with the forces of political Islam. But the election showed that Egypt had entered a different political universe. Egyptians who had been getting pessimistic about the future were re-energized. The act of voting was a vital reminder to its citizens that Egypt had really been changed by the revolution. But the violence that was happening in the region, especially in Syria, made it clear that the road ahead would be long and hard, and that it would be years, not months, before the Arabs and their neighbours reached its end.

Different countries moved at different speeds. The most susceptible to revolution were republics, especially Tunisia, Egypt, Libya and Yemen. In the republics the leaders all had cults of personality that identified them utterly with the system, which made them obvious targets. Monarchies, like Jordan and Morocco, were better at bringing in reforms to head off trouble. Kings who had inherited power from a long family line, with the backing of important tribes, had more legitimacy than presidents. They also had the option of changing their governments and prime ministers, which could act as a lightning rod for dissent. In the third category were countries that were not caught up in the early rush of enthusiasm for change. They were Algeria, Iraq, Lebanon and the Palestinian territories. Their caution came from the shared experience of long and bitter wars. They knew the potential consequences of trying to overturn the established order. Longer term, though, they too cannot be immune to what is happening around them, whether they like it or not. The Lebanese, especially, are feeling the hot breath of Syria.

Countries take years, even generations, to get over dictatorships and civil wars. Arab countries where the uprisings became revolutions are not going to settle back into the political quiet that the old tyrants were able to impose. The way they deal with the legacy of the bad years will determine their futures. Syrians, at the time of writing, face terrifying violence. In Bahrain, Yemen and elsewhere there is terrible uncertainty. But after so many years of decline, millions of Arabs have had an injection of hope, a feeling that they were emerging from a troubled half-century and more of decline. My friend the Oxford historian Eugene Rogan found a quotation from the Lebanese writer Samir Kassir, who was assassinated in 2005. Kassir was a leading critic of Syria's influence in Lebanon, so his friends and allies assumed the Assad regime killed him. He caught the essence of what he called the Arab malaise.

> The Arab people are haunted by a sense of powerlessness ... powerlessness to suppress the feeling that you are no more than a lowly pawn on the global chessboard even as the game is being played in your backyard.[10]

When the people saw regimes cracking and tumbling that feeling was swept away. It returned, a bit, when their lives did not improve as quickly as they had hoped. But an idea had taken hold. They were not powerless anymore. They had proved that they could change their lives.

NOTES

PROLOGUE: BEFORE THE SPRING

1 'Tunisia: a country factsheet on youth employment', International Fund for Agricultural Development, 2011.
http://www.ifad.org/events/gc/34/nen/factsheet/tunisia.pdf
2 Max Rodenbeck, *Cairo: The City Victorious*, Picador, London, 1998, pp. 197–200.
3 Eugene Rogan, *The Arabs: A History*, Allen Lane, London, 2009, p. 281.
4 Avi Shlaim, *Lion of Jordan: The Life of King Hussein in War and Peace*, Allen Lane, London, 2007, p. 153.
5 Quoted in Patrick Seale, *Asad: The Struggle for the Middle East*. University of California Press, Berkeley, 1988, p. 165.
6 Quoted in 'Extraordinary Rendition' factsheet, American Civil Liberties Union, 6 December 2005.
http://www.aclu.org/national-security/fact-sheet-extraordinary-rendition
7 Tariq Ramadan, *The Arab Awakening: Islam and the New Middle East*, Allen Lane, London, 2012, p. 10.

1: REVOLUTION

1 'Tunisia: dinner with Sakher al-Materi', leaked cable from Ambassador Robert F. Godec (27 July 2009), *Guardian* online via WikiLeaks, 7 December 2010.
http://www.guardian.co.uk/world/us-embassy-cables-documents/218324
2 Conversation with regime sources, Tripoli.
3 'Corruption in Tunisia: What's Yours is Mine', cable from Ambassador Robert Godec to the State Department (23 June 2008), WikiLeaks, 30 August 2011.
http://wikiLeaks.ch/cable/2008/06/08TUNIS679.html#
4 'Troubled Tunisia: What Shall We Do?', cable from Ambassador Robert Godec to the State Department (17 July 2009), *Guardian* online via WikiLeaks, 7 December 2010.
http://www.guardian.co.uk/world/us-embassy-cables-documents/217138
5 Details of Muhammad Bouazizi's life and death from visit to Sidi Bouzid, July 2011.
6 Yasmine Ryan, 'How Tunisia's revolution began', al-Jazeera online, 26 January 2011.

http://www.aljazeera.com/indepth/features/2011/01/2011126121815985
483.html

7 Conversation with Walid Sattouti, Sidi Bouzid, 5 July 2011.

8 Various timelines of the revolution are available online: see http://
www.aljazeera.com/indepth/spotlight/tunisia/2011/01/201114142223827361.
html and http://www.guardian.co.uk/world/interactive/2011/mar/22/
middle-east-protest-interactive-timeline. Also see Toby Manhire (Ed.), *The Arab
Spring: Rebellion, Revolution and a New World Order*, Guardian Books, London,
2012.

9 Swimming reference in Paul Legg, 'Ben Ali's smooth rise to Power in Tunisia
contrasts with sudden decline', *Guardian* online, 15 January 2011.
http://www.guardian.co.uk/world/2011/jan/15/ben-ali-power-tunisia

10 'Troubled Tunisia: What Shall We Do?', *Op. Cit.*

11 William Burns (then Assistant Secretary of State for Near Eastern Affairs),
2001. Quoted in Caroline Sevier, 'The Costs of Relying on Aging Dictators',
Middle East Quarterly, summer 2008, pp. 13–22.

12 Badra Gaaloul, 'Back to the Barracks: the Tunisian Army Post-Revolution',
Sada, 3 November 2011. http://carnegieendowment.org/2011/11/03/back-
to-barracks-tunisian-army-post-revolution/6lxg

13 Interview with *Le Parisien* reported by Reuters, 1 July 2012.

2: CAPTURING TAHRIR

1 Samantha M. Shapiro, 'Revolution, Facebook-Style', *New York Times* online, 22
January 2009. http://www.nytimes.com/2009/01/25/magazine/25bloggers-
t.html?pagewanted=all

2 Quoted in my book *Six Days: How the 1967 War Shaped the Middle East*, Simon &
Schuster, London, 2003, p. 65.

3 Interview with administrators of We Are All Khaled Said, *Boston Review* online,
3 November 2011. http://www.bostonreview.net/BR36.6/khaled_said_face-
book_egypt_revolution.php

4 Population and literacy figures from www.cia.gov/library/publications/
the-world-factbook/geos/countrytemplate_eg.html, accessed 19 March 2012.

5 http://www.bbc.co.uk/newsbeat/12914113 Rival football ultras 'united' in Egypt
protests by Debbie Randle, 31 March 2011.

6 *The Daily News*, Egypt, 26 January 2011. http://www.thedailynewsegypt.com/
thousands-protest-across-egypt-in-day-of-anger.html

7 Toby Manhire (Ed.), *Op. Cit*, pp. 13–15.

8 Interview with Mohamed ElBaradei by CNN, 25 January 2011. http:
//edition.cnn.com/video/?/video/world/2011/01/25/ctw.intv.elbaradei.cnn

9 The *New York Times* did a great piece on noise levels in Cairo:
http://www.nytimes.com/2008/04/14/world/middleeast/14cairo.html?page-
wanted=all

3: COUNTER-REVOLUTION

1 For an excellent short guide to power in Gaddafi's Libya see Rana Jawad, *Tripoli Witness,* Gilgamesh, London, 2011, pp. 1–21.
2 Ibid., pp. 3–4.
3 Thanks to Rana Jawad, BBC Tripoli correspondent, for this point and for other observations about this chapter.

4: BULLETPROOF DOVES OF PEACE

1 Interview with the *Wall Street Journal,* published 31 January 2011.
2 For an excellent account of Syria and Lebanon see Nicholas Blanford, *Killing Mr Lebanon*, I. B. Tauris, London, 2006; casino story is on p. 63.
3 Report in government-owned *al-Thawra* under heading 'Dar'a residents denounce and condemn subversive acts', BBC Monitoring media survey, 22 March 2011.
4 BBC interview in Lebanon for Radio 4 series *Tales from the Arab Spring*, November 2011.
5 'Syria: "Shoot to Kill" Commanders Named', Human Rights Watch, 15 December 2011.
   http://www.hrw.org/news/2011/12/15/syria-shoot-kill-commanders-named
6 Rania Abouzeid, 'The Syrian President's Speech: Surprise! There's No Surprise', *Time* online, 30 March 2011. http://www.time.com/time/world/article/0,8599,2062225,00.html#ixzz1o8JGAOpX
7 Interview via Skype, BBC *News at Ten*, 30 March 2011.
8 Report by James Hider, *Times* online, 30 March 2011.
   http://www.thetimes.co.uk/tto/news/world/middleeast/article2966870.ece
9 Various conversations on background in Damascus and abroad.

5: TRIPOLI UNDER THE BOMBS

1 Samantha Power, *A Problem From Hell: America and the Age of Genocide*, Perennial, New York, 2003, preface.
2 Ibid, p. 366.
3 NATO press release, 14 May 2012.
4 Background talk, May 2012.
5 Neil MacFarquhar, 'U.N. Faults NATO and Libyan Authorities in Report', *New York Times*, 2 March 2012.
6 'NATO Strikes Military Command and Control Node', NATO statement, 20 June 2011.
7 'Unacknowledged Deaths', Human Rights Watch, 14 May 2012.
   http://www.hrw.org/reports/2012/05/14/unacknowledged-deaths-0
8 *Corriere della Sera* website, Milan, 20 June 2011.

6: GOD AND POLITICS

1 Pew Research Center, http://www.pewglobal.org/2010/12/02/muslims-around-the-world-divided-on-hamas-and-hezbollah/

2 Pew Research Center, http://www.pewglobal.org/2012/05/08/egyptians-remain-optimistic-embrace-democracy-and-religion-in-political-life/

3 Tariq Ramadan, *Op. Cit.*, pp. 75–76.

4 Many thanks to Rana Jawad and Debbie Randle for letting me quote from their reporting for the BBC on Libya.

7: PUT ON YOUR UNIFORM, BASHAR

1 Conversation with Sarit Michaeli, spokesperson for B'Tselem, the Israeli Information Centre for Human Rights in the Occupied Territories, 2 July 2012.

2 Hamad bin Jassim al-Thani. Prime Minister and Foreign Minister of Quatar.

3 Quoted in profile by Roula Khalaf, *Financial Times*, 16 June 2012.

4 David Lesch, *The New Lion of Damascus*, Yale University Press, New Haven and London, 2005, p. 9.

5 http://eurlex.europa.eu/LexUriServ/LexUriServ.do?uri=OJ:L:2011:136:0045:0047:EN:PDF

6 Ahed al-Hendi, 'The Structure of Syria's Repression', *Foreign Affairs* online, 3 May 2011.

7 For much more on the Ba'ath Party see Patrick Seale, *Op. Cit.*, pp. 24–37.

8 For more on Hama 1982 see ibid., pp. 332–334; Robert Fisk, *Pity The Nation: Lebanon at War*, Andre Deutsch, London, 1990, pp. 181–187; Thomas Friedman, *From Beirut to Jerusalem*, Collins, London, 1990, pp. 76–87.

9 'Syria: 30 years on, Hama survivors recount the horror', Amnesty International report, 28 February 2012. http://www.amnesty.org/en/news/syria-30-years-hama-survivors-recount-horror

8: THE FALL

1 Conversation with Jackie Frazier, London, 7 November 2011.

2 http://www.dailymail.co.uk/news/article-1371714/Musa-Kusa-Ministers-hail-Libyans-defection-Gaddafi-regime-coup.html#ixzz1vJsadN1d.

3 http://www.hrw.org/news/2011/09/08/usuk-documents-reveal-libya-rendition-details.

4 http://www.guardian.co.uk/world/2012/apr/08/special-report-britain-rendition-libya

5 I copied the document in Tripoli courtesy of Peter Bouckaert of Human Rights Watch. It is also available at
http://www.guardian.co.uk/world/interactive/2012/apr/08/libya-moussa-koussa.

6 Neither Sir Mark nor Mr Straw were prepared to comment on the case when I approached them.

7 Based on a visit to the improvised prison in Tajoura, 6 September 2011.

8 Kareem Fahim, 'Instead of a Bloody Struggle, a Headlong Rush Into a Cheering Capital', *New York Times* online, 21 August 2011. http://www.nytimes.com/2011/08/22/world/africa/22scene.html?hp

9 Rebel and description of fire fight quoted in Thomas Erdbrink, 'Vaunted Khamis Brigade Fails to Offer Much Resistance to Libyan Rebels', *Washington Post* online, 21 August 2011. http://www.washingtonpost.com/world/middle-east/vaunted-khamis-brigade-fails-to-offer-much-resistance-to-libyan-rebels/2011/08/21/gIQAne7EVJ_story.html

10 'Libya: Evidence Suggests Khamis Brigade Killed 45 Detainees', Human Rights Watch report, 28 August 2001. http://www.hrw.org/news/2011/08/29/libya-evidence-suggests-khamis-brigade-killed-45-detainees

11 Katya Adler, 'Gaddafi: "He died an angry and disappointed man"', BBC News online, 30 October 2011. http://www.bbc.co.uk/news/world-africa-15516678

12 'Muammar al-Gaddafi: How he died', BBC News online, 31 October 2011. http://www.bbc.co.uk/news/world-africa-15390980

13 Reuters report from the scene quoted by BBC News online, 31 October 2011. http://www.bbc.co.uk/news/world-africa-15390980

9: SLIDING INTO CIVIL WAR

1 Details in 'Syria: Jailed Rights Defender Assaulted, Punished Prison', Human Rights Watch, 4 November 2010. http://www.hrw.org/news/2010/11/04/syria-jailed-rights-defender-assaulted-punished-prison

2 Not her real name. She has now left Syria.

3 'Syria: Climate Change, Drought and Social Unrest', Think Progress, 3 March 2012. http://thinkprogress.org/climate/2012/03/03/437051

4 Interviewed by Mark Savage, November 2011 for BBC Radio 4 series 'Tales From the Arab Spring.'

5 David Ignatius, 'A string of detonators cuts through the Middle East', *Daily Star* Lebanon, 24 May 2012. http://www.dailystar.com.lb/Opinion/Columnist/2012/May-24/174466

6 The best recent study of the implications of the uprising in Bahrain is a June 2012 Chatham House paper by Jane Kinninmont: 'Bahrain: Beyond the Impasse'. http://www.chathamhouse.org/sites/default/files/public/Research/Middle%20East/pr0612kinninmont.pdf

7 Report of the Bahrain Commission of Enquiry http://www.bici.org.bh/BICIreportEN.pdf

EPILOGUE: DOWN A FAULT LINE TO THE FUTURE

1 See Chapter 2.

2 For much more detail see Vali Nasr, *The Shia Revival: How Conflicts Within Islam Will Shape the Future.* W. W. Norton, New York, 2006, pp. 31–62.

3 Robert F. Worth and Nada Bakri, 'Hezbollah Ignites a Sectarian Fuse in Lebanon', *New York Times* online, 18 May 2008.
 http://www.nytimes.com/2008/05/18/world/middleeast/18lebanon.html
4 Vali Nasr, *Op. Cit.*, p. 184.
5 Excerpt from Fareed Zakaria's interview with King Abdullah II in Davos, Switzerland, 29 January 2010.
6 'Saudi Arabia: Dissident Voices Stifled in the Eastern Province', Amnesty International, May 2012.
7 Kinninmont, *Op. Cit.*
8 Fawaz Gerges, *The Far Enemy: Why Jihad Went Global*, Cambridge University Press, Cambridge, 2009.
9 Ben Caspit, *Ma'ariv*, 24 June 2012.
10 Quoted in Eugene Rogan, *Op. Cit.*, p. 5.

ACKNOWLEDGEMENTS

The biggest debt I have is to hundreds of people who were prepared to talk to me during some stressful, exciting, sometimes frightening moments in the region and elsewhere since January 2011. Quotes are all as precise as I can make them, based on notebooks and recordings. In some places I have tidied up the English without altering the meaning. Many people did not want their names to be used, including diplomats and officials in various countries who kindly spent a lot of time discussing their views about the Arab Uprisings.

I owe a lot to the people I work with in the news business who have inspired and sustained me during intense times in the Middle East and North Africa. It was always a huge pleasure to see Marie Colvin of the *Sunday Times* when we bumped into each other in Tahrir Square in Cairo, in the Rixos hotel in Tripoli and lots of other places besides. Marie was a friend for more than twenty years, since we met in Baghdad during the 1991 war. Without Marie's help I would never have made it into the room (alongside her and Christiane Amanpour) to interview Colonel Gaddafi. Almost a year later Marie sent me an email from Homs in Syria saying that reporting the story there was why we went into journalism. She was killed the next day, on 22 February 2012.

My colleagues at the BBC are the best in the world at what they do, and I am indebted to them too, especially to all the teams I have worked with in the Middle East over many years. Writing is a solitary business but news is not.

Nothing whatsoever would have been possible without my producer and travelling companion Cara Swift and her predecessor

Jane Logan. I'm also very lucky to have Lina Sinjab and Tima Khalil as my guides to Syria and Lebanon respectively. In Cairo Raouf Ibrahim is always fearless and tireless. Special thanks to Jeannie Assad, Jimmy Michael, Youssef Shomali, Rob Magee, Angy Ghannam, Ian Druce, Jacky Martens, Bas Solanki, Nik Millard, Kim Ghattas, DC, Sarge, Tony Fallshaw, Amr Aboulfath and Fred Scott. I am lucky to work with top professionals and even luckier that some of them have become real friends.

Lina in Damascus and Rana Jawad in Tripoli read sections of the book, suggested improvements and spotted mistakes. Eugene Rogan at St Antony's College, Oxford, the author of the brilliant and essential book *The Arabs: A History* kindly read part of my manuscript and gave me advice and encouragement. I take full responsibility for any inaccuracies that remain.

I would like to thank the management at BBC News for their help and support, especially Helen Boaden, Fran Unsworth and Jon Williams. Generously, Helen gave me time off to finish this book. James Stephenson and Paul Royall, and the rest of the team at the BBC's *News at Ten* gave me a lot of airtime and encouragement. Paul Danahar, the BBC's Middle East bureau chief, made sure that I was able to concentrate on the Ten during the overthrow of Hosni Mubarak.

Tony Grant, the editor of *From Our Own Correspondent*, and Tarik Kafala, Middle East editor at the BBC's website, encouraged me to write about the turbulence in the Middle East. The results have been blended, I hope seamlessly, into this book. Some of the interviews that feature in this book were done for a BBC Radio 4 series called *Tales from the Arab Spring*. Many thanks to Mark Savage who co-produced the series with Cara and to Tony Phillips and Gwyn Williams who commissioned it.

Over the years I have had a lot of help in the Middle East from Human Rights Watch, who do great work. Special thanks to Peter Bouckaert, Fred Abrahams and Emma Daly. Peter directed me towards Musa Kusa's correspondence with MI6 and the CIA. I was able to report it because Nik Millard had persuaded me to stay on in Tripoli.

Stimulating conversation and ideas came from Sir John Holmes and participants in a Ditchley Foundation conference on change in the Middle East and North Africa held in November 2011.

Thanks once again to my agent, Julian Alexander at LAW, and to the team at Simon and Schuster, especially Emma Harrow, Mike Jones, Briony Gowlett, Lewis Csizmazia and Ian Chapman. Thanks too to Monica Hope for copy editing.

I'd like to thank all my family for their support, and apologise to Mattie, Boatie and Julia for being away in the Middle East or locked in my office writing.

INDEX

Jeremy Bowen is Middle East Editor for the BBC and has covered the majority of breaking news and stories from the Middle East since the 1991 Gulf War. He is the author of two previous books: *Six Days* and *War Stories*.